Fully Updated as per Latest NCERT Textbook

NCERT SOLUTIONS

with Chapterwise **Study Notes**

PHYSICS 12th

Author
Dr. Sanjeev Varshney
Mukesh Kumar

arihant
SUCCESS AND NOTHING LESS

Including Selected Questions of **DIKSHA**

arihant
SUCCESS AND NOTHING LESS

ARIHANT PRAKASHAN (Series), MEERUT

卐 **Administrative & Production Offices**

Regd. Office

'Ramchhaya' 4577/15, Agarwal Road, Darya Ganj, New Delhi -110002
Tele: 011- 47630600, 43518550

卐 **Head Office**

Kalindi, TP Nagar, Meerut (UP) - 250002
Tel: 0121-7156203, 7156204

卐 **Sales & Support Offices**

Agra, Ahmedabad, Bengaluru, Bareilly, Chennai, Delhi, Guwahati, Hyderabad, Jaipur, Jhansi, Kolkata, Lucknow, Nagpur & Pune.

卐 **PRICE** ₹225.00

卐 **PO No. :** TXT-59-T070821-5-26

Published by Arihant Publications (India) Ltd.

For further information about the books published by Arihant, log on to www.arihantbooks.com or e-mail at info@arihantbooks.com

Follow us on

Preface

Feeling the immense importance and value of NCERT books, we are presenting this book, having the **NCERT Exercises Solutions**. For the overall benefit of the students we have made this book unique in such a way that it presents not only solutions but also detailed explanations. Through these detailed and through explanations, students can learn the concepts which will enhance their thinking and learning abilities.

We have introduced some Additional Features with the solutions which are given below:

- **Explanatory Solutions** Along with the solutions to questions we have given all the points that tell how to approach to solve a problem. Here we have tried to cover all those loopholes which may lead to confusion. All formulae and hints are discussed in full detail.
- Also included **Thinking Process** and **Mistake Alert** to understanding 'How to solve question' and points of mistakes.
- **Note** We have provided notes also to solutions in which special points are mentioned which are of great value for the students.

Apart from all those who helped in the compilation of this book a special note of thanks to all. With the hope that this book will be of great help to the students, we wish great success to our readers.

Dr. Sanjeev Varshney
Mukesh Kumar

Contents

1.	Electric Charges and Fields	1-20
2.	Electrostatic Potential and Capacitance	21-37
3.	Current Electricity	38-50
4.	Moving Charges and Magnetism	51-63
5.	Magnetism and Matter	64-72
6.	Electromagnetic Induction	73-84
7.	Alternating Current	85-97
8.	Electromagnetic Waves	98-108
9.	Ray Optics and Optical Instruments	109-149
10.	Wave Optics	150-160
11.	Dual Nature of Radiation and Matter	161-172
12.	Atoms	173-183
13.	Nuclei	184-192
14.	Semiconductor Electronics : Materials, Devices and Simple Circuits	193-204

Electric Charges and Fields

CHAPTER 01

Important Points

01 Quantisation Principle $q = \pm ne$, where n is the number of electrons lost or gained by body.

02 Coulomb's Law $F_{vac} = \dfrac{1}{4\pi\varepsilon_0} \dfrac{|q_1 q_2|}{r^2}$;

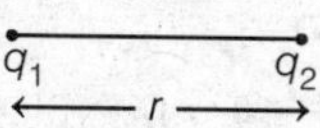

$$F_{med} = \frac{1}{4\pi\varepsilon_0 K} \frac{q_1 q_2}{r^2}$$

03 Superposition Principle Resultant force on a point charge due to a number of other point charges is equal to vector sum of all the forces due to individual charges on that charge, taken one at a time.

$$\mathbf{F}_0 = \mathbf{F}_{01} + \mathbf{F}_{02} + \mathbf{F}_{03} + \dots + \mathbf{F}_{0n}$$

04 Electric field due to a point charge at r distance is

$$E = \frac{1}{4\pi\varepsilon_0} \frac{q}{r^2}, \; \mathbf{F}(r) = q_0\, \mathbf{E}(r)$$

05 Superposition Principle Resultant electric field on a point due to a number of point charges is equal to vector sum of electric field due to individual charges

$$\mathbf{E}(r) = \mathbf{E}_1(r) + \mathbf{E}_2(r) + \mathbf{E}_3(r) + \dots + \mathbf{E}_n(r)$$

06 Electric Dipole Moment $\mathbf{p} = q \times 2\mathbf{a}$

Its direction is from negative charge to positive charge and its unit is C-m.

07 Electric field intensity on axial line of dipole

$$\mathbf{E}_{axial} = \frac{1}{4\pi\varepsilon_0} \cdot \frac{2\,\mathbf{p}r}{(r^2 - a^2)^2}$$

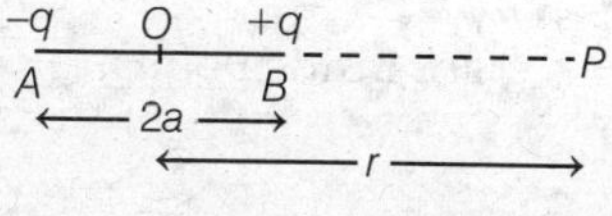

With short dipole approximation, i.e., $r >> a$ $\mathbf{E}_{\text{axial}} = \dfrac{2\mathbf{p}}{4\pi\varepsilon_0 r^3}$.

08 Electric field intensity on equatorial line of dipole

$$\mathbf{E}_{\text{eq}} = -\frac{1}{4\pi\varepsilon_0}\cdot\frac{\mathbf{p}}{(r^2+a^2)^{3/2}}$$

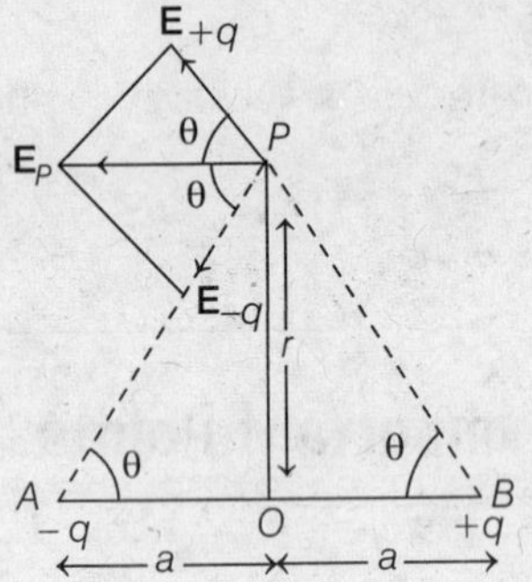

With short dipole approximation, i.e, $r >> a$ $\mathbf{E}_{\text{equatorial}} = -\dfrac{\mathbf{p}}{4\pi\varepsilon_0 r^3}$

09 Electric field intensity at any point due to a short dipole

$$\mathbf{E} = \frac{1}{4\pi\varepsilon_0}\,\mathbf{p}\,\frac{\sqrt{3\cos^2\theta+1}}{r^3}$$

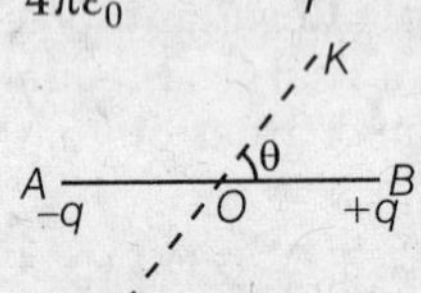

10 Torque on Dipole $\tau = \mathbf{p}\times\mathbf{E}$ or $\tau = pE\sin\theta$

11 Gauss's Theorem $\phi_E = \oint \mathbf{E}\cdot d\mathbf{S} = \int E\,dS\cos\theta = \dfrac{q_{\text{net}}}{\varepsilon_0}$

12 Electric field intensity due to a line charge is $E = \dfrac{|\lambda|}{2\pi\varepsilon_0 r}$

13 Electric field intensity due to a thin infinite plane sheet of charge

$$E = \frac{|\sigma|}{2\varepsilon_0}$$

14 Electric field of two equally and oppositely charged parallel plates

For outside points, $E = 0$

For inside points $E = \dfrac{\sigma}{\varepsilon_0}$

15 **Electric Field Intensity** at a point on the surface or outside a charged spherical shell.

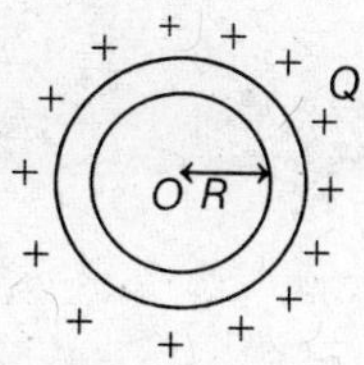

$$E = \frac{1}{4\pi\varepsilon_0} \frac{Q}{r^2}$$

where, $r = R$ on the surface.

16 Electric field intensity inside a charged spherical shell

$$E = 0$$

Exercises

Question 1 What is the force between two small charged spheres having charges of 2×10^{-7} C and 3×10^{-7} C placed 30 cm apart in air?

Sol. According to the question, $q_1 = 2 \times 10^{-7}\text{C}, q_2 = 3 \times 10^{-7}\text{C}$

Distance between q_1 and q_2, $d = 30\text{ cm} = 0.3\text{ m}$

Using Coulomb's law, the force between two charges is given by

$$F = \frac{1}{4\pi\varepsilon_0} \frac{|q_1 q_2|}{d^2}$$

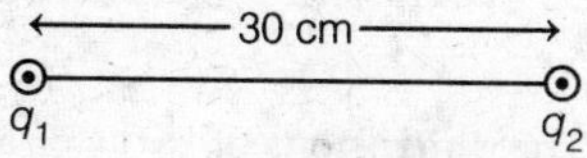

Putting the values of $\frac{1}{4\pi\varepsilon_0}$, q_1, q_2 and d, we get

$$F = \frac{9 \times 10^9 \times 2 \times 10^{-7} \times 3 \times 10^{-7}}{(0.3)^2} = 6 \times 10^{-3}\text{ N}$$

As the two charges q_1 and q_2 both are positive in nature. So, they repel each other as like charges repel each other.

Question 2 The electrostatic force on a small sphere of charge 0.4 μC due to another small sphere of charge −0.8 μC in air is 0.2 N.

(a) What is the distance between the two spheres?

(b) What is the force on the second sphere due to the first?

Sol. According to the question, $q_1 = 0.4\,\mu\text{C}, q_2 = -0.8\,\mu\text{C}$

Let the distance between two charges be r. Force on charge q_1 (0.4 μC) due to another charge q_2 (−0.8 μC) is $F = 0.2\text{ N}$.

(a) We have to find the value of r. Using Coulomb's law, the force between two charges is

$$F = \frac{1}{4\pi\varepsilon_0} \frac{|q_1 q_2|}{r^2}$$

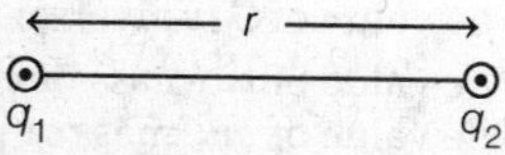

Putting the values of F, $\frac{1}{4\pi\varepsilon_0}$, q_1 and q_2, we get

$$0.2 = 9 \times 10^9 \times \frac{|0.4 \times 10^{-6} \times 0.8 \times 10^{-6}|}{r^2}$$

$$r^2 = 16 \times 9 \times 10^{-4}$$

$$r = 4 \times 3 \times 10^{-2}$$

$$r = 12 \times 10^{-2} \text{ m}, r = 12 \text{ cm}$$

(b) The force of attraction on the second sphere due to the first sphere is 0.2 N.

Question 3 Check that the ratio ke^2/Gm_em_p is dimensionless. Look up a table of physical constants and determine the value of this ratio. What does the ratio signify?

Sol. In the ratio $\frac{ke^2}{Gm_em_p}$, $k = \frac{1}{4\pi\varepsilon_0}$ (constant)

where, G = gravitational constant
m_e = mass of an electron
m_p = mass of a proton

From Coulomb's law

$$F = k\frac{q_1q_2}{r^2}$$

$$\Rightarrow \quad k = \frac{Fr^2}{q_1q_2} \quad \text{or} \quad k = \frac{Fr^2}{q^2}$$

The dimensions of $k = \left(\frac{1}{4\pi\varepsilon_0}\right) = \frac{[MLT^{-2}][L^2]}{[AT]^2} = [ML^3T^{-4}A^{-2}]$

The dimensions of q (electronic charge) = [AT]

The dimensions of G (universal gravitational constant) from the formula $G = \frac{Fr^2}{m^2}$

$$= \frac{[MLT^{-2}][L^2]}{[M^2]}$$

$$= [M^{-1}L^3T^{-2}]$$

The dimensions of m_e and m_p (mass of electron and mass of proton) = [M]

The dimensions of $\frac{ke^2}{Gm_em_p} = \frac{[ML^3T^{-4}A^{-2}][A^2T^2]}{[M^{-1}L^3T^{-2}][M^2]} = [M^0L^0T^0]$

Thus, the given ratio is dimensionless.

The value of $k = \left(\frac{1}{4\pi\varepsilon_0}\right) = 9 \times 10^9$ N-m^2/C^2

The value of e (charge of an electron) = 1.6×10^{-19} C

The value of G (universal gravitational constant) = 6.67×10^{-11} N-m^2/kg^2

The value of m_e(mass of electron) = 9.1×10^{-31} kg

The value of m_p (mass of proton) = 1.67×10^{-27} kg

The value of $\dfrac{\dfrac{ke^2}{r^2}}{\dfrac{Gm_em_p}{r^2}} = \dfrac{F_e}{F_G} = \dfrac{9 \times 10^9 \times (1.6 \times 10^{-19})^2}{6.67 \times 10^{-11} \times 9.1 \times 10^{-31} \times 1.67 \times 10^{-27}}$

$$= 2.27 \times 10^{39}$$

The given ratio signifies that the electrostatic force between an electron and a proton is approximately 2.27×10^{39} times stronger than the gravitational force between them.

Question 4 (a) Explain the meaning of the statement 'electric charge of a body is quantized'.

(b) Why can one ignore quantization of electric charge when dealing with macroscopic, *i.e.*, large scale charges?

Sol.

(a) The electric charge of a body is quantized means that the charge on a body can occur in integral values only. Charge on any body is the integral multiple of charge on an electron because the charge of an electron is the elementary charge in nature. The charge on any body can be expressed by the formula $q = \pm ne$

where, n = number of electrons transferred

and e = charge on one electron.

(b) The charge on one electron is 1.6×10^{-19}C in magnitude, which is very small as compared to the large scale charges

Question 5 When a glass rod is rubbed with a silk cloth, charges appear on both. A similar phenomenon is observed with many other pairs of bodies. Explain how this observation is consistent with the law of conservation of charge.

Sol. According to the law of conservation of charge, "charge can neither be created nor be destroyed but can be transferred from one body to another body".

Before rubbing the two bodies both were neutral *i.e.*, the total charge of the system was zero. When the glass rod is rubbed with a silk cloth, some electrons from glass rod are transferred to silk cloth hence, glass rod attains positive charge (due to loss of electrons) and silk cloth attains same amount of negative charge (due to gain of electrons).

Again the total charge of the system is zero, *i.e.*, the charge before rubbing is same as the charge after rubbing. This is consistent with the law of conservation of charge.

Question 6 Four point charges $q_A = 2\ \mu C$, $q_B = -5\ \mu C$, $q_C = 2\ \mu C$, and $q_D = -5\ \mu C$ are located at the corners of a square $ABCD$ of side 10 cm. What is the force on a charge of 1 μC placed at the centre of the square?

◎ *Thinking Process* Charge placed at the centre is in the influence field of four charges located at the corners of the square. Therefore, we can find force acting on charge placed at the centre using superposition principle.

Sol. Suppose a square ABCD is with each side as 10cm and centre is at O. At the centre the charge of 1μC is placed.

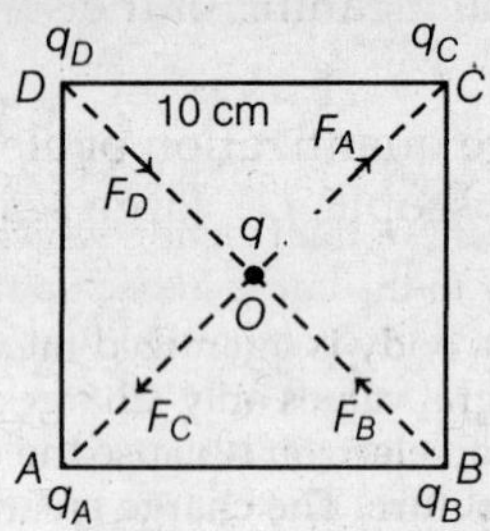

$$\because \quad AB = BC = CD = DA = 10 \text{ cm}$$

$$\therefore \quad AC = \sqrt{10^2 + 10^2}$$

$$= 10\sqrt{2} \text{ cm}$$

$$AC = BD = 10\sqrt{2} \text{ cm}$$

$$AO = BO = CO = DO$$

$$= \frac{10\sqrt{2}}{2} = 5\sqrt{2} \text{ cm}$$

As, $q_A = q_C$, the charge of 1 μ C experiences equal and opposite force F_A and F_C due to charges q_A and q_C. Similarly, the charge 1 μC experiences equal and opposite force. F_B and F_D due to charges q_B and q_D. Thus, the net force on charge 1 μ C due to the given arrangement of charges is zero.

Mistake Alert While solving this, students might make mistakes by taking the wrong direction for individual forces or by not coreectly applying the cancellation of opposite forces.

Remember that opposite forces have the same magnitude and cancel out, resulting in a net force of zero.

Question 7 (a) An electrostatic field line is a continuous curve. That is, a field line cannot have sudden breaks. Why not?

(b) Explain why two field lines never cross each other at any point?

Sol.

(a) An electrostatic field line represents the actual path travelled by a unit positive charge in an electric field. If the line have sudden breaks it means the unit positive test charge jumps from one place to another which is not possible. It also means that electric field becomes zero suddenly at the breaks which is not possible. So, the field line cannot have any sudden breaks.

(b) If two field lines cross each other, then we can draw two tangents at the point of intersection which indicates that (tangent to the curve at each point gives the direction of net electric field at that point) there are two directions of electric field at a particular point, which is not possible at the same instant. Thus, two field lines never cross each other at any point.

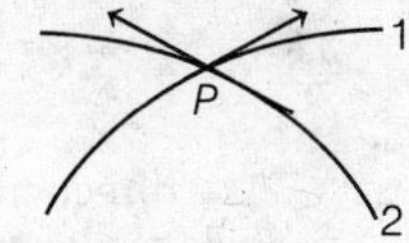

Question 8 Two point charges $q_A = 3\mu C$ and $q_B = -3\mu C$ are located 20 cm apart in vacuum.

(a) What is the electric field at the mid-point O of the line AB joining the two charges?

(b) If a negative test charge of magnitude 1.5×10^{-9} C is placed at this point, what is the force experienced by the test charge?

Thinking Process ◆ First of all calculate the electric fields at mid-point due to both charges and then find the resultant electric field by vector addition.

◆ Force on a charge in an electric field is $F = qE$.

Sol. (a) $AB = 20$ cm

$$AO = OB = 10 \text{ cm} = 0.1 \text{ m}$$
$$q_A = 3\mu C = 3 \times 10^{-6} C,$$
$$q_B = -3\mu C = -3 \times 10^{-6} C$$

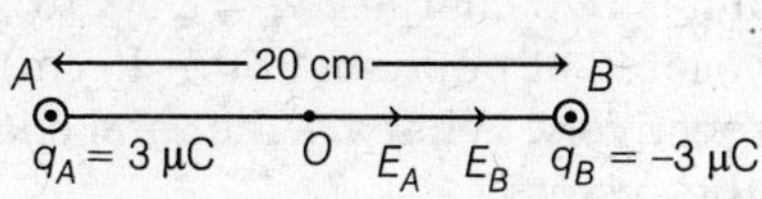

The magnitude of electric field at a point due to a charge q is

$$E = \frac{1}{4\pi\varepsilon_0} \cdot \frac{q}{r^2}$$

where, r is the distance between charge and the point of consideration.
Electric field due to q_A at O is E_A.

$$E_A = \frac{1}{4\pi\varepsilon_0} \cdot \frac{q_A}{(AO)^2}$$

$$E_A = \frac{9 \times 10^9 \times 3 \times 10^{-6}}{(0.1)^2} = \frac{27 \times 10^3}{0.1 \times 0.1} = 2.7 \times 10^{-6} \text{ N/C}$$

The direction of E_A is A to O *i.e.*, towards O or towards OB as the electric field is always directed away from positive charge.
Electric field due to q_B at O is E_B.

$$E_B = \frac{1}{4\pi\varepsilon_0} \cdot \frac{q_B}{(OB)^2}$$

$$E_B = \frac{9 \times 10^9 \times 3 \times 10^{-6}}{(0.1)^2} = \frac{27 \times 10^3}{0.1 \times 0.1} = 2.7 \times 10^6 \text{ N/C}$$

The direction of E_B is O to B *i.e.*, towards O or towards OB as the electric field is always directed towards the negative charge.
Now, we see that both E_A and E_B are in same direction. So, the resultant electric field at O is E. Hence,

$$E = E_A + E_B = 2.7 \times 10^6 + 2.7 \times 10^6 = 5.4 \times 10^6 \text{ N/C}$$

The direction of E (resultant electric field) will be along OB or towards B.

(b) Let us consider, the charge q is placed at the mid-point O. According to the question,

$$q = -1.5 \times 10^{-9} \text{C}$$

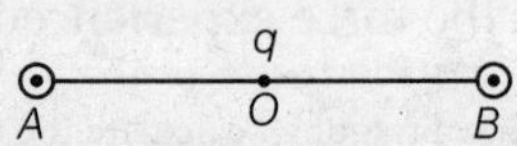

By the basic definition of electric field, $E = \frac{F}{q}$

or $F = qE$, where, E is the net electric field at point O.

$$F = -1.5 \times 10^{-9} \times 5.4 \times 10^6 = -8.1 \times 10^{-3} \text{N}$$

The direction of force is opposite to the direction of field because the charge q is negatively charged. Thus, the direction of force is from O to A.

Question 9 A system has two charges $q_A = 2.5 \times 10^{-7}$ C and $q_B = -2.5 \times 10^{-7}$ C located at points $A(0, 0, -15 \text{ cm})$ and $B(0, 0, +15 \text{ cm})$, respectively. What are the total charge and electric dipole moment of the system?

Sol. Given $A(0, 0, -15 \text{ cm})$ and $B(0, 0, 15 \text{ cm})$

$$q_A = 2.5 \times 10^{-7} \text{C}$$

$$q_B = -2.5 \times 10^{-7} \text{C}$$

The distance between A and B is the length of dipole (because q_A and q_B are same in magnitude and opposite in nature, so they form a dipole).

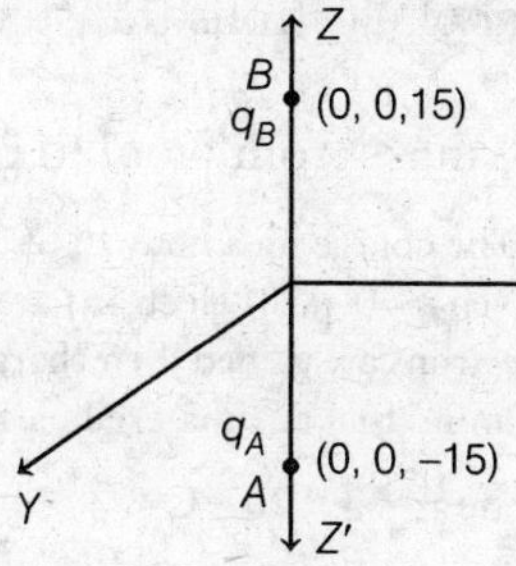

$$AB = 2l = \text{length of the dipole}$$
$$= 30 \text{ cm} = 30 \times 10^{-2}\text{m}.$$

The total charge q on the dipole is

$$q = q_A + q_B = 2.5 \times 10^{-7} - 2.5 \times 10^{-7}\text{C} = 0$$

The electric dipole moment $p =$ Magnitude of any charge $\times$ Length of the dipole

$$p = q_A \times 2l = 2.5 \times 10^{-7} \times 30 \times 10^{-2}$$
$$p = 7.5 \times 10^{-8}\text{C-m}$$

The direction of the dipole moment is always from negative charge to positive charge that is along B to A.

Question 10 An electric dipole with dipole moment 4×10^{-9} Cm is aligned at 30° with the direction of a uniform electric field of magnitude 5×10^4 N/C. Calculate the magnitude of the torque acting on the dipole.

Sol. Given, dipole moment $p = 4 \times 10^{-9}$ C m

Electric field $E = 5 \times 10^4$ N/C

θ = Angle between electric field and the dipole moment = 30°

Torque applied on a dipole in the electric field

$$\tau = \mathbf{p} \times \mathbf{E} = pE \sin \theta$$

or

$$\tau = 4 \times 10^{-9} \times 5 \times 10^4 \sin 30°$$
$$= \frac{20 \times 10^{-5}}{2} = 10^{-4}\text{N-m}$$

Question 11 A polythene piece rubbed with wool is found to have a negative charge of 3×10^{-7} C.

(a) Estimate the number of electrons transferred (from which to which)?

(b) Is there a transfer of mass from wool to polythene?

◎ *Thinking Process* The charge on a body in terms of number of electrons loss or gained by it is given $q = \pm ne$. If electrons are lost then charge obtained will be positive and if electrons are gained then charge obtained will be negative. We should also keep in mind that any material particle always has mass.

Sol. Given, charge on polythene = -3×10^{-7}C

(a) The charge on an object is given by $q = \pm ne$

The number of electrons transferred $n = \dfrac{\text{Total charge } (q)}{\text{Charge of electron } (e)}$

$$n = \frac{3 \times 10^{-7}}{1.6 \times 10^{-19}} = 1.875 \times 10^{12}$$

Thus, the number of electrons transferred is 1.875×10^{12}. Electrons will be transferred from wool to polythene because polythene attains the negative charge that means it gains the electrons.

(b) As the electrons are transferred from wool to polythene, the mass is also transferred because along with the charge each electron will also carry its mass.

The number of electrons transferred = 1.875×10^{12}

The mass of one electron = 9.1×10^{-31} kg

Mass transferred from wool to polythene

= Number of electrons × Mass of one electron

= $1.875 \times 10^{12} \times 9.1 \times 10^{-31} = 1.70 \times 10^{-18}$ kg

Thus, 1.7×10^{-18} kg mass is transferred from wool to polythene.

Question 12 (a) Two insulated charged copper spheres A and B have their centres separated by a distance of 50 cm. What is the mutual force of electrostatic repulsion if the charge on each is 6.5×10^{-7} C? The radii of A and B are negligible compared to the distance of separation.

(b) What is the force of repulsion if each sphere is charged double the above amount and the distance between them is halved?

◎ *Thinking Process* This problem uses a concept of Coulomb's law to find the electrostatic force between two charged spheres.

According to this law, the force between two charges depends directly on the magnitude of each charge and inversely on the square of the distance between them.

Sol. (a) Let us consider, the charge on sphere A is q_A and on sphere B is q_B.

According to the question,

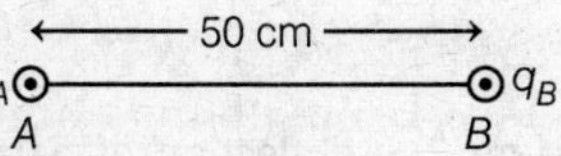

$$q_A = 6.5\times 10^{-7}\text{C}$$
$$q_B = 6.5\times 10^{-7}\text{C}$$

r = distance between A and B = 50 cm = 50×10^{-2}m

From the Coulomb's law, the force between the two spheres is

$$F = \frac{1}{4\pi\varepsilon_0}\cdot\frac{q_A q_B}{r^2} = \frac{9\times 10^9 \times 6.5\times 10^{-7}\times 6.5\times 10^{-7}}{(50\times 10^{-2})^2}$$
$$= \frac{9\times 6.5\times 6.5\times 10^{-5}}{50\times 50\times 10^{-4}} = 1.521\times 10^{-2}\text{ N}$$

Thus, the force between A and B is 1.521×10^{-2}N, this force is repulsive in nature because the charges are similar (positive) in nature.

(b) According to the question, if the charge is doubled

$$q'_A = 2q_A \quad \text{and} \quad q'_B = 2q_B$$

Distance between them is halved *i.e.*, $r' = \frac{r}{2}$

Now, the force between the two spheres is

$$F' = \frac{1}{4\pi\varepsilon_0}\cdot\frac{q'_A q'_B}{r'} = \frac{1}{4\pi\varepsilon_0}\frac{(2q_A)(2q_B)}{(r/2)^2} = \frac{1}{4\pi\varepsilon_0}\cdot\frac{4q_A q_B}{r^2/4}$$
$$= 16\frac{1}{4\pi\varepsilon_0}\frac{q_A q_B}{r^2} = 16\,F = 16\times 1.521\times 10^{-2} = 0.24\text{ N}$$

This force is also repulsive in nature because both the charges are similar (positive) in nature.

Question 13 The given figure shows tracks of three charged particles in a uniform electrostatic field. Give the signs of the three charges. Which particle has the highest charge to mass ratio?

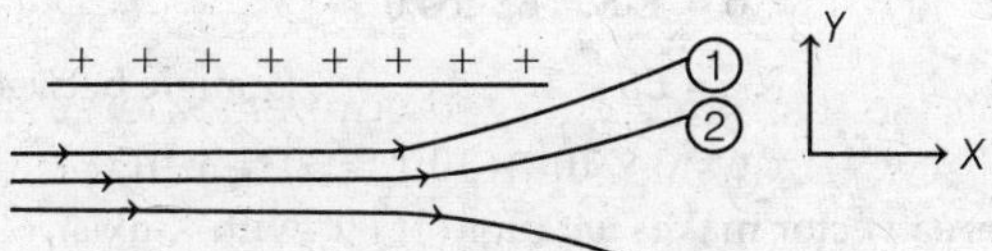

Sol. We know that a positively charged particle is attracted towards the negatively charged plate and a negatively charged particle is attracted towards the positively charged plate.

Here, particle 1 and particle 2 are attracted towards positive plate that means they are negatively charged. Particle 3 is attracted towards negatively charged plate so it is positively charged.

∴ Signs of charges : 1 → Positive (+)
2 → Negative (–)
3 → Positive (+)

As the deflection in the path of a charged particle is directly proportional to the charge/mass ratio i.e.

$$y \propto \frac{q}{m}$$

Here, the deflection of particle 3 is maximum, so the charge to mass ratio of particle 3 is maximum.

Question 14 Consider a uniform electric field $E = 3 \times 10^3\ \hat{\mathbf{i}}$ N/C.

(a) What is the flux of this field through a square of 10 cm on a side whose plane is parallel to the Y-Z plane?

(b) What is the flux through the same square if the normal to its plane makes a 60° angle with the X-axis?

Sol. Electric field $\mathbf{E} = 3 \times 10^3\ \hat{\mathbf{i}}$ N/C, *i.e.*, electric field is directed towards X-axis (due to involvement of $\hat{\mathbf{i}}$).

(a) As the surface is in Y-Z plane, so the area vector (normal to the square) is along X-axis.

$$\text{Area } S = 10 \times 10 = 100\ \text{cm}^2 = 10^{-2}\ \text{m}^2$$

Area vector $\mathbf{S} = 10^{-2}\ \hat{\mathbf{i}}\ \text{m}^2$

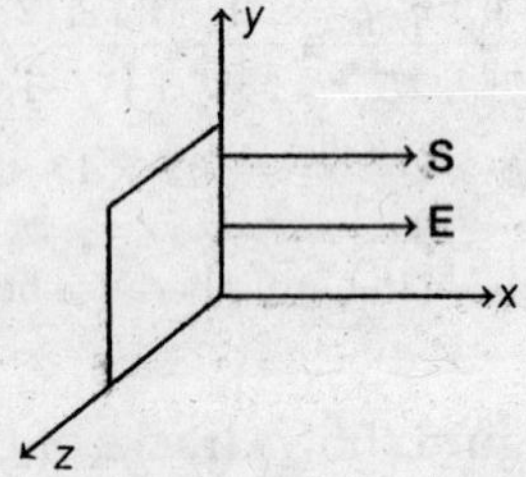

Using the formula of electric flux

$$\phi = \mathbf{E} \cdot \mathbf{S} = ES \cos \theta$$

$$= ES \qquad [\because \text{angle between } \mathbf{E} \text{ and } \mathbf{S} \text{ is } 0°]$$

$$\phi = 3 \times 10^3 \times 10^{-2} = 30\ \text{N-m}^2/\text{C}$$

(b) Now, the area vector makes an angle of 60° with X-axis.

$$\mathbf{E} = 3 \times 10^3\ \hat{\mathbf{i}}\ \text{N/C}$$

$$\mathbf{S} = 100\ \text{cm}^2 = 10^{-2}\ \text{m}^2,\ \theta = 60°$$

Using the formula of electric flux $\phi = \mathbf{E} \cdot \mathbf{S}$

$$\phi = \mathbf{ES} \cos \theta = 3 \times 10^3 \times 10^{-2} \cos 60° = 3 \times 10 \times \frac{1}{2}$$

$$= 15\ \text{N-m}^2/\text{C}$$

Note Remember that the direction of area vector is always perpendicular to the area of a face.

Question 15 What is the net flux of the uniform electric field of Q.14 through a cube of side 20 cm oriented so that its faces are parallel to the coordinate planes?

Sol. As we know that the number of lines entering in the cube is the same as that the number of lines leaving the cube. So, no flux is remained in the cube and hence, the net flux over the cube is zero.

Question 16 Careful measurement of the electric field at the surface of a black box indicates that the net outward flux through the surface of the box is 8.0×10^3 N-m^2/C.

(a) What is the net charge inside the box?

(b) If the net outward flux through the surface of the box were zero, could you conclude that there were no charges inside the box? Why or why not?

Sol. Using the concept of Gauss's theorem,

(a) Given, Net outward flux $\phi = 8.0 \times 10^3$ N-m^2/C

We know that

$$\text{Net flux } \phi = \frac{\text{Net charge}}{\varepsilon_0} = \frac{q}{\varepsilon_0} \Rightarrow q = \varepsilon_0 \phi = 8.854 \times 10^{-12} \times 8 \times 10^3$$

$$\left(\because \varepsilon_0 = 8.854 \times 10^{-12} \frac{C^2}{Nm^2}\right)$$

$$q = 0.07 \times 10^{-6} \text{ C} = 0.07 \mu\text{C}$$

The flux is outward hence, the charge is positive in nature.

(b) If net outward flux = 0

Then, we can conclude that the net charge inside the box is zero, *i.e.*, the box may have either zero charge or have equal amount of positive and negative charges so that net charge inside the box is zero.

It means we cannot conclude that there is no charge inside the box or the box can contain an electric dipole as well.

Question 17 A point charge $+10 \mu$C is at a distance 5 cm directly above the centre of a square of side 10 cm, as shown in figure. What is the magnitude of the electric flux through the square?

[**Hint** : Think of the square as one face of a cube with edge 10 cm.]

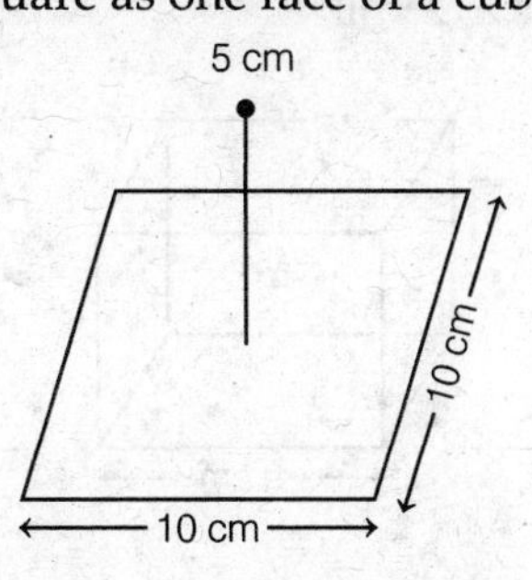

Sol. Now, we imagine an enclosed cubical surface which acts as a Gaussian surface for the given charge and the given square be one face of this cubical surface. Let the charge q is placed at the centre of cube. Now, the figure looks like as shown

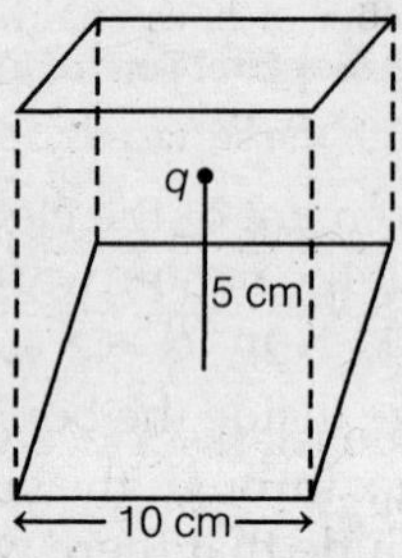

The total electric flux enclosed through the cube is

$$\phi = \frac{q_{net}}{\varepsilon_0} \quad \text{...(i)}$$

[According to Gauss's theorem]

Here, $q = 10\ \mu C = 10 \times 10^{-6}$ C

The flux enclosed by one face *i.e.*, square is 1/6 of total flux (because the cube has six square shaped faces), so

The flux linked with each square

$$\phi' = \frac{\phi}{6} = \frac{1}{6} \cdot \frac{q_{net}}{\varepsilon_0} \quad \text{[From Eq. (i)]}$$

$$\phi' = \frac{1}{6} \times \frac{10 \times 10^{-6}}{8.854 \times 10^{-12}}$$

$$= 1.88 \times 10^5 \text{ N-m}^2/\text{C}$$

Thus, the flux linked with the square is 1.88×10^5 N-m^2/C.

Question 18 A point charge of 2.0 μ C is at the centre of a cubic Gaussian surface 9.0 cm on edge. What is the net electric flux through the surface?

Sol. Let us consider a charge q is placed at the centre of a cubic Gaussian surface. As per the question, $q = 2\mu C = 2 \times 10^{-6}$ C

Length of edge = 9 cm

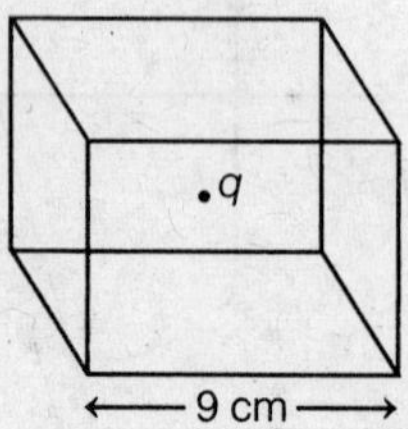

According to Gauss's theorem, the net electric flux (ϕ) through the surface is

$$\phi = \frac{q_{net}}{\varepsilon_0} = \frac{2 \times 10^{-6}}{8.854 \times 10^{-12}}$$

$$\approx 2.26 \times 10^5 \text{ N-m}^2/\text{C}$$

Thus, the net electric flux through the surface is 2.26×10^5 N-m^2/C.

Question 19 A point charge causes an electric flux of -1.0×10^3 N-m^2/C to pass through a spherical Gaussian surface of 10.0 cm radius centred on the charge.

(a) If the radius of the Gaussian surface were doubled, how much flux would pass through the surface?

(b) What is the value of the point charge?

Sol.

(a) The electric flux through a closed surface depends only on the net charge enclosed within the surface and not no its size. Therefore, even if the radius of the Gaussian surface is doubled, the electric flux remains same.

(b) $\phi = -1.0 \times 10^3$ N-m^2/C

Radius = 10.0 cm

Using Gauss's theorem,

The flux linked $\phi = \frac{q_{net}}{\varepsilon_0}$

$$q = \phi\varepsilon_0 = -1.0 \times 10^3 \times 8.854 \times 10^{-12}$$
$$= -8.85 \times 10^{-9} \text{ C}$$

Thus, the value of point charge is -8.85×10^{-9}C.

Question 20 A conducting sphere of radius 10 cm has an unknown charge. If the electric field 20 cm from the centre of the sphere is 1.5×10^3 N/C and points radially inwards, what is the net charge on the sphere?

Sol. Let the value of unknown charge be q.

Electric field at 20 cm away is $E = 1.5 \times 10^3$ N/C, $r = 20$ cm $= 20 \times 10^{-2}$ m (radially inwards)

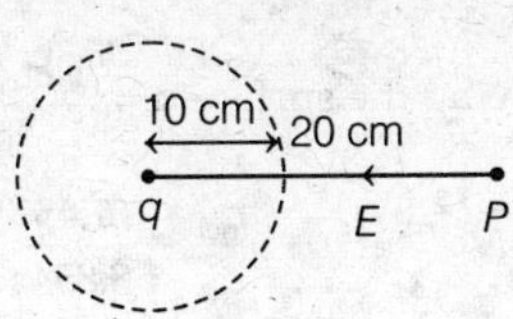

From the formula, electric field

$$E = \frac{1}{4\pi\varepsilon_0} \cdot \frac{q}{r^2} \qquad (r = \text{distance})$$

$$1.5 \times 10^3 = \frac{9 \times 10^9 \times q}{(20 \times 10^{-2})^2}$$

$$q = \frac{1.5 \times 10^3 \times 20 \times 20 \times 10^{-4}}{9 \times 10^9} = 6.67 \times 10^{-9} \text{ C}$$

As, the electric field is radially inwards which shows that the nature of the unknown charge q is negative.

Question 21 A uniformly charged conducting sphere of 2.4 m diameter has a surface charge density of 80.0 $\mu C/m^2$.

(a) Find the charge on the sphere.

(b) What is the total electric flux leaving the surface of the sphere?

Sol. Given, diameter of sphere = 2.4 m

Radius of sphere $r = \frac{2.4}{2} = 1.2$ m

Surface charge density $\sigma = 80 \mu C/m^2$

$= 80 \times 10^{-6} C/m^2$

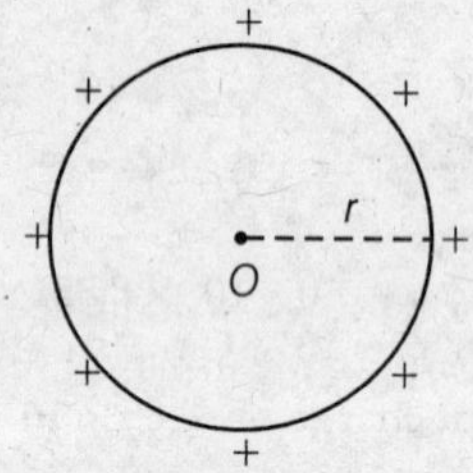

(a) Surface charge density $= \frac{\text{Charge}}{\text{Surface area}}$

$$\sigma = \frac{q}{4\pi r^2}$$

$$q = \sigma \times 4\pi r^2 = 80 \times 10^{-6} \times 4 \times 3.14 \times 1.2 \times 1.2$$

$$q = 1.45 \times 10^{-3} \text{C}$$

(b) Using Gauss's theorem,

Total electric flux leaving the surface $\phi = \frac{\text{Net charge}}{\varepsilon_0}$

$$\phi = \frac{q_{net}}{\varepsilon_0} = \frac{1.45 \times 10^{-3}}{8.854 \times 10^{-12}}$$

$$\phi = 1.6 \times 10^8 \text{ N-m}^2/\text{C}$$

Thus, the electric flux leaving the surface of sphere is 1.6×10^8 N-m^2/C.

Question 22 An infinite line charge produces a field of 9×10^4 N/C at a distance of 2 cm. Calculate the linear charge density.

Sol. Let λ be the linear charge density.

Given, distance $r = 2$ cm $= 2 \times 10^{-2}$ m

Electric field $E = 9 \times 10^4$ N/C.

Using the formula of electric field due to an infinite line charge

$$E = \frac{\lambda}{2\pi\varepsilon_0 r}$$

$$\lambda = 2\pi\varepsilon_0 r E$$

Putting the values, we get

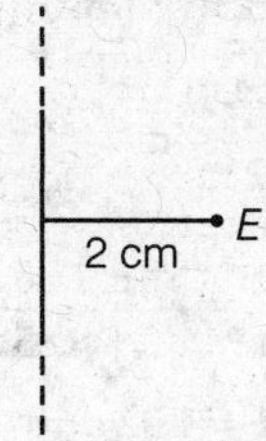

$$\lambda = 2 \times 3.14 \times 8.85 \times 10^{-12} \times 2 \times 10^{-2} \times 9 \times 10^4$$

$$\lambda = 10^{-7} \text{ C/m}$$

Thus, the linear charge density is 10^{-7} C/m.

Mistake Alert Verify each step when substituting values to ensure no missteps in arithmetic particularly when isolating λ.

Question 23 Two large, thin metal plates are parallel and closed to each other. On their inner faces, the plates have surface charge densities of opposite signs and of magnitude 17.0×10^{-22} C/m^2. What is E

(a) in the outer region of the first plate?

(b) in the outer region of the second plate?

(c) between the plates?

Sol. There are two plates A and B having surface charge densities $\sigma_A = 1.70 \times 10^{-22}$ C/m^2 on A and $\sigma_B = -17.0 \times 10^{-22}$ C/m^2 on B respectively.

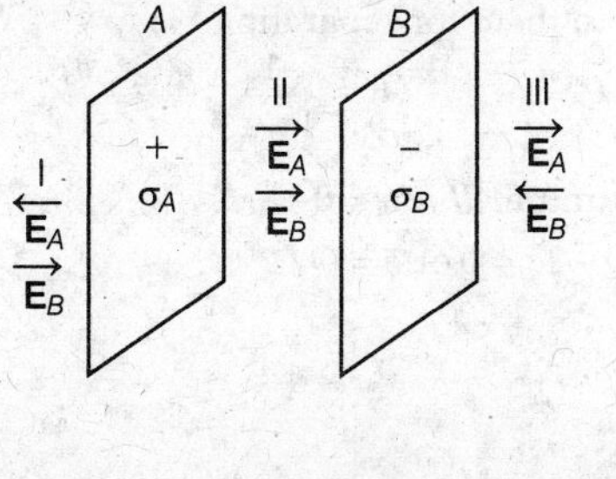

There are three regions

Region I is the outer region of first plate.

Region II is the region between the plates.

Region III is the outer region of the second plate.

(a) According to Gauss's theorem, if the plates have same surface charge density but having opposite signs, then the electric field in region I is zero.

$$\mathbf{E}_\mathrm{I} = \mathbf{E}_A - \mathbf{E}_B = \frac{|\sigma|}{2\varepsilon_0} - \left(\frac{|\sigma|}{2\varepsilon_0}\right) = 0 \text{ (as } \mathbf{E}_A \text{ and } \mathbf{E}_B \text{ are in opposite direction)}$$

(b) Similarly, the electric field in region III is also zero.

$$\mathbf{E}_\mathrm{III} = \mathbf{E}_A - \mathbf{E}_B = \frac{|\sigma|}{2\varepsilon_0} - \left(\frac{|\sigma|}{2\varepsilon_0}\right) = 0$$

(c) In region II, the electric field $= \frac{|\sigma|}{2\varepsilon_0} + \frac{|\sigma|}{2\varepsilon_0}$

$$= \frac{|\sigma|}{\varepsilon_0} = \frac{17.0 \times 10^{-22}}{8.85 \times 10^{-12}}$$

$$E = 1.92 \times 10^{-10} \text{ N/C}$$

DIKSHA APP Questions

☐ Very Short Answer Type

Q.1 In which orientation a dipole placed in uniform electric field is in (a) Stable, (b) unstable Equilibrium?

Sol. (a) For stable equilibrium the angle between p and E must be 0°

(b) For unstable equilibrium the angle between p and E must be 180°

Q.2 A charge Q is to be divided into two such parts, so that force between them when placed at some separation is maximum. Find the values of charges.

Sol. Let one of the part is q the other will be $(Q-q)$.

The force between them for separation r is

$$F = \frac{1}{4\pi \epsilon_0} \frac{q(Q-q)}{r^2}$$

For, F to be maximum, $dF/dq = 0$

or $\quad Q - 2q = 0$ or $q = Q/2$

□ Short Answer Type

Q.1 A glass rod rubbed with silk is brought close to two uncharged metallic spheres in contact with each other, inducing charges on them as shown in figurs. Describe what happens when

(i) the spheres are slightly separated, and

(ii) the glass rod is subsequently removed, and

(iii) the sphere are separated far apart.

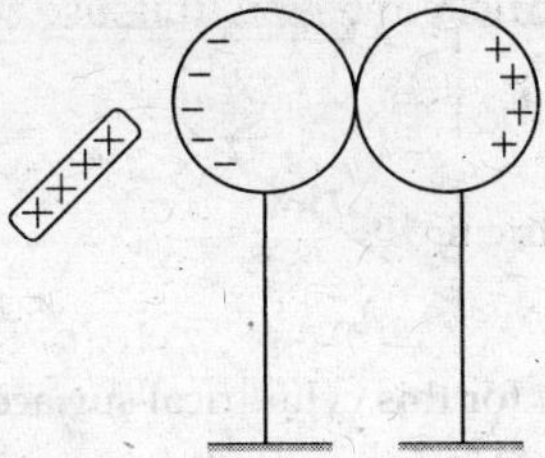

Sol.

(i) When spheres are slightly separated there will be little change in the distribution of charges.

(ii) When the glass rod is subsequently removed, the charges on the sphere are redistributed; positive and negative charges will face each other.

(iii) When spheres are separated far apart, charge on each sphere will be uniformly distributed.

□ Long Answer Type

Q.1 (a) Define electric flux. Write its SI units.

(b) Using Gauss's law, prove that electric field at a point due to uniformly charged infinite plane sheet is independent of the distance from it.

(c) How is the field directed if (i) the sheet is positively charged (ii) negatively charged

Sol.

(a) Electric flux is defined as the total number of electric field lines passing through a given surface area.
SI units: Nm^2C^{-1}

(b) Consider a uniformly charged infinite plane sheet of charge density σ. Consider a cylindrical Gaussian surface of cross- sectional area A and length 2π with its axis perpendicular to the sheet.

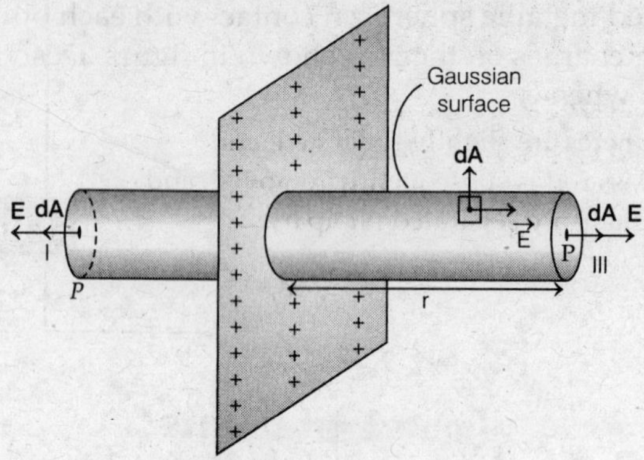

Applying Gauss Law for this cylindrical surface

$$\phi_E = \oint \mathbf{E} \cdot d\mathbf{A} = \frac{q}{\varepsilon_0}$$

$$= \oint_{1} \mathbf{E} \cdot d\mathbf{A} + \oint_{\text{II}} \mathbf{E} \cdot d\mathbf{A} + \oint_{\text{III}} \mathbf{E} \cdot d\mathbf{A} = \frac{q}{\varepsilon_0}$$

$$= \oint Ed\ A\ \cos 0^\circ + EdA \cos 90^\circ + EdA\ \cos 0^\circ = \frac{q}{\varepsilon_0}$$

$$= E \int dA + E \int dA = \frac{q}{\varepsilon_0}$$

$$= 2Ea = \frac{q}{\varepsilon_0} \quad \text{....(i)}$$

Total charge enclosed by the cylinder

$$q = \sigma A \quad \text{....(ii)}$$

From equation (i) and (ii)

$$2EA = \frac{\sigma A}{\varepsilon_0}$$

$$E = \frac{\sigma}{2\varepsilon_0}$$

(c) (i) If the sheet is positively charged *i.e.,* $\sigma > 0$ the field is directed away from it.

(ii) If the sheet is negatively charged *i.e.,* $\sigma < 0$ the field is directed towards it.

Electrostatic Potential and Capacitance

CHAPTER 02

Important Points

01 Electrostatic potential at a distance r from charge q,

$$V = \frac{1}{4\pi\varepsilon_0}\frac{q}{r} \quad \text{(volt)}$$

02 Electrostatic potential difference, $V_B - V_A = \frac{1}{4\pi\varepsilon_0} q\left[\frac{1}{r_B} - \frac{1}{r_A}\right]$

$$= \frac{W_{AB}}{q}$$

03 Electrostatic potential at a point due to a group of N charges,

$$V = \frac{1}{4\pi\varepsilon_0}\sum_{i=1}^{n}\frac{q_i}{r_i}$$

04 Relation between electric field and potential gradient is

$$E = -\frac{\partial V}{\partial r} \quad \text{or} \quad E_x = -\frac{\partial V}{\partial x},\ E_y = -\frac{\partial V}{\partial y},\ E_z = -\frac{\partial V}{\partial z}$$

05 Electrostatic potential energy of a system of two point charges,

$$U = \frac{1}{4\pi\varepsilon_0}\cdot\frac{q_1 q_2}{r}$$

(Put values of charges with their signs)

06 Potential energy of a system of three charges

$$U = \frac{1}{4\pi\varepsilon_0}\left[\frac{q_1 q_2}{r_1} + \frac{q_1 q_3}{r_2} + \frac{q_2 q_3}{r_3}\right]$$

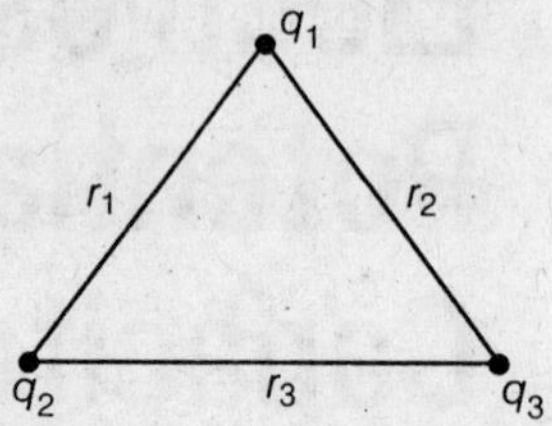

07 Electrostatic potential energy of a system of n point charges,

$$U = \frac{1}{4\pi\varepsilon_0} \cdot \sum_{\substack{i=1,\\ j=2}}^{n} \frac{q_i q_j}{r_{ij}}$$

08 Electrostatic potential due to an electric dipole at axial point,

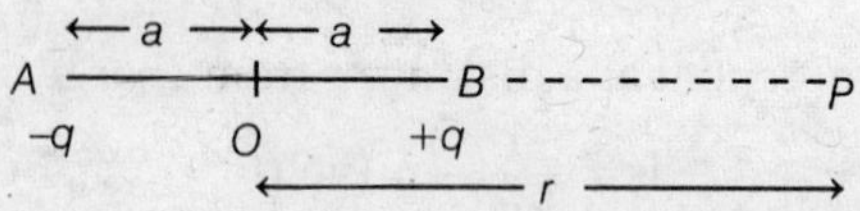

$$V = \frac{1}{4\pi\varepsilon_0} \cdot \frac{p}{r^2}$$

(where p = dipole moment)

09 Electrostatic potential due to an electric dipole at equatorial point,

$$V = \frac{1}{4\pi\varepsilon_0} \frac{q}{\sqrt{r^2 + a^2}} + \frac{1}{4\pi\varepsilon_0} \frac{-q}{\sqrt{r^2 + a^2}}$$

$$V = 0$$

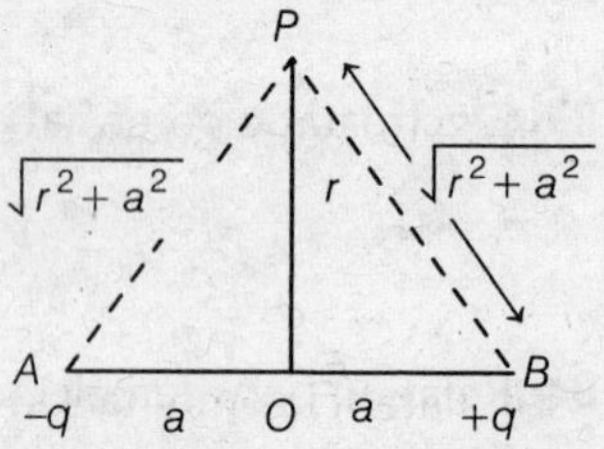

10 Electric potential due to a dipole at any arbitrary point

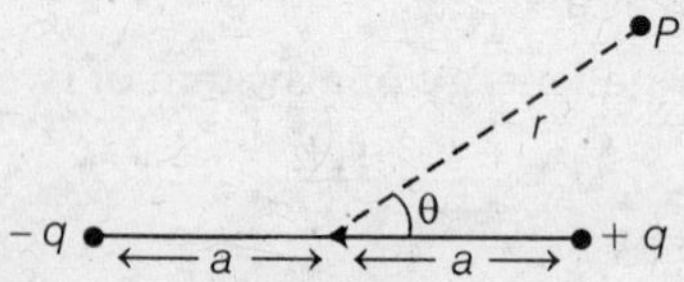

$$V = \frac{1}{4\pi\varepsilon_0} \cdot \frac{P\cos\theta}{(r^2 - a^2\cos^2\theta)}$$

11 Electrostatic potential due to an electric dipole at any arbitrary point, $V = \frac{1}{4\pi\varepsilon_0} \cdot \frac{\mathbf{p} \cdot \hat{\mathbf{r}}}{r^2}$

12 The Potential energy for a charge q in a potential V,

$$U = qV$$

13 The Potential energy of a dipole in electric field

$$U = -\mathbf{p}\cdot\mathbf{E}$$

14 Polarisation of a dielectric material in electric field.

$$p = \varepsilon_0 \chi_e E$$

Where χ_e is electric susceptibility

15 Capacitance $C = \dfrac{q}{V}$

16 Capacitance of a spherical conductor

$$C = 4\pi\varepsilon_0 r \qquad (r = \text{radius})$$

17 Capacitance of a parallel plate capacitor with air as dielectric

$$C = \frac{\varepsilon_0 A}{d}$$

(where A = area of plates and d = distance between plates)

18 Capacity of a parallel plate capacitor with insulating medium as dielectric

$$C = \frac{K\varepsilon_0 A}{d} \qquad (K = \text{dielectric constant})$$

19 Series combination of capacitances,

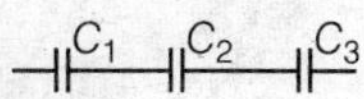

$$\frac{1}{C_s} = \frac{1}{C_1} + \frac{1}{C_2} + \frac{1}{C_3} + \dots \frac{1}{C_n}$$

20 Parallel combination of capacitances

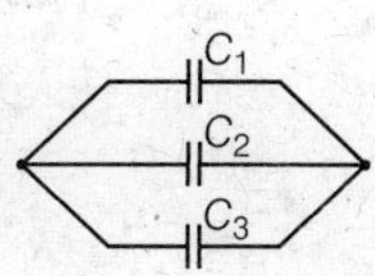

$$C_p = C_1 + C_2 + C_3 + \dots C_n$$

21 Energy stored in a capacitor

$$E = \frac{1}{2}QV = \frac{1}{2}\frac{Q^2}{C} = \frac{1}{2}CV^2$$

The electric energy density $\mu_E = \dfrac{1}{2} E_0 E^2$

22 Common potential $V = \dfrac{\text{total charge}}{\text{total capacitance}} = \dfrac{C_1 V_1 + C_2 V_2}{C_1 + C_2}$

23 Loss of energy on sharing charges $E_1 - E_2 = \dfrac{C_1 C_2 (V_1 - V_2)^2}{2(C_1 + C_2)}$

Exercises

Question 1 Two charges 5×10^{-8} C and -3×10^{-8} C are located 16 cm apart. At what point(s) on the line joining the two charges is the electric potential zero? Take the potential at infinity to be zero.

◎ ***Thinking Process*** Potential is zero at two points

- At line joining charges, between charges.
- At line joining charges, outside charges.

Sol.

(i) Let the potential be zero at point C at a distance x from point B.
Let us consider two charges q_1 and q_2. According to the question,
$q_1 = 5 \times 10^{-8}$ C, $q_2 = -3 \times 10^{-8}$ C, $AB = 16$ cm $= 16 \times 10^{-2}$ m

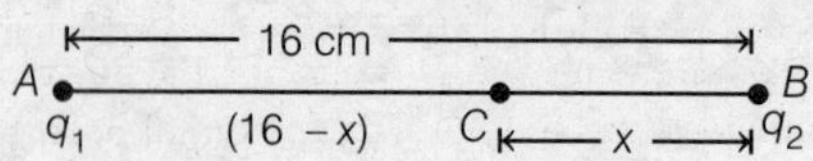

The potential at point C due to charge q_1

$$V_A = \frac{1}{4\pi\varepsilon_0} \cdot \frac{q_1}{AC} = \frac{9 \times 10^9 \times 5 \times 10^{-8}}{(16 - x) \times 10^{-2}} \quad \ldots\text{(i)}$$

The potential at point C due to charge q_2

$$V_B = \frac{1}{4\pi\varepsilon_0} \cdot \frac{q_2}{BC} = \frac{9 \times 10^9 \times (-3) \times 10^{-8}}{x \times 10^{-2}} \quad \ldots\text{(ii)}$$

Now the net potential at point C is zero *i.e.*, $V_A + V_B = 0$
Putting the values from Eqs. (i) and (ii), we get

$$\frac{9 \times 10^9 \times 5 \times 10^{-8}}{(16 - x) \times 10^{-2}} + \left(\frac{-9 \times 10^9 \times 3 \times 10^{-8}}{x \times 10^{-2}}\right) = 0$$

$$\frac{5}{16 - x} - \frac{3}{x} = 0$$

or $\quad 5x - 3(16 - x) = 0$

or $\quad 5x - 48 + 3x = 0$

or $\quad 8x = 48$

or $\quad x = 6$ cm

Thus, the electric potential is zero at the distance of 6 cm from $q_2 (= -3 \times 10^{-8}$ C).

(ii) Let potential is zero at a point C distance x from -3×10^{-8} C charge on line joining two charges outside the system of charges

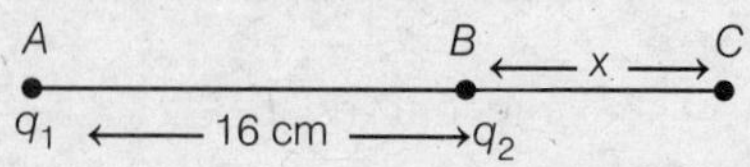

$$V_A = \frac{kq_1}{AC} = \frac{9 \times 10^9 \times 5 \times 10^{-8}}{(16 + x)}$$

$$V_B = \frac{kq_2}{BC} = \frac{9 \times 10^9 \times (-3 \times 10^{-8})}{x}$$

$$V_A + V_B = O \text{ (at C)}$$

$\therefore$ $$\frac{9 \times 10^9 \times 5 \times 10^{-8}}{16 + x} - \frac{9 \times 3 \times 10^9 \times 10^{-8}}{x} = 0$$

$\Rightarrow$ $$\frac{5}{16 + x} - \frac{3}{x} = 0 \Rightarrow 5x - 48 - 3x = 0$$

$\Rightarrow$ $$x = 24 \text{ cm}$$

The net potential is zero at the distance of 24cm from B.

Question 2 A regular hexagon of side 10 cm has a charge 5 μC at each of its vertices. Calculate the potential at the centre of the hexagon.

◎ **Thinking Process** It is based on the potential due to n number of charges and total potential is equal to the algabraic sum of potential produced by individual charges.

Sol. $ABCDEF$ is a regular hexagon of side 10 cm each. At each corner the charge $q = 5\mu C$ is placed. O is the centre of the hexagon.

Given, $$AB = BC = CD = DE = EF = FA = 10 \text{ cm}$$

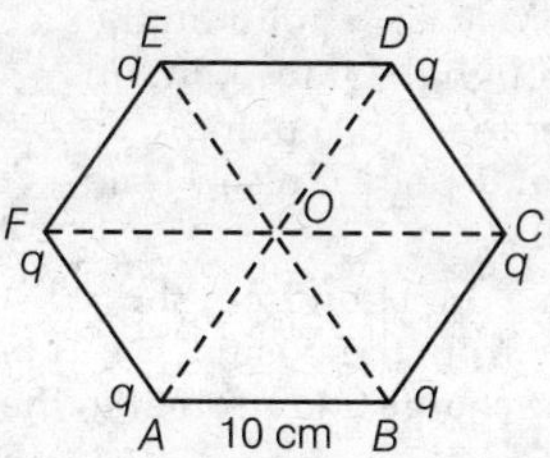

As the hexagon has six equilateral triangles, so the distance of centre O from every vertex is 10 cm.

i.e. $$OA = OB = OC = OD = OE = OF = 10 \text{ cm} = 10 \times 10^{-2} \text{m}$$

Potential at point O = Algabraic sum of potential at centre O due to individual point charges.

$\therefore$ $$V_O = V_A + V_B + V_C + V_D + V_E + V_F$$

$$V_O = \frac{1}{4\pi\varepsilon_0} \cdot \left[\frac{q}{OA} + \frac{q}{OB} + \frac{q}{OC} + \frac{q}{OD} + \frac{q}{OE} + \frac{q}{OF}\right] \quad \left(\because V = \frac{1}{4\pi\varepsilon_0} \cdot \frac{q}{r}\right)$$

Putting the values,

$$V_O = 9\times10^9\left[\frac{5\times10^{-6}}{10\times10^{-2}}+\frac{5\times10^{-6}}{10\times10^{-2}}+\frac{5\times10^{-6}}{10\times10^{-2}}+\frac{5\times10^{-6}}{10\times10^{-2}}+\frac{5\times10^{-6}}{10\times10^{-2}}+\frac{5\times10^{-6}}{10\times10^{-2}}\right]$$

or $$V_O = 9\times10^9\times\frac{5\times10^{-6}\times6}{10\times10^{-2}}$$

$$V_O = 2.7\times10^6\ \text{V}$$

Question 3 Two charges 2 μC and – 2 μC are placed at points A and B; 6 cm apart.

(a) Identify an equipotential surface of the system.

(b) What is the direction of the electric field at every point on this surface?

Sol. (a) Equipotential surface means the surface where potential remains same at each point.

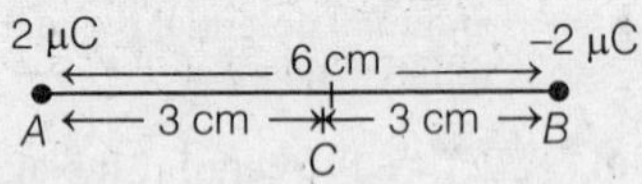

∴ The potential at C

$$V=\frac{1}{4\pi\varepsilon_0}\left[\frac{2\times10^{6}}{0.03}+\frac{(-2\times10^{-6})}{0.03}\right]=0$$

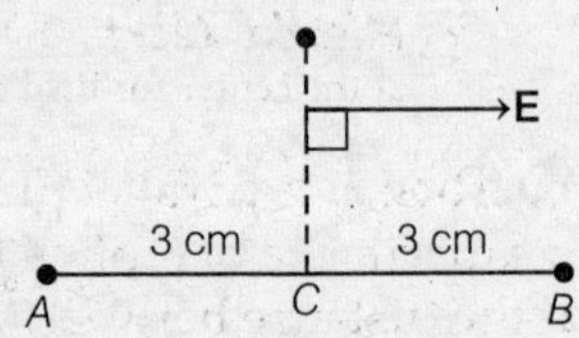

So, the potential is zero at each point on the line which passes through the mid-point of AB and perpendicular to it. So, a plane passing through the mid-point C of AB is an equipotential surface.

(b) The electric field is in a direction from the point A to point B i.e., from the positive charge to the negative charge and normal to the equipotential surface.

Question 4 A spherical conductor of radius 12 cm has a charge of 1.6×10^{-7} C distributed uniformly on its surface. What is the electric field

(a) inside the sphere?

(b) just outside the sphere?

(c) at a point 18 cm from the centre of the sphere?

◎ ***Thinking Process*** Charge uniformly distributed over a spherical conductor behaves as total charge is present at its centre.

Sol. Radius of spherical conductor $(r) = 12$ cm $= 0.12$ m and charge on conductor $(q) = 1.6 \times 10^{-7}$ C.

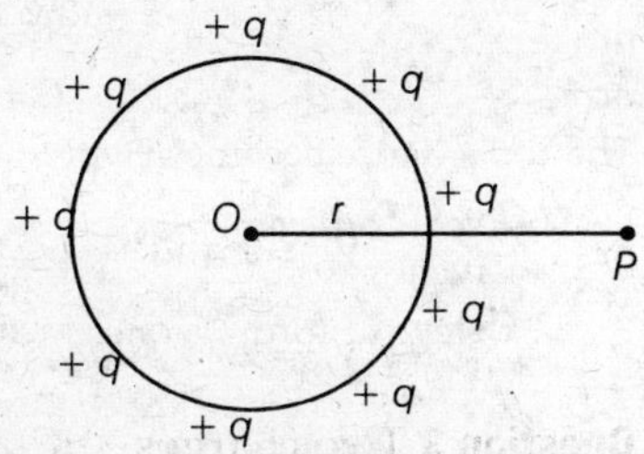

(a) The electric field inside a sphere is zero because the net enclosed charge within any internal gaussian surface is zero.

(b) For a point just outside the sphere or for a point lying on the surface of the sphere, the charge may be supposed to be concentrated on the centre of the sphere by using the formula of electric field.

$$E = \frac{1}{4\pi\varepsilon_0} \cdot \frac{q}{r^2} = \frac{9 \times 10^9 \times 1.6 \times 10^{-7}}{0.12 \times 0.12}$$

$$= 1 \times 10^5 \text{ N/C}$$

(c) Now, we have to find the electric field at point P, where $OP = 18$ cm $= 0.18$ m

Using the formula of electric field

$$E = \frac{1}{4\pi\varepsilon_0} \frac{q}{(OP)^2} = \frac{9 \times 10^9 \times 1.6 \times 10^{-7}}{0.18 \times 0.18} = 4.4 \times 10^4 \text{ N/C}$$

Mistake Alert Outside the conductor, treat the charge as it is concentrated at the center for field calculations.

Question 5 A parallel plate capacitor with air between the plates has a capacitance of 8 pF (1 pF $= 10^{-12}$ F). What will be the capacitance, if the distance between the plates is reduced by half and the space between them is filled with a substance of dielectric constant 6?

Sol. Let initially the distance between the plates be d and air be filled between the plates. Now, the capacitance is C_0.

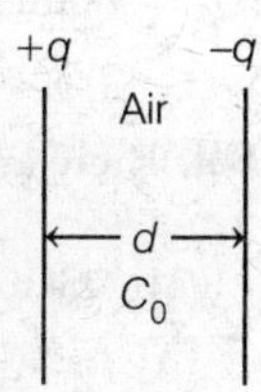

$$C_0 = 8 \text{ pF} = 8 \times 10^{-12} \text{ F}$$

Using the formula of capacitance of a parallel plate capacitor, we get

$$C_0 = \frac{\varepsilon_0 A}{d}$$

(where A is the area of plates and d is the distance between two plates)

$$8 \times 10^{-12} = \frac{\varepsilon_0 A}{d} \quad \text{...(i)}$$

Now, the distance between the plates is reduced to half, $d' = \frac{d}{2}$ and the space between the plates is filled with a dielectric of dielectric constant $K = 6$. Now, let the new capacitance be C. In this condition area remains same.

$$\therefore \quad C = \frac{K\varepsilon_0 A}{d'} \quad \text{(where } K \text{ is the dielectric constant)}$$

$$C = \frac{\varepsilon A}{d} \cdot 2$$

or $$C = 12 \times 8 \times 10^{-12}$$ [From Eq. (i)]

or $$C = 96 \times 10^{-12} \text{ F} = 96$$

The capacitance becomes 96 pF.

Quick Solution

Given $C = 8pF = 8 \times 10^{-12} F$

Using the formula of capacitance of parallel plate capacitor, we get

$$C_0 = \frac{\epsilon_0 A}{d}$$

if $d' = \frac{d}{2}$ and $k = 6$

$$\therefore \quad C = 12 \frac{\epsilon_0 A}{d'} = 12C_0 \qquad [\because C = KC_0]$$

$$C = 12 \times 8 \times 10^{-12} = 96 \times 10^{-12} F = 96 \text{ pF}$$

Mistake Alert Do not avoid skipping the relation $d' = \frac{d}{2}$ as its crucial for correct calculations. Do not forget to multiply by K after considering the dielectric material.

Question 6 Three capacitors each of capacitance 9 pF are connected in series.

(a) What is the total capacitance of the combination?

(b) What is the potential difference across each capacitor, if the combination is connected to a 120 V supply?

Thinking Process Use the formula of equivalent capacitance when two or more capacitors are connected in series and remember that charges at the plates of each capacitor in series remain same and potential across each capacitor is different.

Sol. There are three capacitors each of capacitance 9 pF.

$$\therefore \quad C_1 = C_2 = C_3 = 9 \text{ pF} \text{ and voltage } V = 120 \text{ V}$$

(a) The total capacitance in series combination

$$\frac{1}{C_s} = \frac{1}{C_1} + \frac{1}{C_2} + \frac{1}{C_3} = \frac{1}{9} + \frac{1}{9} + \frac{1}{9}$$

$$\frac{1}{C_s} = \frac{3}{9} \Rightarrow C_s = 3 \text{ pF}$$

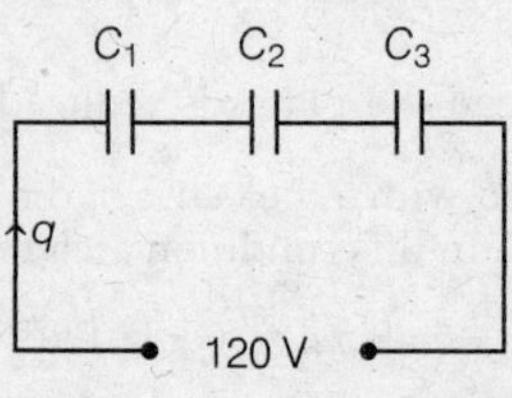

(b) Let the charge across the system be q and potentials across C_1, C_2 and C_3 be V_1, V_2 and V_3 respectively.

Charge $q = C_s . V = 3 \times 120 = 360$ pC

Potential difference across C_1, $(V_1) = \frac{q}{C_1} = \frac{360}{9} = 40$ V

Potential difference across C_2, $(V_2) = \frac{q}{C_2} = \frac{360}{9} = 40$ V

Potential difference across C_3, $(V_3) = \frac{q}{C_3} = \frac{360}{9} = 40$ V

Thus, the potential difference across each capacitor is 40 V.

Mistake Alert In this type of problem remember that charge Q is constant in a series combination, while potential divides among capacitors. Carefully apply $Q = CV$ for individual capacitors to avoid mixing up C_{total} with C_1, C_2, C_3.

Question 7 Three capacitors of capacitances 2 pF, 3 pF and 4 pF are connected in parallel.

(a) What is the total capacitance of the combination?

(b) Determine the charge on each capacitor, if the combination is connected to a 100 V supply.

Thinking Process Use the formula of equivalent capacitance when two or more capacitors are connected in parallel and remember that potential difference across the plates of each capacitor remains same in parallel and charge at plates of each capacitor is different.

Sol. Given, $C_1 = 2$ pF, $C_2 = 3$ pF and $C_3 = 4$ pF

(a) The total capacitance of the parallel combination is given by

$$C_p = C_1 + C_2 + C_3 = 2 + 3 + 4 = 9 \text{ pF}.$$

(b) Let the charges on the capacitors C_1, C_2 and C_3 be q_1, q_2 and q_3 respectively. The potential difference across each of the capacitors is same as 100 V.

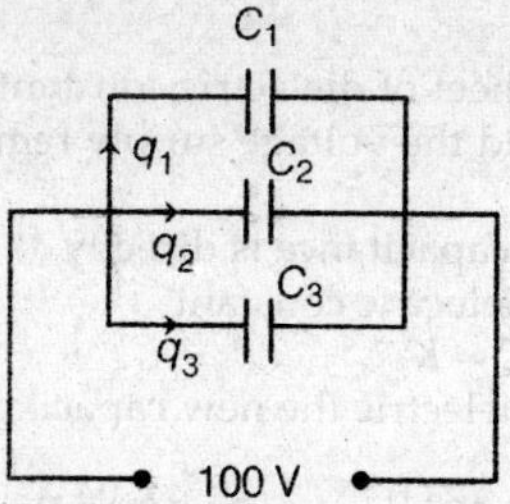

Charge q_1 at $C_1 = C_1 V = 2 \times 100 = 200$ pC

Charge q_2 at $C_2 = C_2 V = 3 \times 100 = 300$ pC

Charge q_3 at $C_3 = C_3 V = 4 \times 100 = 400$ pC

Question 8 In a parallel plate capacitor with air between the plates, each plate has an area of 6×10^{-3} m^2 and the distance between the plates is 3 mm. Calculate the capacitance of the capacitor. If this capacitor is connected to a 100 V supply, what is the charge on each plate of the capacitor?

◎ ***Thinking Process*** To calculate the capacitance of a parallel plate capacitor.

capacitance is $C = \dfrac{\varepsilon_0 A}{d}$.

Sol. Area of plates $(A) = 6 \times 10^{-3}$ m^2

Distance between plates $(d) = 3$ mm $= 3 \times 10^{-3}$ m

and potential $V = 100$ V

Capacitance of a parallel plate capacitor

$$C = \frac{\varepsilon_0 A}{d} = \frac{8.854 \times 10^{-12} \times 6 \times 10^{-3}}{3 \times 10^{-3}}$$

$$C = 1.77 \times 10^{-11} \text{ F}$$

When the capacitor is connected to a 100 V supply, charge on each plate of the capacitor $q = CV = 1.77 \times 10^{-11} \times 100$

$$q = 1.77 \times 10^{-9} \text{ C}$$

Question 9 Explain what would happen, if in the capacitor given in above Q.8, a 3 mm thick mica sheet (of dielectric constant = 6) were inserted between the plates,

(a) while the voltage supply remained connected?

(b) after the supply was disconnected?

◎ ***Thinking Process*** Whenever a dielectric is placed in between the plates of a parallel plate capacitor, then its capacitance increases (it becomes K times the capacitance when there is air in between the plates, where K = dielectric constant).

Sol.

(a) As we insert a mica sheet of dielectric constant $K = 6$ between the plates and the voltage supply remained connected.

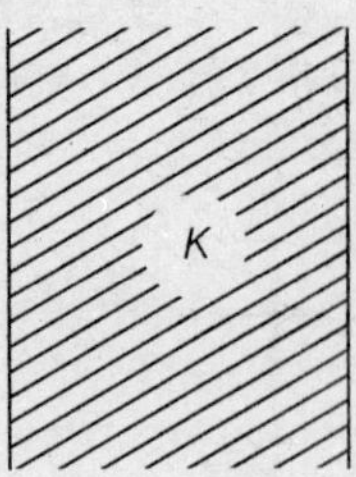

As we know that the capacitance is directly proportional to the dielectric constant.

$$C \propto K$$

So, as we insert the dielectric the new capacitance becomes

$$C' = CK = 6 \times 1.77 \times 10^{-11} = 1.062 \times 10^{-10} \text{ F}$$

Now, we see that the capacitance increases, so the charge will also increase.

Charge on the capacitor is $q' = C'V = 1.062 \times 10^{-10} \times 100$

or $q' = 1.062 \times 10^{-8}$ C

(b) When the voltage supply was disconnected, charge of the capacitor remains the same.
New capacitance after inserting the dielectric $C' = CK = 6 \times 1.77 \times 10^{-11}$ $= 1.062 \times 10^{-10}$ F

$$C' = 1.062 \times 10^{-10} \text{ F}$$

The potential difference across the plates of the capacitor

$$V' = \frac{q'}{C'} = \frac{1.77 \times 10^{-9}}{1.062 \times 10^{-10}} = 16.67 \text{ V}$$

or use $$V' = \frac{V}{K} = \frac{100}{6} = 16.67 \text{ V}$$

Note When the battery remains connected and dielectric is inserted between plates of capacitor the capacity of the capacitor and charge stored is changed. When the battery disconnected and dielectric is inserted between plates of capacitor, charge remains same but the capacitance and potential change.

Question 10 A 12 pF capacitor is connected to a 50 V battery. How much electrostatic energy is stored in the capacitor?

Sol. Given, voltage connected across the capacitor $V = 50$ V and Capacitance of the capacitor $C = 12 \text{ pF} = 12 \times 10^{-12}$ F

Energy stored in the capacitor

$$E = \frac{1}{2}CV^2 = \frac{1}{2} \times 12 \times 10^{-12} \times 50 \times 50 = 1.5 \times 10^{-8} \text{ J}$$

Question 11 A 600 pF capacitor is charged by a 200 V supply. Then, it is disconnected from the supply and is connected to another uncharged 600 pF capacitor. How much electrostatic energy is lost in the process?

◎ **Thinking Process** When one charged and another uncharged capacitor connected, the energy is transferred from charged capacitor to another uncharged capacitor. In this process, there is a loss in energy in the form of heat in connecting wire.

Sol. Given, capacitance of capacitor $C_1 = 600 \text{ pF} = 600 \times 10^{-12}$ F and supply voltage $V_1 = 200$ V

$$C_2 = 600 \text{ pF} = 600 \times 10^{-12} \text{ F and } V_2 = 0 \text{ (uncharged)}$$

$$\text{Loss in energy } (E) = \frac{C_1C_2(V_1 - V_2)^2}{2(C_1 + C_2)}$$

$$E = \frac{600 \times 10^{-12} \times 600 \times 10^{-12} (200 - 0)^2}{2(600 + 600) \times 10^{-12}} = 6 \times 10^{-6} \text{ J}$$

Thus, the 6×10^{-6} J amount of electrostatic energy is lost in the sharing of charges.

DIKSHA APP Questions

☐ Multiple Choice Questions

Q.1 Work done for bringing a charge q from infinity to a point in space is

(a) Positive

(b) Negative

(c) Zero

(d) Depends on the presence of electric field

Sol. (d) The work done in bringing a charge from infinity to a point depends on the electric field at that point. If the point is in the field of another charge, work is done either against or with the field, depending on the nature of the charge and the direction of movement.

Q.2 Which of the following condition leads to negative potential energy between two charges ?

(a) One charge is negative and other charge is positive

(b) Repulsive electrostatic force

(c) Both (a) and (b)

(d) None of the above

Sol. (a) $U = \frac{1}{4\pi\varepsilon_0}\frac{q_1 q_2}{r}$

When one charge is negative and the other is positive, they attract each other. The potential energy between them is negative because work is required to separate the charges, indicating an attractive interaction. Repulsive forces lead to positive potential energy.

Q.3 Potential in the equatorial plane of the dipole is

(a) Negative

(b) Positive

(c) Zero

(d) Depends on distance from the centre of dipole

Sol. (c) $V = V_1 + V_2 = \frac{1}{4\pi\varepsilon_0}\frac{q}{r} + \frac{1}{4\pi\varepsilon_0}\frac{-q}{r} = 0$

Q.4 For system of charges, the total potential at a point depends upon

(a) Charges

(b) Position of point with respect to charges

(c) Nature of medium

(d) All of the above

Sol. (d) The total potential at a point in a system of charges depends on the magnitudes and positions of the charges, the location of the point with respect to the charges and the nature of the medium.

Q.5 Two point charges q and $-2q$ are kept at distance d apart. At what point, potential due to the charges is zero ?

(a) At a distance $d/2$ from charge q
(b) At a distance $d/2$ from charge $-2q$
(c) At a distance $d/3$ from charge q
(d) At a distance $d/3$ from charge $-2q$

Sol. (c) Let potential be zero at point C, which is at distance x from charge q.

$$V_C = V_A + V_B = 0$$

$$\frac{1}{4\pi\varepsilon_0}\frac{q}{x} + \frac{1}{4\pi\varepsilon_0}\frac{2q}{d-x} = 0$$

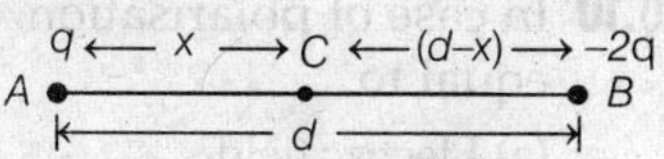

$$\frac{1}{4\pi\varepsilon_0}\frac{q}{x} = \frac{1}{4\pi\varepsilon_0}\frac{2q}{d-x}$$

$$d - x = 2x \Rightarrow d = 3x \Rightarrow x = \frac{d}{3}$$

Q.6 Which of the following is true about electrostatic potential for a point charge ?

(a) It is inversely proportional to distance
(b) it is the product of charge and work done
(c) Electric field and potential can never be equal in magnitude
(d) Both 1 and 3

Sol. (a) $V = \frac{1}{4\pi\varepsilon_0}\frac{q}{r} \Rightarrow V \propto \frac{1}{r}$

Q.7 Which of the following is true for brining a positive test charge close to a negative charge Q ?

(a) $W > 0, V > 0$
(b) $W > 0, V > 0$
(c) $W < 0, V < 0$
(d) None of these

Sol. (c) $W = U = \frac{1}{4\pi\varepsilon_0}\frac{(-Q)q}{r} = -W < 0$

$$V = \frac{1}{4\pi\varepsilon_0}\frac{(-Q)}{r} = -V_e < 0$$

Q.8 For constant potential on the surface, the value of electric field is

(a) Zero
(b) Negative
(c) Positive
(d) Infinity

Sol. (a) $E = \frac{-dV}{dr}$

If $$0 = \frac{-dV}{dr}$$

$\Rightarrow$ $$V = \text{constant}$$

Q.9 Which of the following is NOT a equipotential surface ?

(a) Sphere with a point charge at its centre
(b) Infinitely long sheet with charge at the centre
(c) Non-interesting spheres in case of a dipole
(d) All of the above

Sol. (b) Option (b) is correct.

Q.10 In case of polarisation, polarisation density is numerically equal to

(a) Electric field
(b) Charge induced per unit area
(c) Dielectric constant
(d) Electrical susceptibility

Sol. (b) Polarisation density $= \frac{\text{induced dipole moment}}{\text{Volume}} = \frac{q' \times 2a}{A \times 2a} = \frac{q'}{A}$

Q.11 Under what condition, non-polar dielectric behaves as polar dielectric ?

(a) In the absence of electric field
(b) In the presence of large external electric field
(c) In the presence of small external electric field
(d) None of the above

Sol. (b) Non polar dielectric become polarised in presence of large external electric field as electric force on charges separate the non polar molecules.

Q.12 Two point charges $+10\,\mu C$ and $-10\,\mu C$ are separated by a distance of 2 cm in water of dielectric constant 80. The potential energy of the system is

(a) -45 J (b) -0.56 J
(c) $+45$ J (d) $+0.56$ J

Sol. (b) $U = \frac{1}{4\pi\varepsilon_0 k} \frac{q_1 q_2}{r}$

$$= \frac{9 \times 10^9 \times 10 \times 10^{-6} \times (-10 \times 10^{-6})}{80 \times 2 \times 10^{-2}}$$

$$= \frac{-90 \times 10^{-1}}{16} = -0.56 \text{ J}$$

Q.13 Which of the following angle has minimum potential energy when dipole is placed in uniform electric field ?

(a) 0° (b) 180°
(c) 90° (d) 45°

Sol. (a) $U = -pE\cos\theta$

$= -pE\cos\theta = -pE = \text{Minimum}$

Q.14 Two plates have net charge 70 pC and −70 pC connected to a potential of 20 V. The capacitance of the system is

(a) 3.5 pF (b) 7 pF (c) 7 pC (d) 10.5 pF

Sol. (a) Capacitance is given by

$$C = \frac{q}{V} = \frac{70\,pC}{20} = 3.5\text{ pF}$$

Q.15 Which form of energy is stored in a capacitor during its charging ?

(a) Chemical energy (b) Heat energy
(c) Electrical potential energy (d) Sound energy

Sol. (c) Electrical potential energy $U = \frac{1}{2}CV^2$ or $\frac{1}{2}\frac{q^2}{C}$ or $\frac{1}{2}qV$ Joule.

☐ Short Answer Type

Q.1 How the energy of parallel plate capacitor changes if area of the plate reduces to half, the distance between the plate increases to four times and medium is replaced fro vacuum to a medium of dielectric constant 5.

Sol. New area $= A/2$

New distance $= 4d$ dielectric constant, $K = 5$

Initial energy of parallel plate capacitor

$$U_1 = \frac{1}{2}CV^2 \quad \ldots\text{(i)}$$

where $C = \frac{A\varepsilon_0}{d}$

Change in capacitance

$$C_2 = \frac{K\frac{A}{2}\varepsilon_0}{4d} = \frac{K}{8}\frac{A\varepsilon_0}{d} = \frac{5}{8}\frac{A\varepsilon_0}{d} = \frac{5}{8}C$$

Final energy of parallel plate capacitor

$$U_2 = \frac{1}{2}C_2V^2 = \frac{1}{2}\times\frac{5}{8}CV^2 = \frac{5}{8}\times\frac{1}{2}CV^2 = \frac{5}{8}U_1$$

Hence, we obtain new energy $\frac{5}{8}$ times the initial energy.

Q.2 Can two equipotential surfaces intersect each other ?

Sol. No, two equipotential surfaces never intersect each other as at point of intersection there will be two values of potential which is impossible.

Q.3 What would be work done if a point charge $+q$, is taken from one point to another point on an equipotential surface ?

Sol.

$$V_B - V_A = \frac{W_{AB}}{q_0} \quad [\because V_A = V_B \text{ (equipotential surface)}]$$

$$0 = \frac{W_{AB}}{q_0} \Rightarrow W_{AB} = 0$$

Q.4 Does the electric potential increases or decreases along the electric field lines ?

Sol. Electric potential decreases along the electric field lines as $E = \frac{-dV}{dr}$.

Q.5 Sixty-four drops of same size are charged at 110 volt each. They coalesce to form a bigger drop. Calculate the potential of the bigger drop.

Sol. Let the radius of small drops be r and radius of big drop be R volume of 64 small drops = Volume of 1 big drop

$$64 \times \frac{4}{3}\pi r^3 = \frac{4}{3}\pi R^3$$

$$4r = R \quad \text{...(i)}$$

Potential of small drop

$$V = \frac{1}{4\pi\varepsilon_0}\frac{q}{r} = 110 \text{ V} \quad \text{...(ii)}$$

potential of big drop $V = \frac{1}{4\pi\varepsilon_0}\frac{64q}{R} = \frac{1}{4\pi\varepsilon_0}\frac{64q}{4r}$ by using Eq. (i)

$$V = \frac{1}{4\pi\varepsilon_0}\frac{q}{R} \times 16 = 110 \times 16 = 1760 \text{ V}$$

Q.7 In a parallel plate capacitor, the capacitance increases from 3 micro farad to 30 micro farad, on introducing a dielectric medium between the plates. What is the dielectric constant of the medium ?

Sol. Given : Capacitance without dielectrics $C_0 = 3\ \mu F$

Capacitance with dielectrics $C = 30\ \mu F$

Dielectric constant $K = \frac{C}{C_0} = \frac{30\mu F}{3\mu F} = 10$

Q.8 How would you connect two capacitors across a battery, in series or parallel, so that they store greater (i) total charge and (ii) total energy ?

Sol. Total charge, $q = CV \quad \therefore q \propto C$

Total energy, $U = \frac{1}{2}CV^2 \quad \therefore U \propto C$

Since equivalent capacitance C_p in parallel combination ($C_p = C_1 + C_2 + ... C_n$) is greater than equivalent capacitance in series combination $\left(\frac{1}{C_S} = \frac{1}{C_1} + \frac{1}{C_2} + ... \frac{1}{C_n}\right)$

$\therefore$ Capacitors must be connected in parallel combination.

Q.9 n identical capacitors are joined in parallel and the combination is given a potential difference V. If these capacitors be disconnected and joined in series, what potential difference will be obtained across the combination ?

Sol. When the capacitors are connected in parallel then the potential difference across each capacitor will be same V. When the capacitors are connected in series, the potential difference across each capacitor will be added. The potential difference across the series combination will be nV.

Current Electricity

CHAPTER 03

Important Points

01 Electric current $I = \frac{q}{t} = \frac{ne}{t}$

02 Current density $\mathbf{J} = \frac{I}{\mathbf{A}}$

03 Drift velocity of electrons

$$v_d = \frac{eE\tau}{m} = \frac{ve\tau}{ml} \qquad \left[\because E = \frac{v}{l}\right]$$

04 Mobility of free electrons $\mu = \frac{\mathbf{v}_d}{\mathbf{E}} = \frac{e\tau}{m}$

05 Relation between drift velocity v_d and free electrons density (n),

$$v_d = \frac{I}{Ane}$$

06 Ohm's law $\frac{V}{I} = R = \frac{ml}{Ane^2\tau} = \text{constant}$

where, R is called electrical resistance.

or vector form of ohm's law $\mathbf{J} = \sigma\mathbf{E}$

07 Resistivity or specific resistance $\rho = \frac{RA}{l} = \frac{m}{ne^2\tau}$

08 In series combination of resistors,

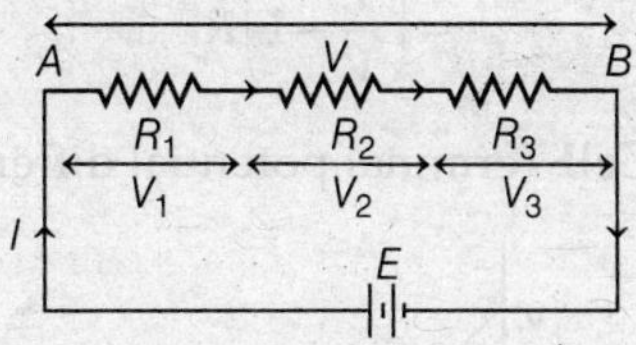

$$R_{eq} = R_1 + R_2 + R_3$$

and total potential drop $V = V_1 + V_2 + V_3$.

09 In parallel combination of resistors,

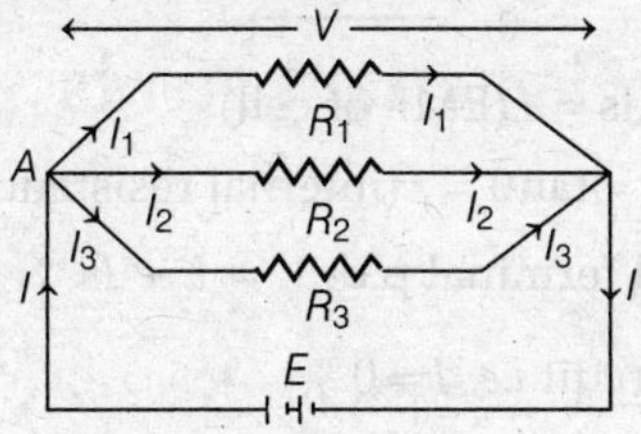

$$\frac{1}{R_{eq}} = \frac{1}{R_1} + \frac{1}{R_2} + \frac{1}{R_3}$$

Total current drawn $I = I_1 + I_2 + I_3$

10 Temperature dependence of resistance $R_2 = R_1 (1 + \alpha \Delta t)$

[$R_2 \to$ Resistance at t_2° C, $R_2 \to$ Resistance at t_1°C]

and temperature coefficient of Resistance $\alpha = \dfrac{R_2 - R_1}{R_1(t_2 - t_1)}$

11 Current from cell in closed circuit $I = \dfrac{E}{(R + r)}$

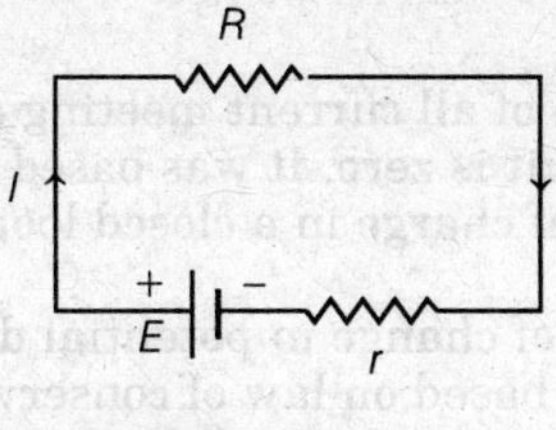

12 Internal Resistance of Cell Resistance offered by electrolyte of cell

$$r = \left(\frac{E}{V} - 1\right)R$$

13 Discharging of Cell Terminal potential difference $V = E - Ir$

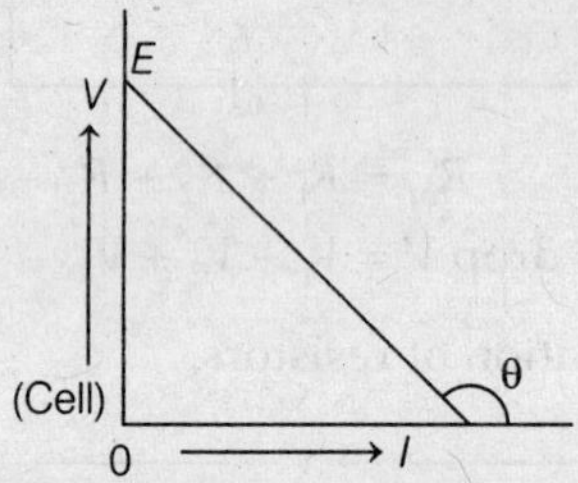

intercept on Y-axis = E(EMF of cell)

negative slope $m = \tan\theta = r$ (internal resistance of cell).

14 Charging of Cell terminal p.d. $V = E + Ir$

15 Cell is in open circuit *i.e.* $I = 0$

terminal potential difference V = EMF of cell (E)

16 Conductance $G = \frac{1}{\text{Electrical resistance } (R)} \Omega^{-1}$

17 Conductivity $\sigma = \frac{1}{\text{Resistivity } (\rho)} (\Omega \text{m})^{-1}$

18 Joule's law of heating

$$H = I^2 Rt = VIt = \frac{V^2}{R} t \text{ joule} \qquad [\because V = IR]$$

19 Power dissipated

$$P = \frac{W}{t} = I^2 R = VI = \frac{V^2}{R} \text{ watt}$$

20 Kirchhoff's Laws

(a) **Algebraic sum of all current meeting at a junction of an electrical circuit is zero. It was based on law of conservation of charge in a closed loop of an electrical circuit.**

(b) **Algebraic sum of change in potential difference is zero in *a* closed loop. It based on law of conservation of energy.**

(i) Junction law, $\Sigma I = 0$; (ii) Loop law, $\Sigma \Delta V = 0$

21 Wheatstone bridge $\frac{P}{Q} = \frac{R}{S}$ (Balanced Condition)

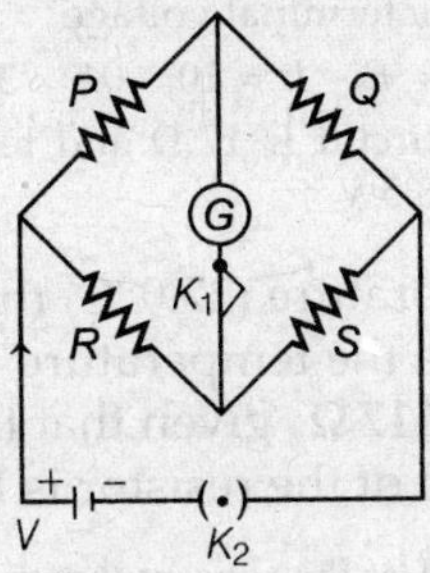

Exercises

Question 1 The storage battery of a car has an emf of 12 V. If the internal resistance of the battery is 0.4 Ω, what is the maximum current that can be drawn from the battery?

◎ *Thinking Process* To find the maximum current, use the concept that the current is maximum, if the external load resistance is zero.

Sol. Given, emf $E = 12$ V, internal resistance $r = 0.4\Omega$

$\therefore$ Current drawn from the battery $I = \frac{E}{R + r}$

In case of maximum current, $R = 0$

$$\therefore \quad I_{max} = \frac{E}{r} = \frac{12}{0.4} = 30 \text{ A}$$

Question 2 A battery of emf 10 V and internal resistance 3 Ω is connected to a resistor. If the current in the circuit is 0.5 A, what is the resistance of the resistor? What is the terminal voltage of the battery when the circuit is closed?

Sol. Given, emf of battery, $E = 10$ V

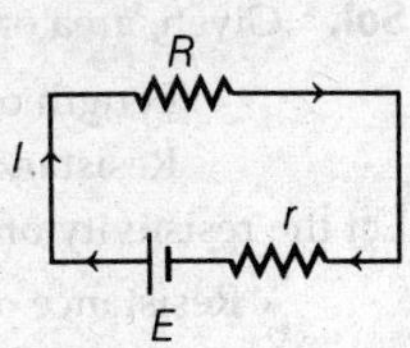

Internal resistance, $r = 3\ \Omega$

Current in circuit, $I = 0.5$ A

The current in the circuit $= \frac{\text{emf}}{\text{Total resistance of the circuit}}$

$$I = \frac{E}{R + r}$$

$$\therefore \quad 0.5 = \frac{10}{R + 3}$$

or $R + 3 = 20$

$R = 17\Omega$

When the circuit is closed, the terminal voltage

$$V = E - Ir = 10 - 0.5 \times 3 = 10 - 1.5 = 8.5\text{ V}$$

Thus, the resistance in the circuit is 17 Ω and terminal voltage of the battery when the circuit is closed, is 8.5 V.

Question 3 At room temperature (27.0°C) the resistance of a heating element is 100 Ω. What is the temperature of the element, if the resistance is found to be 117 Ω, given that the temperature coefficient of the material of the resistor is $1.70 \times 10^{-4}\ °C^{-1}$.

◎ ***Thinking Process*** Use the concept that the resistance of a heating element increases with increase in temperature.

Sol. Given, the resistance of heating element at temperature 27 °C

$$R_{27} = 100\Omega$$

Resistance of heating element at temperature $t°C = R_t = 117\Omega$

Temperature coefficient of resistance $\alpha = 1.70 \times 10^{-4}\ °C^{-1}$

Temperature coefficient of resistance

$$\alpha = \frac{R_t - R_{27}}{R_{27}(t - 27)}$$

$$1.70 \times 10^{-4} = \frac{117 - 100}{100\,(t - 27)}$$

or

$$t - 27 = \frac{17}{100 \times 1.70 \times 10^{-4}}$$

or

$$t = 1000 + 27 = 1027\ °C$$

Thus, the temperature of element is 1027 °C when its resistance is 117 Ω.

Question 4 A negligibly small current is passed through a wire of length 15 m and uniform cross-section $6.0 \times 10^{-7}\ m^2$ and its resistance is measured to be 5.0 Ω. What is the resistivity of the material at the temperature of the experiment?

Sol. Given, area of cross-section of wire $(A) = 6.0 \times 10^{-7}\ m^2$

Length of the wire $l = 15$ m

Resistance of wire $R = 5\ \Omega$

Let the resistivity of the material be ρ.

Resistance of wire $R = \rho \dfrac{l}{A}$

or

$$\rho = \frac{RA}{l} = \frac{5 \times 6.0 \times 10^{-7}}{15} = 2 \times 10^{-7}\ \Omega\text{-m}$$

Thus, the resistivity of the material at the temperature of the experiment is $2 \times 10^{-7}\Omega$-m.

Question 5 A silver wire has a resistance of 2.1 Ω at 27.5 °C and a resistance of 2.7 Ω at 100 °C. Determine the temperature coefficient of resistivity of silver.

Sol. Given, resistance of silver wire at 27.5 °C, $R_{27.5} = 2.1\,\Omega$

Resistance of silver wire at 100 °C, $R_{100} = 2.7\,\Omega$

Let the temperature coefficient of silver be α.

$$\alpha = \frac{R_{t_2} - R_{t_1}}{R_1\,(t_2 - t_1)}$$

$$\alpha = \frac{R_{100} - R_{27.5}}{R_{27.5}\,(100 - 27.5)} = \frac{2.7 - 2.1}{2.1 \times 72.5}$$

$$\alpha = 0.0039\ {}^\circ\text{C}^{-1}$$

Thus, the temperature coefficient of resistivity of silver is $0.0039\ {}^\circ\text{C}^{-1}$.

Note The temperature coefficient of resistivity indicates how much the resistivity of silver increases for every 1°C rise in temperature.

Question 6 A heating element using nichrome connected to a 230 V supply draws an initial current of 3.2 A which settles after a few seconds to a steady value of 2.8 A. What is the steady temperature of the heating element, if the room temperature is 27.0°C? Temperature coefficient of resistance of nichrome averaged over the temperature range involved is $1.70 \times 10^{-4}\ {}^\circ\text{C}^{-1}$.

Sol. Given, potential difference = 230 V

Initial current at 27°C = $I_{27^\circ\text{C}} = 3.2$

Final current at t°C = $I_{t^\circ\text{C}} = 2.8$

Room temperature = 27°C

Temperature coefficient of resistance,

$$\alpha = 1.70 \times 10^{-4}\ {}^\circ\text{C}^{-1}$$

Temperature coefficient of resistance

$$\alpha = \frac{R_t - R_{27}}{R_{27}\,(t - 27)}$$

$$= \frac{\dfrac{V}{I_{t^\circ\text{C}}} - \dfrac{V}{I_{27^\circ\text{C}}}}{\dfrac{V}{I_{27^\circ\text{C}}}(t - 27)} = \frac{I_{27^\circ\text{C}} - I_{t^\circ\text{C}}}{I_{t^\circ\text{C}}(t - 27)}$$

$$1.7 \times 10^{-4} = \frac{3.2 - 2.8}{2.8\,(t - 27)}$$

$$t - 27 = \frac{0.4}{2.8 \times 1.7 \times 10^{-4}} = 840.3$$

or $$t = 840.3 + 27 = 867.3^\circ\text{C}$$

Thus, the steady temperature of heating element is 867.3 °C.

Question 7 Determine the current in each branch of the network shown in given figure.

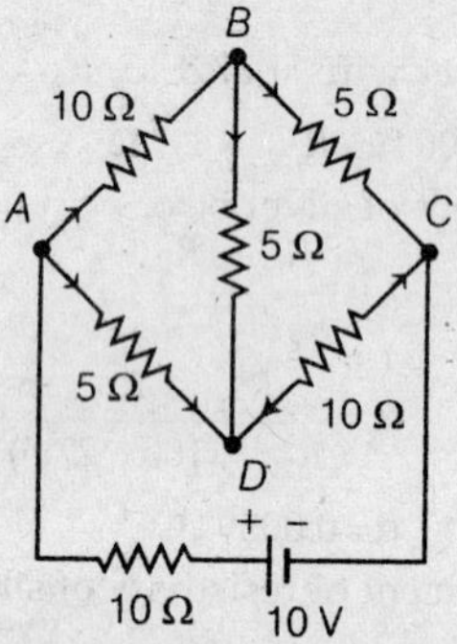

◎ *Thinking Process* **Here, the given circuit is closed having two closed loops, so to calculate the current in the circuit we have to apply Kirchhoff's laws.**

Sol.

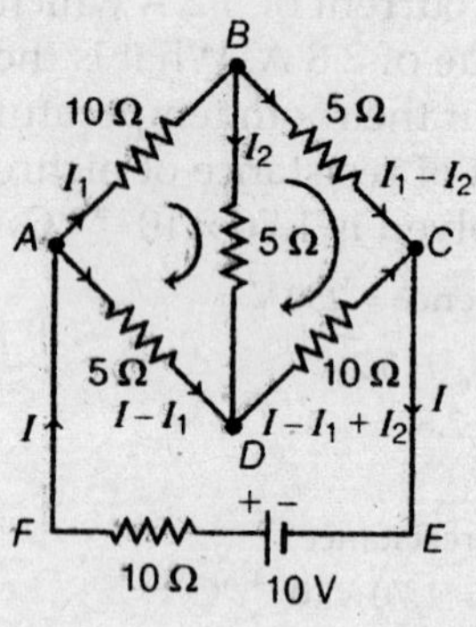

In loop $ABDA$ applying kirchhoff's voltage law

$$\Sigma \Delta V = 0$$

$$10I_1 + 5I_2 - 5(I - I_1) = 0$$

$$2I_1 + I_2 - I + I_1 = 0$$

$$3I_1 + I_2 = I \qquad \text{...(i)}$$

In loop *BCDB* applying kirchhoff's voltage law

$$\Sigma \Delta V = 0$$

$$5(I_1 - I_2) - 10(I - I_1 + I_2) - 5I_2 = 0$$

$$I_1 - I_2 - 2I + 2I_1 - 2I_2 - I_2 = 0$$

$$3I_1 - 4I_2 = 2I \qquad \text{...(ii)}$$

By solving the Eq. (i) and Eq. (ii), we get

$$I_1 = \frac{2I}{5} \text{ and } I_2 = -\frac{I}{5} \qquad \text{...(iii)}$$

In loop *ABCEFA* applying kirchhoff's voltage law

$$\Sigma \Delta V = 0$$

$$10I_1 + 5(I_1 - I_2) - 10 + 10I = 0$$

$$2 = 2I + 3I_1 - I_2 \qquad \text{...(iv)}$$

Putting the values of I_1 and I_2 from Eq. (iii) in Eq. (iv), we get

$$2 = 2I + 3\left(\frac{2I}{5}\right) - \left(-\frac{I}{5}\right)$$

or $$2 = \frac{17}{5} I$$

or $$I = \frac{10}{17} \text{ A}$$

Current in branch *AB*, $I_1 = \frac{2}{5} \times \frac{10}{7} = \frac{4}{17}$ A

Current in branch *BD*, $I_2 = -\frac{I}{5} = -\frac{2}{17}$ A

Current in branch *BC* is $I_1 - I_2 = \frac{4}{17} - \left(-\frac{2}{17}\right) = \frac{6}{17}$ A

Current in branch *AD* is $I - I_1 = \frac{10}{17} - \frac{4}{17} = \frac{6}{17}$ A

Current in branch *DC* is $(I - I_1) + I_2 = \frac{6}{17} + \left(-\frac{2}{17}\right) = \frac{4}{17}$ A

Mistake Alert Misapplication of kirchoff's voltage or current laws (KVL/KCL) in the loops or junctions can lead to incorrect current values. Ensure all signs and directions are consistent.

- Misreading the polarity of the battery or voltage source may lead to wrong current direction assumptions.

Question 8 A storage battery of emf 8.0 V and internal resistance 0.5 Ω is being charged by a 120 V DC supply using a series resistor of 15.5 Ω. What is the terminal voltage of the battery during charging? What is the purpose of having a series resistor in the charging circuit?

Thinking Process Use the formula of terminal potential difference in charging a cell. $E = V + Ir$

Sol. Emf of the battery $E = 8$ V, emf of DC supply $V = 120$ V

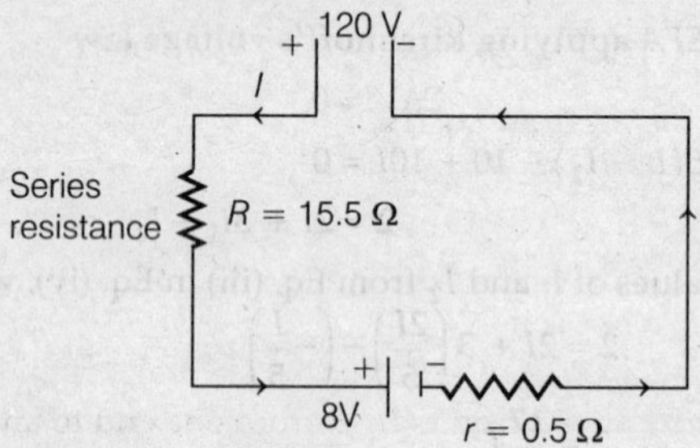

Since, the battery is bring charged, so effective emf in the circuit

$$E_{eff} = V - E = 120 - 8 = 112\text{ V}$$

Current in circuit, $$I = \frac{\text{Effective emf}}{\text{Total resistance}} = \frac{E}{r + R}$$

$$= \frac{112}{0.5 + 15.5} = \frac{112}{16} = 7\text{ A}$$

The battery of 8 V is being charged by 120 V, so the terminal potential across battery of 8 V will be greater than its emf

Terminal potential difference $V = E + Ir = 8 + 7(0.5) = 11.5$ V

The purpose of the series resistance is to control the current drawn from the external supply, otherwise the current in the circuit will be very high.

Mistake Alert A common mistake is forgetting to include the internal resistance of the battery while calculating the current or terminal voltage.

Question 9 The number density of free electrons in a copper conductor estimated at $8.5 \times 10^{28}\ \text{m}^{-3}$. How long does an electron take to drift from one end of a wire 3.0 m long to its other end? The area of cross-section of the wire is $2.0 \times 10^{-6}\ \text{m}^2$ and it is carrying a current of 3.0 A.

Thinking Process To find the time for the electrons to drift from one end to other, we have to calculate the drift velocity of the electrons first.

Sol. Given, number density of electrons $n = 8.5 \times 10^{28} m^{-3}$

Length of wire $l = 3$ m

Area of cross-section of wire $A = 2 \times 10^{-6} m^2$

Current $I = 3$ A and charge on electron $e = 1.6 \times 10^{-19}$ C

Time taken by electron to drift from one end to another of the wire,

$$t = \frac{\text{Length of the wire}}{\text{Drift velocity}} = \frac{l}{v_d} \quad \text{...(i)}$$

Using the relation, $I = ne A v_d$

or $$v_d = \frac{I}{ne A} \quad \text{...(ii)}$$

Putting the value in Eq. (ii) from Eq. (i),

$$t = \frac{l \, ne \, A}{I}$$

$$= \frac{3 \times 8.5 \times 10^{28} \times 1.6 \times 10^{-19} \times 2 \times 10^{-6}}{3}$$

or $t = 2.72 \times 10^4 \text{ s} = 7 \text{ h } 33 \text{ min}$

Thus, the time taken by an electron to drift from one end to another end is 7 h 33 min.

DIKSHA APP Questions

☐ Multiple Choice Questions

Q.1 The unit of mobility is

(a) ms^{-1} (b) $ms^{-1}V$

(c) $m^2V^{-1}s^{-1}$ (d) $m^2V^{-1}s$

Sol. (c) $\mu = \frac{V_d}{E} = \frac{ms^{-1}}{Vm^{-1}} = m^2V^{-1}s^{-1}$

Q.2 In the current against voltage curve in Ohm's law, the slope gives

(a) resistance (b) conductance

(c) resistivity (d) conductivity

Sol. (b) Slope $= \frac{I}{V} = \frac{1}{R}$ = Conductance

Q.3 The resistance of a wire is 10 ohm. What will be the new resistance, if it is stretched uniformly 8 times its original length ?

(a) 640 ohm (b) 64 ohm

(c) 10 ohm (d) 6400 ohm

Sol. (a) Since, $R \propto l^2$ (when volume is constant)

Therefore, $$\frac{R_1}{R_2} = \left(\frac{l_1}{l_2}\right)^2 = \frac{10}{R_2} = \left(\frac{l}{8l}\right)^2 = \frac{1}{64}$$

$$R_2 = 640 \text{ ohm.}$$

Q.4 There are n numbers of resistors with resistance as R ohm. What is the ratio of effective resistances of series and parallel combinations ?

(a) $R^2 : 1$ (b) $1 : 1$ (c) $1 : n^2$ (d) $n^2 : 1$

Sol. (d) $R_S = R + R + \ldots n$ times $= nR$

$$\frac{1}{R_P} = \frac{1}{R} + \frac{1}{R} + \ldots n \text{ times} = \frac{n}{R}$$

$$R_P = \frac{R}{n}$$

$$\frac{R_S}{R_P} = \frac{nR}{\frac{R}{n}} = \frac{n^2}{1}$$

Q.5 There are three copper wires of equal length and the ratio of their radii is 1 : 2 : 3. What is the ratio of their resistivity ?

(a) 1 : 2 : 3 (b) 3 : 2 : 1 (c) 1 : 1 : 1 (d) 1 : 4 : 9

Sol. (c) Resistvity is independent of length and area (radius) of wire.

Q.6 There are two unknown resistors. When they are connected in series and parallel their effective resistances are 10 ohm and 2.4 ohm respectively what are the resistance of individual resistance of each resistor ?

(a) 10 ohm and 2.4 ohm (b) 6 ohm and 4 ohm
(c) 6 ohm and 6 ohm (d) 1 ohm and 2.4 ohm

Sol. (b) $R_S = R_1 + R_2 = 10$ ...(i)

$$R_P = \frac{R_1 R_2}{R_1 + R_2} = 2.4 \quad \ldots\text{(ii)}$$

From Eq. (i) $R_2 = 10 - R_1$ put in Eq. (ii)

$$\frac{R_1(10 - R_1)}{R_1 + 10 - R_1} = 2.4$$

$$10R_1 - R_1^2 = 2.4 \times 10 = 24$$

$$R_1^2 - 10R_1 + 24 = 0$$

Solving we get $R_1 = 6\Omega$

Put R_1 in Eq. (i) $6 + R_2 = 10$

$$R_2 = 4\Omega$$

Q.7 What is the internal resistance of a 2.1 V cell which gives a current of 0.2 A through a resistance of 10 ohm ?

(a) 1 ohm (b) 0.5 ohm
(c) 2 ohm (d) 3 ohm

Sol. (b) $\because I = \dfrac{E}{R + r}$

$$0.2 = \frac{2.1}{10 + r}$$

$$10 + r = \frac{2.1}{0.2} = 10.5 \Rightarrow r = 0.5\Omega$$

Q.8 Charge through a conductor is given as a function of time t as $q = 4t^2 + 4t + 4$ coulomb. At 2 s, what is the current flowing ?

(a) 12 A (b) 8 A
(c) 20 A (d) 28 A

Sol. (c) $\because I = \dfrac{dq}{dt} = \dfrac{d}{dt}(4t^2 + 4t + 4) = 8t + 4$

put $t = 2\,\text{s}$

$$I = 8 \times 2 + 4 = 20\text{ A}$$

☐ Very Short Answer Type

Q.1 Why nichrome is preferred in electric heaters ?

Sol. Nichrome is an alloy and has high resistivity and can withstand very high temperature without oxidation.

Q.2 A wire is cut into half. What is the effect on its specific resistance ?

Sol. Specific resistance will be same as independent of area of cross-section and length of the wire.

Q.3 Two wires of equal length, one of copper and other of manganin have seen same resistance. Which is thicker ?

Sol. So, manganin will be thicker.

$$R_{cu} = R_{mang.}$$

$$\rho_{cu}\frac{l}{A_{cu}} = \rho_{mang.}\frac{l}{A_{mang.}} \Rightarrow \frac{\rho_{cu}}{\rho_{mang.}} = \frac{A_{cu}}{A_{mang.}}$$

$\because$ $\rho_{mang.} > \rho_{cu}$ (manganin is alloy and Cu is metal)

$\therefore$ $A_{mang.} > A_{cu}$

Q.4 In metals why the resistivity is increased with the increase in temperature ?

Sol. When the temperature of metals is increased the average time τ between the collision decreases and the number of free electrons is independent of temperature. So as per the following formula resistivity $\rho = m/ne^2 \tau$ is increased with increase in temperature.

Q.5 At transition temperature what happens to the resistivity and conductivity of a superconductor ?

Sol. For the superconductors, at transition temperature, the resistivity becomes zero and conductivity becomes infinity.

Q.6 Why Kirchhoff's voltage rule follows from the law of conservation of energy ?

Sol. Kirchhoff's voltage rule follows from the law of conservation of energy since the energy supplied by the emf sources is equal to the sum of energy delivered to all the resistors of the circuit.

Q.7 State Ohm's law.

Sol. If the physical conditions of conductor (temperature, length etc.) do not change, then the current in the conductor is directly proportional to the potential difference across the conductor *i.e.* $I \propto V$.

Moving Charges and Magnetism

CHAPTER 04

Important Points

01 Force on a charge particle q moving with velocity $\mathbf{v}$ in uniform magnetic field $\mathbf{B}$ making an angle θ with field direction is
$\mathbf{F} = q(\mathbf{v} \times \mathbf{B}) = qvB\sin\theta$

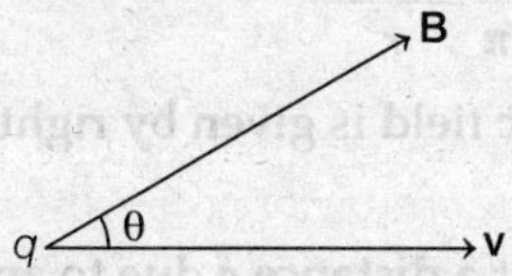

02 Direction of magnetic force on charge particle in uniform magnetic field is given by fleming's left hand rule

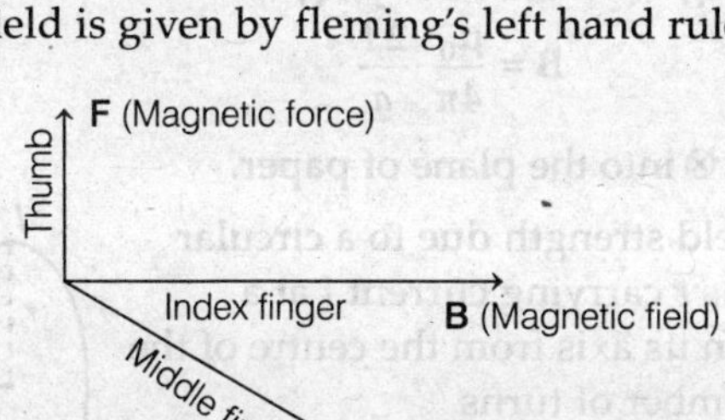

03 The total force F experienced by charge (q) when it is moving with velocity v in the presence of electric field $\mathbf{E}$ and magnetic field $\mathbf{B}$,

$$\mathbf{F} = q\,(v \times \mathbf{B} + \mathbf{E})$$

This is called **Lorentz force.**

04 Force experienced by a current carrying conductor having current I and length l, when placed in a magnetic field B is, (θ is angle between **I** and **B**.)

$$\mathbf{F} = I\,\mathbf{l} \times \mathbf{B} = IlB \sin\theta$$

05 Radius of circular path when charge particle q enters perpendicular to uniform magnetic field $r = \frac{mv}{q\mathbf{B}}$ and time period

$$T = \frac{2\pi m}{q\mathbf{B}}$$

The pitch of the helix $p = \frac{2\pi\, mv \cos\theta}{q\mathbf{B}}$

06 **The Biot-Savart law** The magnetic field dB due to an element of length dl carrying a current I at a point P at a distance r from the conductor is

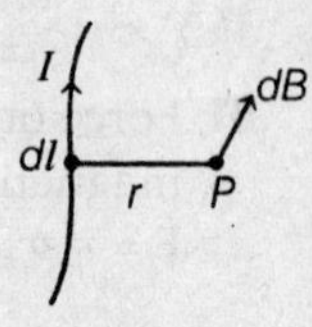

$$d\mathbf{B} = \frac{\mu_0}{4\pi} \frac{Id\mathbf{l} \times \mathbf{r}}{r^3}$$

The direction of magnetic field is given by right hand palm rule or right hand screw rule.

07 **Magnetic field strength at a distance a due to an infinitely long conductor carrying current is**

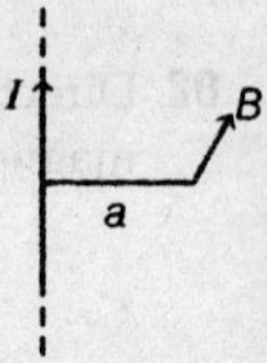

$$\mathbf{B} = \frac{\mu_0}{4\pi} \cdot \frac{2I}{a}$$

direction → ⊗ into the plane of paper.

08 Magnetic field strength due to a circular coil of radius r carrying current I at a distance x on its axis from the centre of the coil of N number of turns

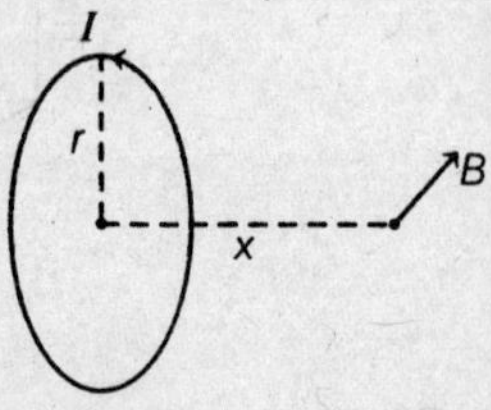

$$\mathbf{B} = \frac{\mu_0 N I r^2}{2(r^2 + x^2)^{3/2}}$$

Direction of magnetic field is away from centre when current is anticlockwise and is towards centre when current is clockwise.

09 Magnetic field strength at the centre of the circular coil having radius r current I and N number of turns in the coil, is

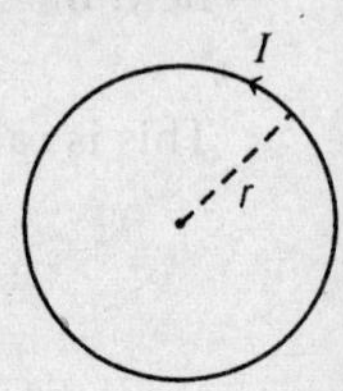

$$\mathbf{B} = \frac{\mu_0 N I}{2r}$$

10 Magnetic field strength at the centre of an arc of radius r subtending an angle θ and carrying current I is

$$B = \frac{\mu_0}{4\pi} \cdot \frac{I}{r}\theta$$

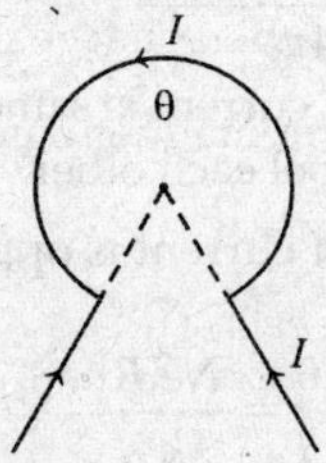

11 **Ampere's circuital law** $\oint \mathbf{B}.dl = \mu_0 I$, where B is the magnetic field induction at a point on the closed path and I is the current in the closed path.

12 The magnetic field induction B inside a long solenoid carrying current I is given by

$$B = \mu_0 nI$$

where, n is the number of turns per unit length $= \frac{N}{l}$ and N is the total no. of turns in solenoid.

The magnetic field induction at the ends of solenoid is given by

$$B = \frac{\mu_0 nI}{2}$$

13 Magnetic dipoles moment $\mathbf{M} = NI\mathbf{A}$

where, A is the area N is number of turns and I is the current.

14 The magnetic moment of an electron moving around the nucleus is given by

$$\mu_B = \frac{e}{2m} l, \left[l = mvr = m\left(\frac{2\pi r}{T}\right)r = \frac{2\pi mr^2}{T} \right]$$

where, l is the magnitude of angular momentum.

The smallest value of μ is called the Bohr magneton is given by

$$\mu_B = 9.27 \times 10^{-24} \text{ J/T}$$

15 Torque on a current loop of any shape $\tau = \mathbf{M} \times \mathbf{B} = MB\sin\theta$, where $M = NI\vec{\mathbf{A}}$ is magnetic dipole moment and θ is angle between normal to plane of coil and magnetic field.

16 Force between the two parallel long currents carrying conductors placed r distance apart in vacuum

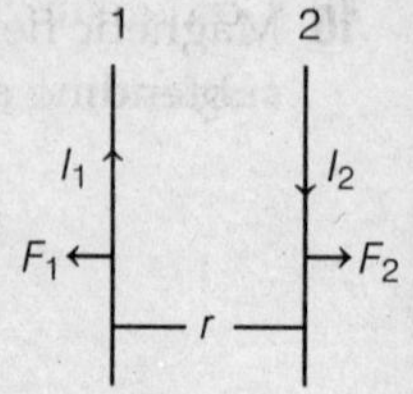

$$F = \frac{\mu_0}{4\pi} \cdot \frac{2 I_1 I_2}{r}$$

If the direction of flow of current is same in both conductors, then they repel each other.

If the direction of flow of current is opposite in both conductors they attract each other.

17 Current sensitivity $I_S = \frac{\theta}{I} = \frac{NAB}{k}$

where, k is the spring constant SI unit of I_S is rad/A or div/A.

18 Voltage sensitivity $V_S = \frac{\theta}{V} = \frac{\theta}{IR} = \frac{I_S}{R} = \frac{NAB}{kR}$

where, k is the spring constant, R is the resistance SI unit of V_S is rad/V or div/V.

19 Conversion of a Galvanometer into Ammeter

Small resistance (shunt) is connected in parallel to galvanometer

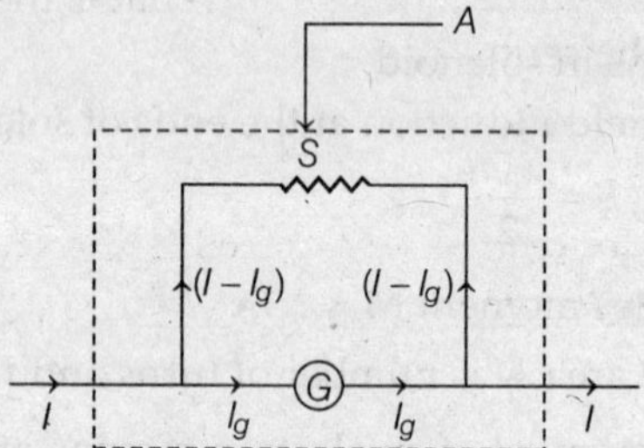

$$S = \frac{G I_g}{I - I_g}$$

S = Shunt

G = Galvanometer resistance

I_g = Full scale deflection current

I = Range of ammeter

Resistance of Ammeter $\frac{1}{R_a} = \frac{1}{S} + \frac{1}{G}$.

20 Conversion of Galvanometer into Voltmeter

High resistance connected in series to galvanometer

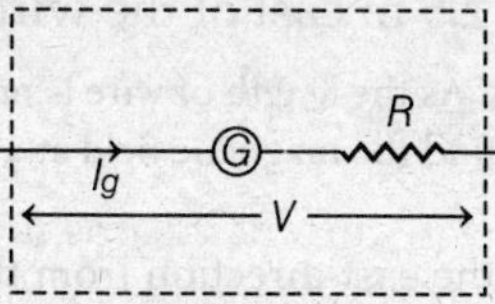

$$R = \frac{V}{I_g} - G$$

R = High resistance
G = Galvanometer resistance
I_g = Full scale deflection current
V = Range of voltmeter.

Exercises

Question 1 A circular coil of wire consisting of 100 turns, each of radius 8.0 cm carries a current of 0.40 A. What is the magnitude of the magnetic field **B** at the centre of the coil?

Sol. Here, $N = 100$, $r = 8 \text{ cm} = 8 \times 10^{-2}$ m

and $I = 0.40$ A

The magnetic field B at the centre of circular coil.

$$\mathbf{B} = \frac{\mu_0 NI}{2r} = \frac{4\pi \times 10^{-7} \times 100 \times 0.40}{2 \times 8 \times 10^{-2}} = 3.1 \times 10^{-4} \text{ T}$$

Question 2 A long straight wire carries a current of 35 A. What is the magnitude of the field **B** at a point 20 cm away from the wire?

◎ ***Thinking Process*** Use the formula for magnetic field produced by a current carrying infinite long wire. Here the length of the wire is not given so we can consider it of infinite length.

Sol. Here, we have to find the magnetic field at point P.

$I = 35$ A and $r = 20$ cm $= 0.2$ m

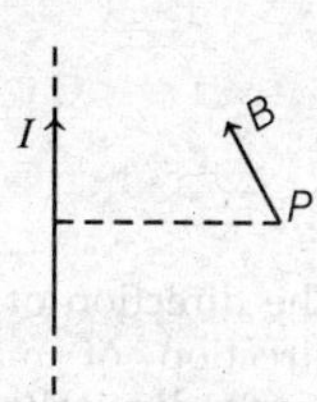

The wire is long and it is considered as an infinite length wire. The magnetic field

$$\mathbf{B} = \frac{\mu_0}{4\pi} \cdot \frac{2I}{r} = \frac{10^{-7} \times 2 \times 35}{0.2} = 3.5 \times 10^{-5} \text{ T}$$

Question 3 A long straight wire in the horizontal plane carries a current of 50 A in north to south direction. Give the magnitude and direction of **B** at a point 2.5 m east of the wire.

◎ *Thinking Process* As the length of wire is not mentioned in the question, so use the formula to find the magnetic field at a point due to infinite length wire.

Sol. Here, the point P is in the east direction from the wire which is placed in north-south direction and in the horizontal plane.

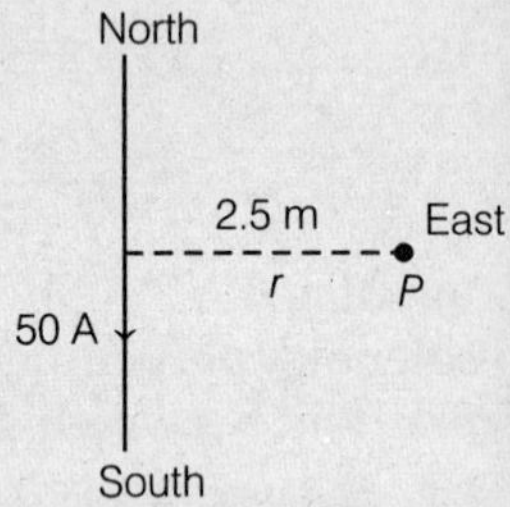

Given, $I = 50$ A and $r = 2.5$ m

The magnitude of magnetic field

$$\mathbf{B} = \frac{\mu_0}{4\pi} \cdot \frac{2I}{r} = 10^{-7} \times \frac{2 \times 50}{2.5}$$

$$= 4 \times 10^{-6} \text{ T}$$

The direction of magnetic field at point P is given by Maxwell's right hand rule. The current flows from north to south, *i.e.*, downwards, then the direction of magnetic field at P is perpendicularly outwards to the horizontal plane.

Question 4 A horizontal overhead power line carries a current of 90 A in east to west direction. What are the magnitude and direction of the magnetic field due to the current 1.5 m below the line?

◎ *Thinking Process* The overhead power line is considered as an infinite length wire so use the formula to find the magnetic field at a point due to infinite length wire.

Sol. Given, $I = 90$ A and $r = 1.5$ m

Here, point P is below the power line, where we have to find the magnetic field and its direction.

The magnitude of magnetic field

$$\mathbf{B} = \frac{\mu_0}{4\pi} \cdot \frac{2I}{r} = \frac{10^{-7} \times 2 \times 90}{1.5}$$

$$= 1.2 \times 10^{-5} \text{ T}$$

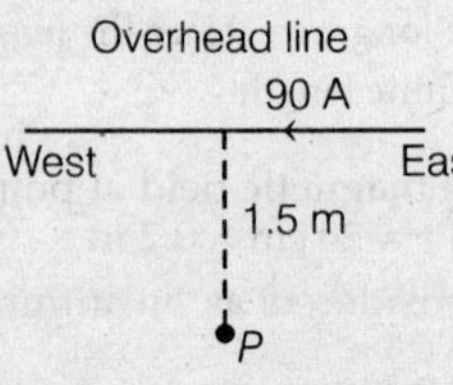

The direction of magnetic field is given by Maxwell's right hand rule. So, the direction of magnetic field at point P due to the flowing current is perpendicularly outwards to the plane of paper *i.e.* southward.

Question 5 What is the magnitude of magnetic force per unit length on a wire carrying a current of 8 A and making an angle of 30° with the direction of a uniform magnetic field of 0.15 T?

Sol. According to the question, $I = 8$ A, $\theta = 30°$, $\mathbf{B} = 0.15$ T, $l = 1$ m

The magnitude of magnetic force

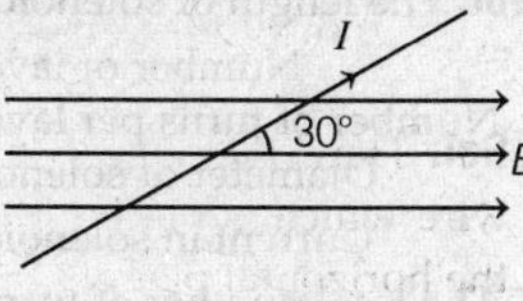

$$\mathbf{F} = I(\mathbf{l} \times \mathbf{B}) = I\, l\, B \sin\theta$$

$$\frac{\mathbf{F}}{l} = 8 \times 0.15 \times \sin 30°$$

$$\frac{\mathbf{F}}{l} = \frac{8 \times 0.15}{2} = 0.6 \text{ N}m^{-1}$$

Question 6 A 3.0 cm wire carrying a current of 10 A is placed inside a solenoid perpendicular to its axis. The magnetic field inside the solenoid is given to be 0.27 T. What is the magnetic force on the wire?

Sol. Here, the angle between the magnetic field and the direction of flow of current is 90°. Because the magnetic field due to a solenoid is along the axis of the solenoid and the wire is placed perpendicular to the axis.

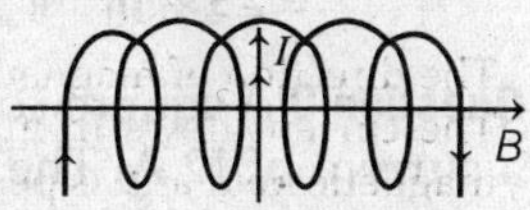

Given, $l = 3$ cm $= 3 \times 10^{-2}$ m, $I = 10$ A, $B = 0.27$ T,

The magnitude of magnetic force on the wire

$$F = I\, l\, B \sin 90° = 10 \times 3 \times 10^{-2} \times 0.27 \times \sin 90° = 8.1 \times 10^{-2} \text{ N} \quad [\because \theta = 90°]$$

Direction of magnetic force is given by Fleming's left hand rule. For the given diagram, it is into the plane of the paper.

Question 7 Two long and parallel straight wires A and B carrying currents of 8.0 A and 5.0 A in the same direction are separated by a distance of 4.0 cm. Estimate the force on a 10 cm section of wire A?

Sol. Given, $I_1 = 8$ A, $I_2 = 5$ A and $r = 4$ cm $= 0.04$ m,

$l = 10$ cm $= 0.1$ m

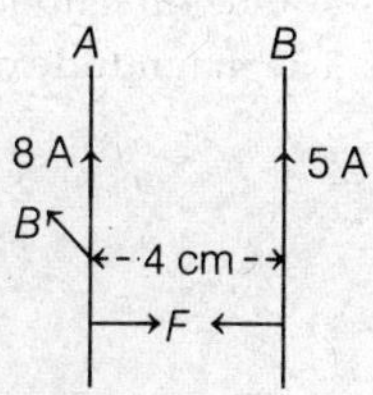

Force per unit length on two parallel wire carrying current

$$\frac{F}{l} = \frac{\mu_0}{4\pi} \cdot \frac{2I_1 \cdot I_2}{r}$$

$$= \frac{10^{-7} \times 2 \times 8 \times 5}{0.04} = 2 \times 10^{-4} \text{ N/m}$$

The force on length 10 cm of wire A is $F \times l = F \times 0.1$ ($\because$ 1m = 100 cm)

$$\Rightarrow \quad F' = 2 \times 10^{-4} \times 0.1 = 2 \times 10^{-5} \text{ N}$$

Using Maxwell's right hand rule the direction of magnetic field due to B on A is perpendicularly outwards to the plane of paper.

According to Fleming's left hand rule, the direction of force is towards B and the nature of force is attractive.

Mistake Alert The direction of the force depends on the direction of the currents; in this case, they are in the same direction, so the force will be attractive.

Question 8 A closely wound solenoid 80 cm long has 5 layers of windings of 400 turns each. The diameter of the solenoid is 1.8 cm. If the current carried is 8.0 A, estimate the magnitude of B inside the solenoid near its centre.

Sol. The length of solenoid, l = 80 cm = 0.8 m

Number of layers = 5

Number of turns per layer = 400

Diameter of solenoid = 1.8 cm

Current in solenoid I = 8 A

$\therefore$ The total number of turns $N = 400 \times 5 = 2000$

and number of turns/length, $n = \frac{N}{l} = \frac{2000}{0.8} = 2500$

The magnitude of magnetic field inside the solenoid

$$B = \mu_0 nI = 4\pi \times 10^{-7} \times 2500 \times 8$$
$$= 2.5 \times 10^{-2}\ \text{T}$$

Question 9 A square coil of side 10 cm consists of 20 turns and carries a current of 12 A. The coil is suspended vertically and the normal to the plane of the coil makes an angle of 30° with the direction of a uniform horizontal magnetic field of magnitude 0.80 T. What is the magnitude of torque experienced by the coil?

Sol. Given, side of square coil = 10 cm = 0.1 m

Number of turns (N) = 20

Current in square field coil I = 12 A

Angle made by normal to the coil with magnetic field coil $\theta = 30°$

Magnetic field $B = 0.80$ T

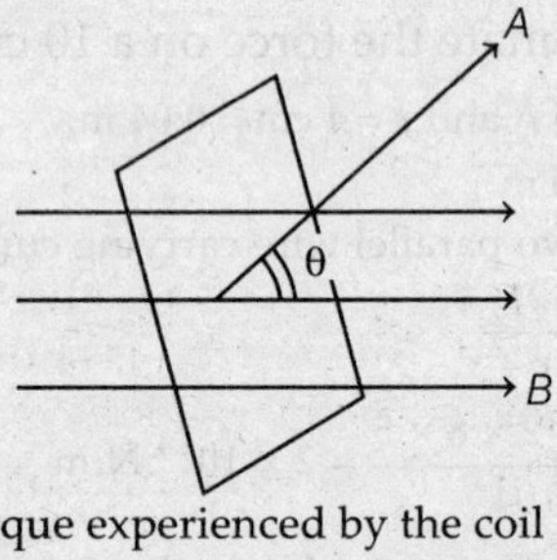

The magnitude of torque experienced by the coil

$$\tau = NI\,AB \sin\theta$$
$$= 20 \times 12 \times (10 \times 10^{-2})^2 \times 0.80 \times \sin 30°$$
$$\tau = 2.4 \times 0.80 \sin 30° = \frac{2.4 \times 0.80}{2} = 0.96 \text{ N-m (Joule)}$$

Note
- The torque is maximum when the plane of the coil is parallel to the magnetic field (*i.e.*, $\theta = 90°$). In this case, the torque is reduced because $\theta = 30°$, and the $\sin\theta$ term influences the magnitude.
- The direction of the torque can be determined using the right-hand rule, and it tends to rotate the coil to align the normal with the magnetic field.

Question 10 Two moving coil meters M_1 and M_2 having the following particulars :
$R_1 = 10\ \Omega, N_1 = 30, A_1 = 3.6 \times 10^{-3}\ m^2, B_1 = 0.25$ T
$R_2 = 14\ \Omega, N_2 = 42, A_2 = 1.8 \times 10^{-3} m^2, B_2 = 0.50$ T
(The spring constants are identical for the two meters).
Determine the ratio of (a) current sensitivity and (b) voltage sensitivity of M_2 and M_1.

◎ **Thinking Process** In this problem, we use the concept of a formula for current sensitivity and voltage sensitivity.

$$I_s \text{ (current sensitivity)} = \frac{NBA}{k}$$

$$V_s \text{ (voltage sensitivity)} = \frac{NBA}{kR}$$

where, N be the number of turns in the coil, B be the magnetic field, A be the area of cross-section of the coil, R be the resistance and k is the spring constant.

Sol. Given, $R_1 = 10\ \Omega, N_1 = 30, A_1 = 3.6 \times 10^{-3} m^2, B_1 = 0.25$ T
$R_2 = 14\ \Omega, N_2 = 42, A_2 = 1.8 \times 10^{-3} m^2, B_2 = 0.50$ T
$k_1 = k_2$ (spring constants are same)

(a) Using the formula of current sensitivity,

$$I_S = \frac{NAB}{k}$$

$$\therefore \quad \frac{I_{S_2}}{I_{S_1}} = \frac{N_2 B_2 A_2 . k_1}{N_1 B_1 A_1 k_2} = \frac{42 \times 0.50 \times 1.8 \times 10^{-3}}{30 \times 0.25 \times 3.6 \times 10^{-3}} = \frac{7}{5} \qquad (k_1 = k_2)$$

(b) Using the formula of voltage sensitivity,

$$V_S = \frac{NAB}{kR} = \frac{I_S}{R}$$

$$\frac{V_{s_1}}{V_{s_2}} = \frac{I_{S_1}}{I_{S_2}} \times \frac{R_2}{R_1} = \frac{5}{7} \times \frac{14}{10} = \frac{1}{1}$$

Question 11 In a chamber, a uniform magnetic field of 6.5 G ($1G = 10^{-4}$ T) is maintained. An electron is shot into the field with a speed of 4.8×10^6 m/s normal to the field. Explain why the path of the electron is a circle. Determine the radius of the circular orbit. ($e = 1.6 \times 10^{-19}$ C, $m_e = 9.1 \times 10^{-31}$ kg)

◎ **Thinking Process** As the charge particle enters perpendicularly in a uniform magnetic field, it acquires a circular path as the required centripetal force is provided by the magnetic force acting on the charged particle.

Sol. Given, magnetic field $B = 6.5\ G = 6.5 \times 10^{-4}$ T

Charge $e = -1.6 \times 10^{-19}$ C

Speed of electron $v = 4.8 \times 10^6$ m/s

Mass of electron $m_e = 9.1 \times 10^{-31}$ kg

Angle between magnetic field and electron velocity is $\theta = 90°$

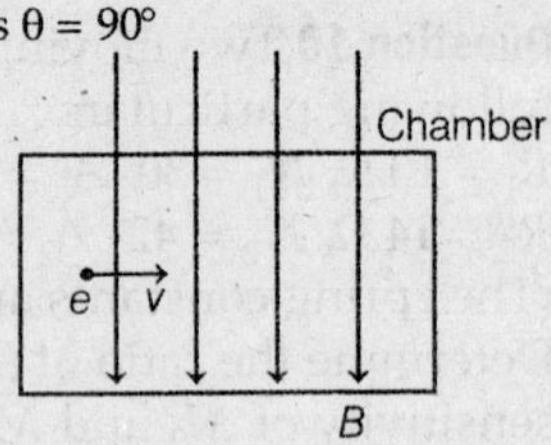

The force on the charge particle entering in the magnetic field is

$$\mathbf{F} = q\,(\mathbf{v} \times \mathbf{B}) = evB\sin 90° = evB$$

According to Fleming's left hand rule, the direction of force is perpendicular to both velocity and magnetic field.

So, the force will only change the direction of motion without changing the magnitude of velocity. So, the electron attains a circular path and the necessary centripetal force is provided by the magnetic force.

$$\therefore \quad evB = \frac{mv^2}{r}$$

or $$r = \frac{mv}{eB}$$

or $$= \frac{9.1 \times 10^{-31} \times 4.8 \times 10^{6}}{1.6 \times 10^{-19} \times 6.5 \; 10^{-4}}$$

$$= 4.2 \times 10^{-2} \text{ m}$$

$$= 4.2 \text{ cm}$$

Question 12 In Q. 11 obtain the frequency of revolution of the electron in its circular orbit. Does the answer depend on the speed of the electron? Explain.

Sol. Given, $B = 6.5 \text{ G} = 6.5 \times 10^{-4}$ T $\quad [\because 1\text{G} = 10^{-4} \text{ T}]$

$v = 4.8 \times 10^{6}$ m/s, $e = 1.6 \times 10^{-19}$ C

and $m_e = 9.1 \times 10^{-31}$ kg

We know that when an electron (charged particle) moves on a circular path in unifrom magnetic field, then the required centripetal force is provided by the magnetic force on it.

$$\frac{mv^2}{r} = qvB \Rightarrow \frac{mv}{r} = qB$$

If angular velocity of electron is ω, then

$$v = r\omega$$

$$\therefore \quad \frac{m\,(r\omega)}{r} = qB$$

$$\omega = \frac{qB}{m}$$

(if frequency of revolution is ν then $\omega = 2\pi\nu$)

$$\therefore \quad 2\pi\nu = \frac{qB}{m} \Rightarrow \nu = \frac{qB}{2\pi m}$$

Frequency of revolution of electron in the orbit

$$\nu = \frac{Bq}{2\pi m} = \frac{Be}{2\pi m_e} = \frac{6.5 \times 10^{-4} \times 1.6 \times 10^{-19}}{2 \times 3.14 \times 9.1 \times 10^{-31}} \quad (\because \text{For electron } q = e)$$

$$= 18.18 \times 10^6 \text{ Hz}$$

Here, we observe that the frequency of electron is independent to the velocity.

Question 13

(a) A circular coil of 30 turns and radius 8.0 cm carrying a current of 6.0 A is suspended vertically in a uniform horizontal magnetic field of magnitude 1.0 T. The field lines make an angle of 60° with the normal of the coil. Calculate the magnitude of the counter torque that must be applied to prevent the coil from turning.

(b) Would your answer change, if the circular coil were replaced by a planar coil of some irregular shape that encloses the same area? (All other particulars are also unaltered.)

Sol. (a) Given, number of turns $N = 30$, radius $(r) = 8$ cm $= 0.08$ m

Current in the coil $I = 6$ A

Magnetic field $B = 1.0$ T

Angle made by magnetic field with the normal of the coil, $\theta = 60°$

Magnitude of counter torque = Magnitude of torque acting on the current carrying coil due to the magnetic field

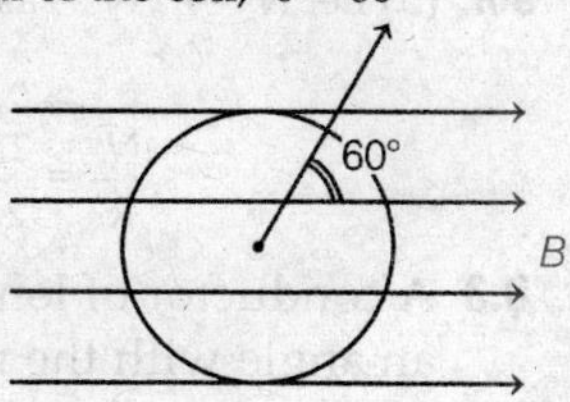

$$\tau = NIAB \sin\theta$$

$$= 30 \times 6 \times \pi\,(0.08)^2 \times 1 \times \sin 60°$$

$$= 30 \times 6 \times 3.14 \times 0.08 \times 0.08 \times \sqrt{\frac{3}{2}}$$

$$= 3.133 \text{ N-m (Joule)}$$

(b) From the formula, it is clear that the torque on the loop does not depend on the shape if area remains constant. So, the torque remains constant (all other particulars are unaltered).

Mistake Alert Use the the formula for the area of a circle correctly. For irregular shapes, ensure the area enclosed is given. Use the sine of the angle between the field and the normal to the coil, not the angle with the plane of the coil.

DIKSHA APP Questions

Multiple Choice Questions

Q.1 Two wires are kept parallel and carry equal currents separated by 2 cm apart. They experience an attractive force of 16×10^{-5} newton per unit length. Find the current flowing in the two wires.

(a) 16×10^5 A (b) 16 A (c) 4 A (d) 1 A

Sol. (c) $\because \left(\frac{F}{l}\right) = \frac{\mu_0}{4\pi}\frac{2I_1I_2}{r} = \frac{10^{-7} \times 2 \times I \times I}{r}$

$$16 \times 10^{-5} = \frac{2 \times 10^{-7} \times I^2}{0.02} \Rightarrow I = 4 \text{ A}$$

Q.2 Among the following which cannot be used to increase the voltage sensitivity of the galvanometer ?

(a) By increasing the area of the coil
(b) By increasing the magnetic field
(c) By decreasing the couple per unit twist
(d) By increasing the number of turns

Sol. (d) Let $N' \rightarrow 2\text{N} \rightarrow$ as $V_S = \frac{NBA}{KR}$

$$R' \rightarrow 2R$$
$$\frac{N'}{R'} = \frac{2N}{2R} = \frac{N}{R} = \text{Constant}$$

Q.3 A conductor of length 20 cm carries a current of 1 A is kept at an angle with the magnetic field of 4 T. Find the angle between the conductor and the magnetic field if it experiences a force of 0.4 N.

(a) 0° (b) 30° (c) 60° (d) 90°

Sol. (b) $\because \mathbf{F} = \mathbf{B}Il\sin\theta$

$$0.4 = 4 \times 1 \times 0.20 \times \sin\theta$$
$$\sin\theta = \frac{1}{2} \Rightarrow \theta = 30°$$

Q.4 The magnitude of the magnetic field of a long straight wire carrying a current of 1 A at a distance of 2 cm is

(a) 10^{-5} T (b) 10^{-7} T
(c) 2×10^{-7} T (d) 2×10^{-5} T

Sol. (a) Since, $B = \frac{\mu_0}{4\pi}\frac{2I}{r}$

$$= 10^{-7} \times \frac{2 \times 1}{0.02} = 10^{-5} \text{ T}$$

☐ Very Short Answer Type

Q.1 If a charged particle is moving perpendicular to the magnetic field what is the work done ? Explain.

Sol. The work done is zero. Because in a perpendicular magnetic field the charge will execute a circular path and the velocity of the particle and the force are perpendicular to each other.

$$W = F s \cos\theta = F s \cos 90° = 0.$$

Q.2 Why Phosphor-Bronze wire is used for suspension of the coil in a moving coil galvanometer ?

Sol. Phosphor-Bronze wire is used in a moving coil galvanometer since it provides small couple per unit twist and high tensile strength.

Q.3 Increasing the number of turns increases the current sensitivity and not the voltage sensitivity, why ?

Sol. $V_s = NBA/(KR_g)$. According to the given formula, increasing the number of turns will simultaneously increase the length of the coil which in turn increase the resistance of the coil R_g. Therefore, the voltage sensitivity remains the same.

Q.4 Define one ampere.

Sol. One ampere is defined as that current when it is passed through each of the two infinitely long straight conductors kept at a distance of one meter apart in vacuum causes ~ach conductor to experience a force of 2×10^{-7} newton per meter length of the conductor.

Q.5 What is velocity selector ?

Sol. By proper choice of electric and magnetic fields the particle with particular speed is selected. Here the force due to electric and magnetic fields are the same and we can calculate the velocity using $v = E / B$. Such an arrangement is called velocity selector.

CHAPTER 05

Magnetism and Matter

Important Points

01 The magnetic moment of a bar magnet of pole strength m and of length $2l$ is given by

$$\mathbf{m} = qm \times 2l = m \times 2l \text{ SI unit is Am}^2$$

02 The magnetic force between the two poles of a magnet of pole strength m_1, m_2 and separated by r is given by

$$\mathbf{F} = \frac{\mu_0}{4\pi} \cdot \frac{m_1 m_2}{r^2}$$

03 Magnetic field strength at a point on axial line of a bar magnet is given by

$$\mathbf{B}_{\text{axial}} = \frac{\mu_0}{4\pi} \cdot \frac{2\,\mathbf{m}d}{(d^2 - l^2)^2}$$

when $l << d$, $\mathbf{B}_{\text{axial}} = \frac{\mu_0}{4\pi} \cdot \frac{2\,\mathbf{m}}{d^3}$

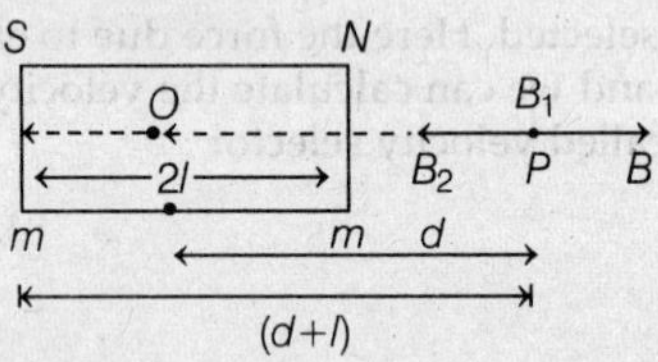

where, d is the distance from the centre of magnet to the point p and $2l$ be the length of the magnet. m is the dipole moment.

04 Magnetic field strength at a point on equitorial line of a bar magnet is give by

$$\mathbf{B}_{\text{eq}} = -\frac{\mu_0}{4\pi} \cdot \frac{\mathbf{m}}{(d^2 + l^2)^{3/2}}$$

when $l << d$, $B_{eq} = -\frac{\mu_0}{4\pi}\frac{\mathbf{m}}{d^3}$

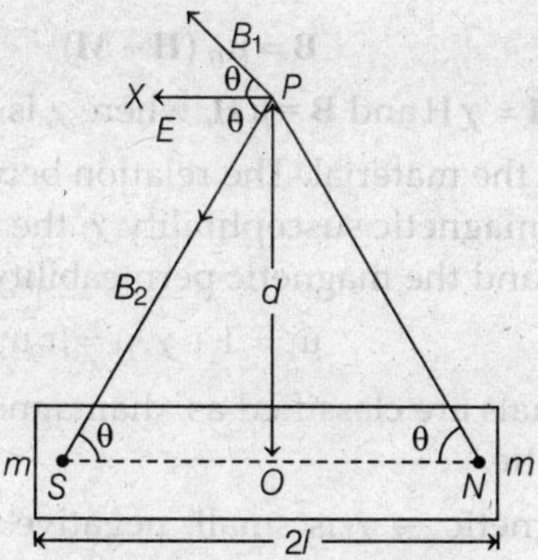

where, d is the distance from the centre of the magnet to the point P and $2l$ be the length of magnet. m is the dipole moment.

05 The magnetic moment of a current loop is given by

$$\mathbf{m} = N I \mathbf{A}$$

It's SI unit is A-m^2

where, N = number of turns, I = current,   = area vector.

06 When a bar magnet of dipole moment $\mathbf{m}$ is placed in a uniform magnetic field $\mathbf{B}$, then

(i) force on the magnet (magnetic dipole) is zero.

(ii) torque on the magnet (magnetic dipole)

$$\tau = \mathbf{m} \times \mathbf{B} = mB\sin\theta \text{ J}$$

(iii) potential energy $U = -\mathbf{m}\cdot\mathbf{B} = -mB(\cos\theta_2 - \cos\theta_1)$
$= MB[\cos\theta_1 - \cos\theta_2)\text{J}$

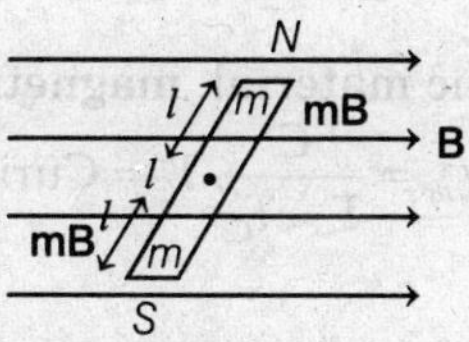

07 Gauss's law in magnetism states that the net magnetic flux through any closed surface is zero *i.e.*, monopole do not exist.

$$\int_S \mathbf{B}.d\mathbf{S} = 0$$

08 A material placed in an external magnetic field B_0. The magnetic intensity is defined as $\mathbf{H} = \frac{\mathbf{B}_0}{\mu_0}$

09 If the magnetization **M** of the material is its net dipole moment per unit volume, then the magnetic field **B** in the material is

$$\mathbf{B} = \mu_0 (\mathbf{H} + \mathbf{M})$$

10 For a material $\mathbf{M} = \chi \mathrm{H}$ and $\mathbf{B} = \mu \mathbf{H}$, where χ is called the magnetic susceptibility of the material. The relation between three quantities—the magnetic susceptibility χ, the relative magnetic permeability μ_r and the magnetic permeability μ is given by

$$\mu_r = 1 + \chi, \mu = \mu_0 \mu_r$$

11 Magnetic materials are classified as, diamagnetic, paramagnetic and ferromagnetic.

(i) For diamagnetic $\rightarrow \chi$ is small, negative and independent of temperature.

(ii) For paramagnetic $\rightarrow \chi$ is small positive and inversely proportional to absolute temperature T .

(iii) For ferromagnetic $\rightarrow \chi$ is large and they are characterized by non-linear relation between **B** and **H.** They show the property of hysteresis.

12 **Curie Law** (i) For paramagnetic material, Magnetic succeptibility

$$\chi_m = \frac{C}{T}$$

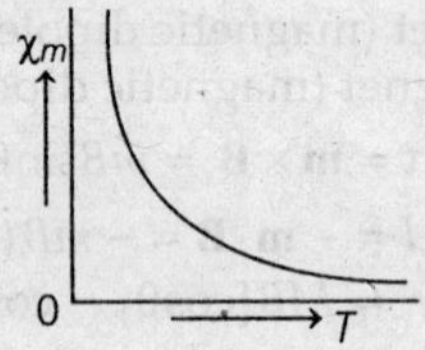

(ii) **For ferromagnetic material, magnetic succeptibility**

$$\chi_m = \frac{C}{T - T_C}, T_C = \text{Curie temperature}$$

Exercises

Question 1 A short bar magnet placed with its axis at 30º with a uniform external magnetic field of 0.25 T experiences a torque of magnitude equal to 4.5×10^{-2} J. What is the magnitude of magnetic moment of the magnet?

◎ ***Thinking Process*** To find the magnitude of magnetic moment of the magnet, use the concept of torque acting on magnetic dipole when placed in a magnetic field.

Sol. Given, uniform magnetic field $B = 0.25$ T

The magnitude of torque $\tau = 4.5 \times 10^{-2}$ J

Angle between magnetic moment and magnetic field $\theta = 30°$

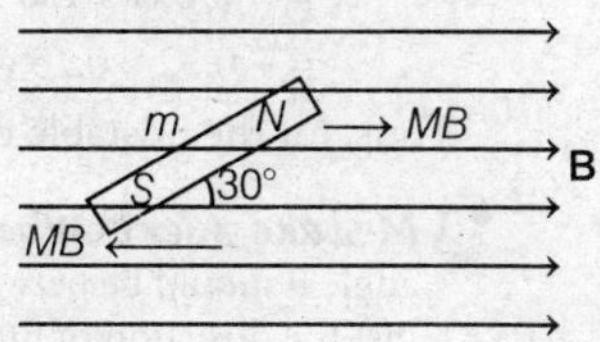

Torque experienced on a magnet placed in external magnetic field

$$\tau = \mathbf{m} \times \mathbf{B}$$

$$\tau = mB \sin \theta \qquad (\because \mathbf{A} \times \mathbf{B} = AB \sin \theta)$$

$$4.5 \times 10^{-2} = M \times 0.25 \times \sin 30°$$

$$m = \frac{4.5 \times 10^{-2}}{0.25 \times \sin 30°}$$

$$= \frac{4.5 \times 10^{-2} \times 2}{0.25 \times 1} \qquad \left(\because \sin 30° = \frac{1}{2}\right)$$

$$= 0.36 \text{ J/T}$$

Thus, the magnitude of magnetic moment of the magnet is 0.36 J/T.

Question 2 A short bar magnet of magnetic moment $m = 0.32$ J/T is placed in a uniform magnetic field of 0.15 T. If the bar is free to rotate in the plane of the field, which orientation would correspond to its (a) stable and (b) unstable equilibrium? What is the potential energy of the magnet in each case?

Sol. Given, magnetic moment of magnet $\mathbf{m} = 0.32$ J/T

The magnitude of magnetic field $\mathbf{B} = 0.15$ T

(a) For stable equilibrium, the angle between magnetic moment ($\mathbf{m}$) and magnetic field ($\mathbf{B}$) is $\theta = 0°$

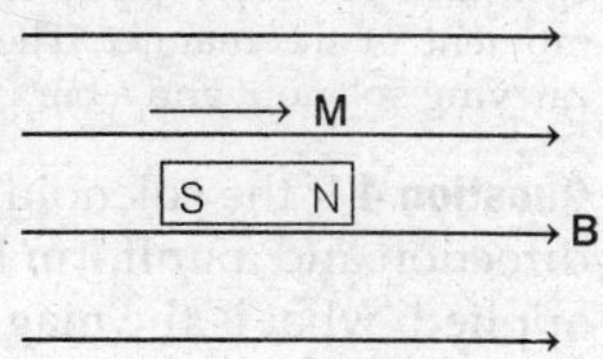

($\because$ In this position, magnetic dipole moment will be in a direction parallel to magnetic field thus no torque will act on it.) $\tau = mB\sin 0° = 0$

∵ The potential energy of the magnet

$$U = -\mathbf{m} \cdot \mathbf{B}$$

$$= -mB\cos\theta \qquad (\because \mathbf{A}\cdot\mathbf{B} = AB\cos\theta)$$

$$= -0.32 \times 0.15 \cos 0^\circ = -4.8 \times 10^{-2}\ \text{J}$$

Thus, for the stable equilibrium the potential energy is -4.8×10^{-2}J.

(b) For the unstable equilibrium, the angle between the magnetic moment and magnetic field is 180°.

Thus, no torque will act on it

$$\tau = mB\sin 180^\circ = 0$$

$$\theta = 180^\circ$$

Potential energy of the magnet

$$U = -mB\cos 180^\circ$$

$$= -0.32 \times 0.15\,(-1) = 4.8 \times 10^{-2}\ \text{J}$$

Thus, for the unstable equilibrium the potential energy is 4.8×10^{-2} J.

Mistake Alert When using the potential energy formula, remember the angle θ should be between the magnetic moment and the magnetic field, not just the direction of motion. Misplacing the angle leads to incorrect energy values.

Question 3 A closely wound solenoid of 800 turns and area of cross-section 2.5×10^{-4} m^2 carries a current of 3.0 A. Explain the sense in which the solenoid acts like a bar magnet. What is its associated magnetic moment?

Sol. Given, number of turns $N = 800$

Area of cross-section of solenoid $A = 2.5 \times 10^{-4}$ m^2

Current through solenoid $I = 3$ A

As a current passes through a solenoid, a magnetic field is produced. By the use of Maxwell's right hand grip rule, the magnetic field is along the axis of the solenoid. Using the formula of magnetic moment.

$$\mathbf{m} = NIA$$

$$= 800 \times 3 \times 2.5 \times 10^{-4}$$

$$= 0.6\ \text{J/T along the axis of the solenoid}$$

A current carrying solenoid of closely wound turns act as a bar magnet because each turn provide a dipole moment and all turns together provides the dipoles moment of the magnet. The pattern of magnetic field lines due to a current carrying solenoid and a bar magnet is same.

Question 4 If the solenoid in Q. 3 is free to turn about the vertical direction and a uniform horizontal magnetic field of 0.25 T is applied, what is the magnitude of torque on the solenoid when its axis makes an angle of 30° with the direction of applied field?

Sol. Given, magnetic field $B = 0.25$ T

Angle between magnetic moment and the magnetic field $\theta = 30^\circ$

from the Q. 3 We get, Magnetic moment $\mathbf{m} = 0.6$ J/T

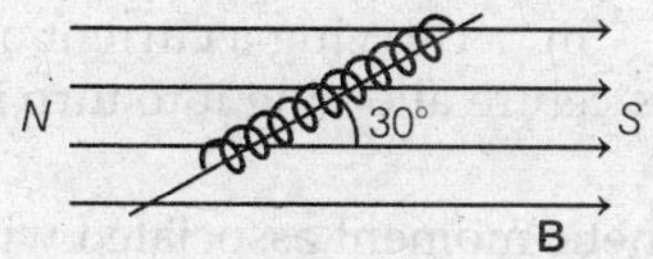

Torque acting on the solenoid when it is placed at an angle θ with the magnetic field.

$$\tau = \mathbf{m}B \sin\theta = 0.6 \times 0.25 \sin 30°$$
$$= 0.6 \times 0.25 \times \frac{1}{2}$$
$$= 0.075 \text{ N-m}$$

Thus, the magnitude of the torque on the solenoid is 0.075 N-m.

Question 5 A bar magnet of magnetic moment 1.5 J/T lies aligned with the direction of a uniform magnetic field of 0.22 T.

(a) What is the amount of work required by an external torque to turn the magnet so as to align its magnetic moment: (i) normal to the field direction, (ii) opposite to the field direction?

(b) What is the torque on the magnet in cases (i) and (ii)?

Sol. Given, magnetic moment of magnet $\mathbf{m} = 1.5$ J/T

Uniform magnetic field $B = 0.22$ T

(a) (i) Angle $\theta_1 = 0°$ ($\because$ The magnet lies aligned in the direction of field)

and $\theta_2 = 90°$

($\because$ The magnet is to be aligned normal to the field direction)

Work done in rotating the magnet from angle θ_1 to angle θ_2

$$W = mB(\cos\theta_1 - \cos\theta_2)$$
$$= 1.5 \times 0.22 (\cos 0° - \cos 90°) = 0.33 \text{ J}$$

(ii) Angle $\theta_1 = 0°$ and $\theta_2 = 180°$

($\because$ Magnet is to be aligned opposite to the direction of field)

Work done $W = mB(\cos\theta_1 - \cos\theta_2)$

$$= 1.5 \times 0.22[(1-(-1)]$$
$$= 1.5 \times 0.22 \times 2 = 0.66 \text{ J}$$

(b) Using the formula of torque, $\tau = mB\sin\theta$

(i) $\theta = 90°$ (when magnetic moment normal to the field)

$$\tau = 1.5 \times 0.22 \sin 90° = 0.33 \text{ N-m}$$

(ii) $\theta = 180°$ (when magnetic moment opposite to the field)

$$\tau = 1.5 \times 0.22 \sin 180° = 0$$

Note Torque depends on both the magnitude of the magnetic moment and the sine of the angle between the moment and the magnetic field.

Question 6 A closely wound solenoid of 2000 turns and area of cross-section $1.6 \times 10^{-4}\ m^2$, carrying a current of 4.0 A, is suspended through its centre allowing it to turn in a horizontal plane.

(a) What is the magnetic moment associated with the solenoid?

(b) What are the force and torque on the solenoid, if a uniform horizontal magnetic field of 7.5×10^{-2} T is set up at an angle of 30° with the axis of the solenoid?

Sol. Given, number of turns $N = 2000$

Area of cross-section $A = 1.6 \times 10^{-4}\ m^2$

Current $I = 4$ A

(a) Magnetic moment associated with solenoid

$\mathbf{m} = NIA = 2000 \times 4 \times 1.6 \times 10^{-4} = 1.28$ J/T, along the axis of the solenoid

(b) The force (net) on the solenoid is zero, because two equal and opposite forces (on each of its poles) are acting, but their lines of action are parallel so they form a couple thus a torque (no force) is applied on it.

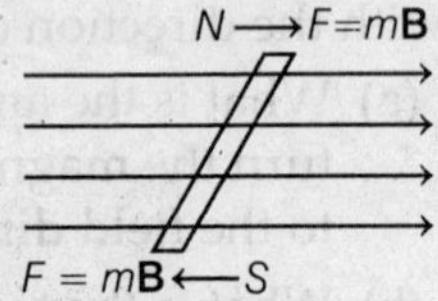

Torque on the solenoid $\tau = \mathbf{m}B \sin\theta$ (given $\theta = 30°$)

$$= 1.28 \times 7.5 \times 10^{-2} \sin 30°$$

$$= 1.28 \times 7.5 \times 10^{-2} \times \frac{1}{2}$$

$$= 4.8 \times 10^{-2} \text{ N-m (J), in a direction } \perp \text{ to } \mathbf{m} \text{ and } \mathbf{B}$$

Question 7 A short bar magnet has a magnetic moment of 0.48 J/T. Give the direction and magnitude of the magnetic field produced by the magnet at a distance of 10 cm from the centre of the magnet on (a) the axis, (b) the equatorial line (normal bisector) of the magnet

Thinking Process Here we have to find out the magnetic field at a point on the axial line and on the equatorial line. So use the formula of magnetic field due to a bar magnet at its axial and equatorial position.

Sol. Given, magnetic moment of bar magnet $\mathbf{m} = 0.48$ J/T

Distance from the centre of magnet $d = 10$ cm $= 0.1$ m

(a) When the point lies on the axial line.

Magnetic field at point P

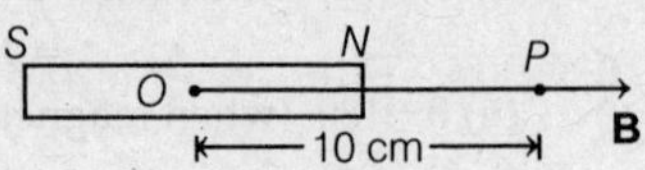

$$\mathbf{B} = \frac{\mu_0}{4\pi} \cdot \frac{2\mathbf{m}}{d^3}$$

$$= \frac{10^{-7} \times 2 \times 0.48}{(0.1)^3}$$

$$= 0.96 \times 10^{-4} \text{ T}$$

The direction of magnetic field is along the direction of magnetic moment. We know that the direction of magnetic moment is from S to N pole. Thus, the direction of magnetic field is from S to N pole of the magnet.

(b) Use the formula of magnetic field due to a short bar magnet on its equatorial line.

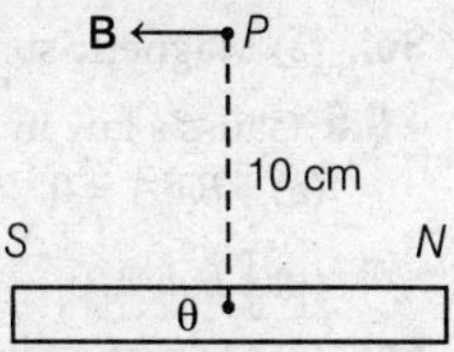

$\therefore$ Magnetic field at point P

$$\mathbf{B} = \frac{\mu_0}{4\pi} \cdot \frac{\mathbf{m}}{d^3}$$

$$= 10^{-7} \times \frac{0.48}{(0.1)^3} = 0.48 \times 10^{-4} \text{ T}$$

The direction of magnetic field on equatorial line is opposite to the direction of magnetic moment. So, the direction of magnetic field is from N to S pole of the magnet.

Note The field on the axial line is stronger than on the equatorial line for the same distance.

DIKSHA APP Questions

☐ Multiple Choice Questions

Q.1 The magnetism of a magnet is due to

(a) earth

(b) cosmic rays

(c) due to pressure of big magnet inside the earth

(d) spin motion of electrons

Sol. (d) The magnetism of magnet is due to the spin motion of electron.

Q.2 Magnetic susceptibility of a diamagnetic substance

(a) decreases with temperature

(b) is not affected by temperature

(c) increases with temperature

(d) first increases then decreases with temeprature

Sol. (b) Magnetic susceptibility x_m of diamagnetic material is small negative which is independent of temperature.

Q.3 Susceptibility of a diamagnetic substance is

(a) zero (b) negative

(c) less than 1 (d) greater than 1

Sol. (b) Susceptibility is negative for a diamagnetic substance.

Q.4 What are the dimensions of magnetic susceptibility

(a) Dimensionless (b) $[L^{-1}A]$

(c) $[MLT^{-2}A^{-2}]$ (d) $[L^{-2}A]$

Sol. (a) Magnetic susceptibility is dimensionless.

Q.5 Gauss's law in magnetism is

(a) $\oint B.dA = 0$ (b) $\oint b.dV = 0$

(c) $\oint B.ds = 0$ (d) $\oint B.ds = u_0 l$

Sol. (c) Magnetic flux through closed surface is zero *i.e.,*

$$\oint \mathbf{B} \cdot \mathbf{ds} = 0$$

it signifies monopole do not exist.

□ Short Answer Type

Q.1 A ball of superconducting material is dipped in liquid nitrogen and placed near a bar magnet. (i) in which direction will it move ? (ii) What will be the direction of its magnetic moment ?

Sol. A superconducting material and nitrogen are diamagnetic in nature. When a ball of superconducting material is dipped in liquid nitrogen, it behaves as a diamagnetic material. When it is placed near a bar magnet, it will be feebly magnetized opposite to the direction of magnetizing field. Due to it, (i) it will be repelled *i.e.,* moving away from magnet (ii) its direction of magnetic moment will be opposite to the direction of the-magnetic field of magnet.

Q.2 From molecular point of view, discuss the temperature evidence of susceptibility for diamagnetism, paramagnetism and ferromagnetism.

Sol. Diamagnetism is due to the orbital motion of electrons in an atom developing magnetic moments opposite to applied field. Thus, the resultant magnetic moment of the diamagnetic material is zero, and hence the susceptibility x of diamagnetic material is not much affected by temperature.

Paramagnetism and ferromagnetism is due to alignments of atomic magnetic moments in the direction of the applied field. As temperature is raised, the alignment is disturbed, resulting in decrease in susceptibility of both with increase in temperature.

Electromagnetic Induction

CHAPTER 06

Important Points

01 The magnetic flux through any surface of area **A** placed in magnetic field **B** is given by

$$\phi = \mathbf{B} \cdot \mathbf{A} = BA \cos \theta$$

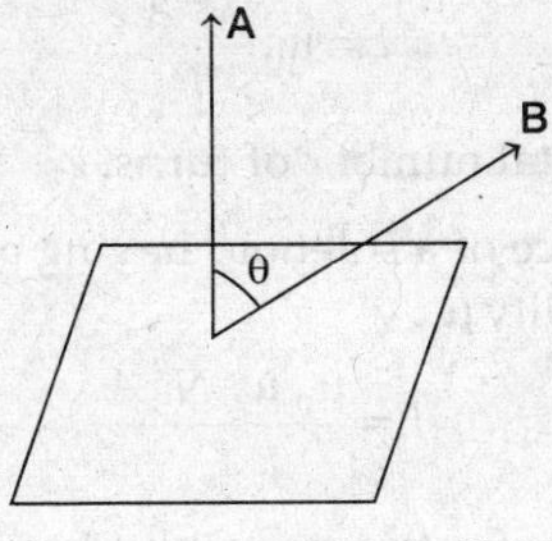

Where, θ is the angle between magnetic field and area vector.

02 According to the Faraday's law of electromagnetic induction, the induced emf is given by

$$\varepsilon = -\frac{d\phi}{dt}$$

or

$$= -\frac{Nd\phi}{dt}$$

Where, N be the number of turns.

03 Lenz's law states that the polarity of the induced emf is such that it tends to produce a current which opposes the change in magnetic flux that produces it. It is based on law of conservation of energy.

04 The motional emf in a rod of length l, placed normally in a uniform magnetic field B and moving with velocity v is

$$\varepsilon = Bvl$$

05 A rod of length l, rotating with angular velocity ω in a uniform magnetic field B perpendicular to the plane of rotation

$$\varepsilon = \frac{1}{2} B\omega l^2$$

06 The self inductance of a coil is given by,

$$\phi = LI$$

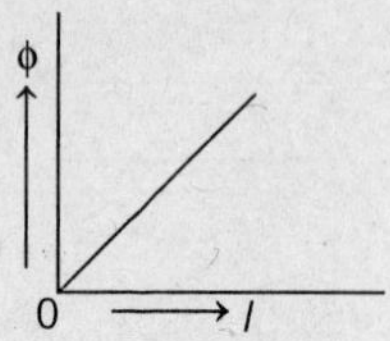

where, L is coefficient of self inductance.

07 Induced emf $\varepsilon = -\dfrac{LdI}{dt}$

where, L is coefficient of self inductance.

08 Induced emf between two neighbouring placed coils

$$\varepsilon = -M\frac{dI}{dt}$$

where, M is coefficient of mutual inductance.

09 For a long solenoid, the self induction coefficient is

$$L = \mu_0 \frac{N^2 A}{l}$$

where, N is the total number of turns.

10 The self-inductance of a solenoid having a magnetic core with relative permeability μ_r.

$$L = \frac{\mu_0\, \mu_r\, N^2 A}{l}$$

11 Mutual inductance for two co-axial solenoids of same length

$$M = \frac{\mu_0 N_1 N_2 A}{l}$$

where, N_1 and N_2 are total number of turns of the two solenoids. A is the area of cross-section of each coil.

12 In an AC generator, the induced emf produced is given by

$$\varepsilon = \quad .n\,\omega t$$

$$\varepsilon_0 = NAB\omega = \text{Maximum emf}$$

Where, $\omega = 2\pi f$ rad/s is angular frequency

$$\varepsilon = NB\,A\,(2\pi f)\sin(2\pi f\,t)$$

where, f is the frequency.

13 Magnetic energy stored in a coil of inductance L is given by

$$U = \frac{1}{2} LI^2$$

Exercises

Question 1 Predict the direction of induced current in the situations described by the following figures.

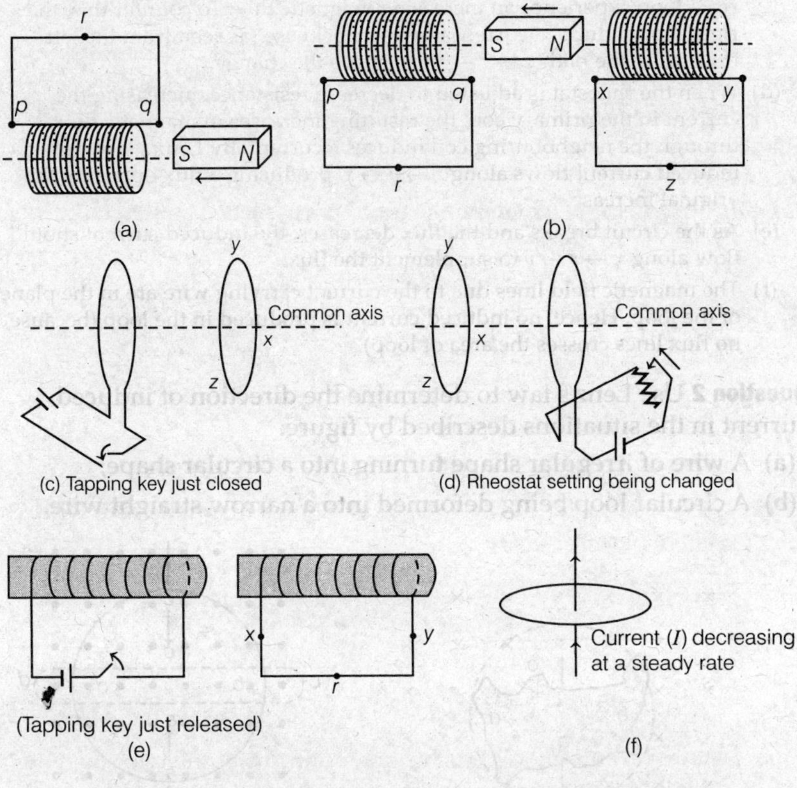

◎ ***Thinking Process*** According to Lenz's law, the direction of induced current is always in such a way that it opposes the cause due to which it is produced

Sol.

(a) When the South pole of the magnet moves toward the coil, the coil induces a current to oppose the increase in magnetic flux. To do this, it generates a South pole at end q, creating a repelling magnetic field as per Lenz's law. This requires a clockwise current when viewed from the magnet's side, flowing along the path $q \rightarrow r \rightarrow p \rightarrow q$.

(b) When the magnet moves so that its South pole approaches coil pq and its North pole moves away from coil xy, induced current develop to oppose these changes. The coil pq forms a South pole at q, and coil xy forms a South pole at x, resulting in clockwise current (from the magnet's view) flowing along $p \rightarrow r \rightarrow q$ and $y \rightarrow z \rightarrow x$ respectively.

(c) When the left loop's circuit is completed and current begins to flow, the right loop experience an increasing magnetic flux. To counter this, the right loop induces a current flowing clockwise (as seen from the left, (following the path $y \rightarrow z \rightarrow x$ to oppose the change.

(d) When the rheostat is adjusted to decrease resistance, increasing the current in the primary coil, the resulting increases in magnetic flux through the neighbouring coil induces a current. By Lenz's law, this induced current flows along $z \rightarrow y \rightarrow x$, producing a flux opposing the original increase.

(e) As the circuit breaks and the flux decreases, the induced current should flow along $x \rightarrow r \rightarrow y$ to supplement the flux.

(f) The magnetic field lines due to the current carrying wire are in the plane of the loop. Hence, no induced current is produced in the loop (because no flux lines crosses the area of loop).

Question 2 Use Lenz's law to determine the direction of induced current in the situations described by figure.

(a) A wire of irregular shape turning into a circular shape;

(b) A circular loop being deformed into a narrow straight wire.

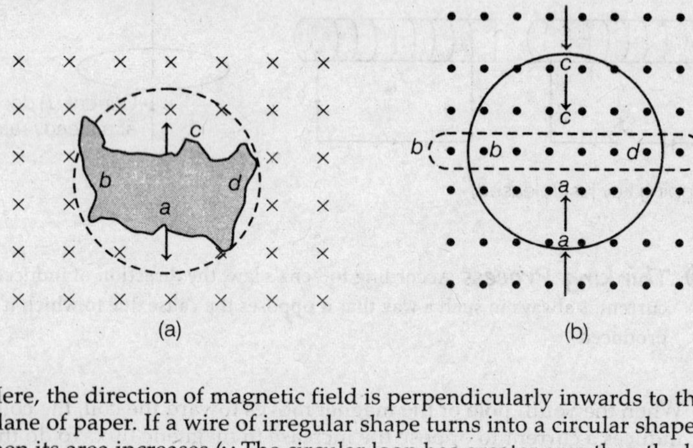

Sol.

(a) Here, the direction of magnetic field is perpendicularly inwards to the plane of paper. If a wire of irregular shape turns into a circular shape then its area increases ($\because$ The circular loop has greater area than the loop of irregular shape.) so, that the magnetic flux linked also increases.

Now, the induced current is produced in a direction such that it decreases the magnetic field [*i.e.*, the current will flow in such a direction so that the wire forming the loop is pulled inward in all directions (to decrease the area)], *i.e.*, current is in anticlockwise direction, i.e., *adcba*.

(b) When a circular loop deforms into a narrow straight wire, the magnetic flux linked with it also decreases. The current induced due to change in flux will flow in such a direction that it will oppose the decrease in magnetic flux so, it will flow anticlockwise, *i.e.*, along $a'd'c'b'a'$, due to which the magnetic field produced will be out of the plane of paper.

Question 3 A long solenoid with 15 turns per cm has a small loop of area 2.0 cm^2 placed inside the solenoid normal to its axis. If the current carried by the solenoid changes steadily from 2.0 A to 4.0 A in 0.1 s, what is the induced emf in the loop while the current is changing?

Sol. Given, number of turns $n = 15$ per cm = 1500 per metre

Area of small loop $A = 2\,\text{cm}^2 = 2\times10^{-4}\,\text{m}^2$

Change in current $\frac{dI}{dt} = \frac{4-2}{0.1} = \frac{2}{0.1} = 20\,\text{A/s}$

Let e be the induced emf,

According to Faraday's law,

$$e = \frac{d\phi}{dt} = \frac{d}{dt}(BA) \qquad (\because \phi = BA)$$

or
$$e = A\frac{dB}{dt} = A\frac{d}{dt}(\mu_0 nI)$$

($\because$ Magnetic field inside the solenoid $B = \mu_0 nI$)

or
$$e = A\mu_0 n\frac{dI}{dt}$$

$$e = 2\times10^{-4}\times4\times3.14\times10^{-7}\times1500\times20$$

$$(\because \mu_0 = 4\pi\times10^{-7})$$

$$e = 7.5\times10^{6}\,\text{V}$$

Thus, the induced emf in the loop is 7.5×10^{6} V.

Mistake Alert Ensure you use the correct formula $\phi_B = \mathbf{B}\times\mathbf{A}$ and that the flux change is correctly computed as the difference in flux for the initial and final magnetic fields.

Note The emf induced is related to the rate of change of current and thus the rate of change of the magnetic field.
The negative sign in Faraday's law indicates the direction of the induced emf opposes the change in flux.

Question 4 A rectangular wire loop of sides 8 cm and 2 cm with a small cut is moving out of a region of uniform magnetic field of magnitude 0.3 T directed normal to the loop. What is the emf developed across the cut if the velocity of the loop is 1 cm/s in a direction normal to the (a) longer side, (b) shorter side of the loop? For how long does the induced voltage last in each case?

◎ *Thinking Process* Use the concept of motional emf as wire loop is moving normal to the magnetic field.

Sol. Given, length of the loop $l = 8 \text{ cm} = 8 \times 10^{-2}$ m

Width of the loop $b = 2 \text{ cm} = 2 \times 10^{-2}$ m

Velocity of the loop = 1 cm/s = 0.01 m/s

Magnitude of magnetic field $B = 0.3$ T

(a) **When velocity is normal to the longer side** ($l = 8 \text{ cm} = 8 \times 10^{-2}$ m)

In this case, motional emf

$$e = Blv = 0.3 \times 8 \times 10^{-2} \times 0.01 = 2.4 \times 10^{-4} \text{ V}$$

$$\text{Time} = \frac{\text{Distance}}{\text{Velocity}} = \frac{\text{Shorter side (width)}}{\text{Velocity}} = \frac{h}{v}$$

$$t = \frac{2 \times 10^{-2}}{0.01} = 2 \text{ s}$$

Hence, the induced voltage is 2.4×10^{-4} V which lasts for 2 sec.

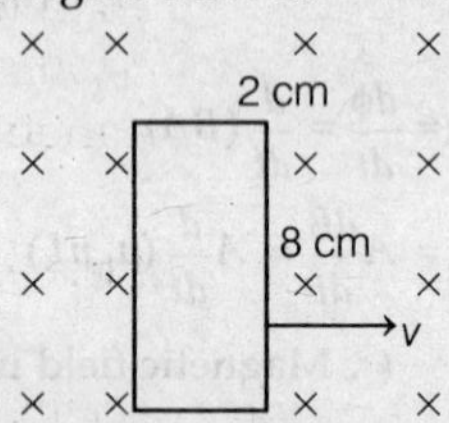

(b) **When velocity is normal to the shorter side** ($l = 2 \text{ cm} = 2 \times 10^{-2}$ m)

In this case, the developed emf

$$e = Blv = 0.3 \times 2 \times 10^{-2} \times 0.01$$

$$e = 0.6 \times 10^{-4} \text{ V}$$

$$\text{Time} = \frac{\text{Longer side (length)}}{\text{Velocity}} = \frac{l}{v} = \frac{8 \times 10^{-2}}{0.01}$$

$$t = 8 \text{ s}$$

Hence, the induced voltage is 0.6×10^{-4} V which lasts for 8 sec.

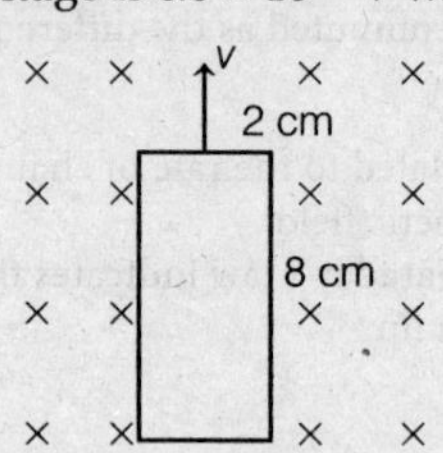

Question 5 A 1.0 m long metallic rod is rotated with an angular frequency of 400 rad/s about an axis normal to the rod passing through its one end. The other end of the rod is in contact with a circular metallic ring. A constant and uniform magnetic field of 0.5 T parallel to the axis exists everywhere. Calculate the emf developed between the centre and the ring.

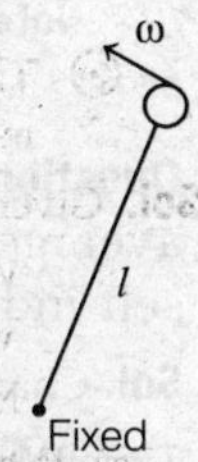

Sol. Length of rod $l = 1\,\text{m}$

Angular frequency of rod $\omega = 400$ rad/s

Magnetic field $B = 0.5$ T

The linear velocity of fixed end = 0

The linear velocity of other end = $l\omega$ $(\because v = r\omega)$

Average linear velocity of the rod, $v = \dfrac{0 + l\omega}{2} = \dfrac{l\omega}{2}$ ...(i)

By using the formula of motional emf,

$$\varepsilon = Bvl = \frac{Bl\omega}{2} \cdot l = \frac{1}{2} Bl^2\omega \qquad \text{[From Eq. (i)]}$$

$$\varepsilon = \frac{0.5 \times (1)^2 \times 400}{2} \Rightarrow \varepsilon = 100\text{ V}$$

Thus, the emf developed between the centre and ring is 100 V.

Question 6 A horizontal straight wire 10 m long extending from east to west is falling with a speed of 5.0 m/s, at right angles to the horizontal component of the earth's magnetic field, 0.30×10^{-4} Wb/m^2.

(a) What is the instantaneous value of the emf induced in the wire?
(b) What is the direction of the emf ?
(c) Which end of the wire is at the higher electrical potential?

Sol. Given, velocity of straight wire = 5 m/s

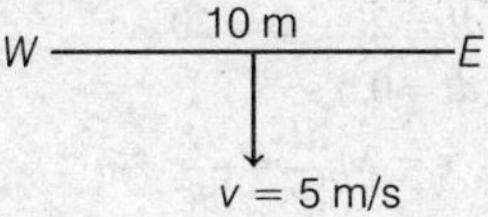

Magnetic field of horizontal component of Earth

$B = 0.30 \times 10^{-4}$ Wb/m^2, directed from South to north

Length of wire $l = 10$ m

(a) Emf induced in the wire $\varepsilon = Blv \sin\theta$

Here, $\theta = 90°$

$\therefore \quad \sin\theta = 1$

($\because$ Wire is falling at right angle to Earth's horizontal magnetic field component)

$$= 0.3 \times 10^{-4} \times 10 \times 5 = 1.5 \times 10^{-3}\text{ V}$$

(b) According to the Fleming's right hand rule, the force is downward, then the direction of induced emf will be from West to East.

(c) As the direction of induced emf or current is from West to East, the West end of the wire is at higher potential.

($\because$ Current always flows from a point at higher potential to a point at lower potential)

Note Since the wire is moving in magnetic field, an induced EMF is generated according to Faraday's Law of induction.

Question 7 Current in a circuit falls from 5.0 A to 0.0 A in 0.1 s. If an average emf of 200 V induced, give an estimate of the self-inductance of the circuit.

Sol. Change in current, $dI = 0 - 5 = -5$ A

Time taken in current change $dt = 0.1$ s

Induced average emf $\varepsilon_{av} = 200$ V

Induced emf in the circuit $\varepsilon = -L\dfrac{dI}{dt}$

$$200 = -L\left(\frac{-5}{0.1}\right)$$

or $$L = \frac{200}{50} = 4\,\text{H}$$

Mistake Alert Always check the signs of the quantities like ΔI and emf. Here, both change in current and induced emf have negative signs, but they cancel out in the formula.

Question 8 A pair of adjacent coils has a mutual inductance of 1.5 H. If the current in one coil changes from 0 to 20 A in 0.5 s, what is the change of flux linkage with the other coil?

Sol. Given, mutual inductance of coil $M = 1.5$ H

Current change in coil $dI = 20 - 0 = 20$ A

Time taken in change $dt = 0.5$ s

Induced emf in the coil $\varepsilon = M\dfrac{dI}{dt} = \dfrac{d\phi}{dt}$

or $$d\phi = M.dI = 1.5 \times 20$$

$$d\phi = 30\,\text{Wb}$$

Thus, the change of flux linkage is 30 Wb.

DIKSHA APP Questions

Multiple Choice Questions

Q.1 If the speed of rotation of a dynamo is doubled, then induced emf will

(a) become four times (b) become half
(c) remain unchanged (d) become double

Sol. (d) The induced emf in a dynamo is directly proportional to the speed of rotation. If the speed is doubled the rate of change of magnetic flux doubled, so the induced emf will become double.

Q.2 In an *AC* generator a coil with *N* turns, each having area *A* and total resistance *R*, rotates with frequency ω in a magnetic field B. The maximum value of emf generated in the coil is

(a) $NBA\omega$ (b) NAB
(c) $NABR\omega$ (d) $NABR$

Sol. (a) $\because \phi = BA\cos\omega t \Rightarrow e = \frac{-Nd\phi}{dt} = -N\frac{d}{dt}(BA\cos\omega t) = -NBA(\omega)(-\sin\omega t)$

$$\varepsilon = NAB\omega \sin\omega t$$

For maximum emf, $\sin\omega t$ = maximum = 1

$$\varepsilon_{max} = NAB\omega.$$

Q.3 The number of turns and length of the solenoid are both doubled, keeping area of cross-section of the solenoid same. Then the self-inductance of the coil will be

(a) halved (b) doubled
(c) $1^{1/2}$ times the original value (d) Unaffected

Sol. (b) $\because L = \frac{\mu_0 N^2 A}{l}$

$$\therefore \quad L' = \frac{\mu_0 (2N)^2 A}{2l} = \frac{4}{2}\frac{\mu_0 N^2 A}{l}$$

$$= \frac{2\mu_0 N^2 A}{l} = 2L$$

Q.4 If *N* is the number of turns in a coil, then the value of self-inductance varies as

(a) N (b) N^2
(c) N^{-2} (d) N^3

Sol. (b) $\because L = \frac{\mu_0 N^2 A}{l} \Rightarrow L \propto N^2$

Q.5 A coil is suspended in a uniform magnetic field. When a current is passed through the coil it starts oscillating. But when an aluminium plate is placed near the coil, it stops. This is due to

(a) development of air current when the plate is placed
(b) induction of electrical charge on the plate
(c) shielding of magnetic lines of force as aluminium is a paramagnetic material
(d) electromagnetic induction in the aluminium plate giving rise to electromagnetic damping

Sol. (d) The oscillating coil produces time variable magnetic field. If causes eddy current in the aluminum plate which causes anti-torque on the coil, due to which it stops. Thus, electromagnetic induction in the aluminium plate gives rise to electromagnetic damping.

Q.6 The magnetic flux through a coil of resistance R changes by an amount $\Delta\phi$ in time Δt. The total quantity of electric charge Q, which passes through any point of the coil is

(a) $Q = \Delta\phi / R$ (b) $Q = \Delta\phi / \Delta t$
(c) $Q = (\Delta\phi / \Delta t) + R$ (d) $Q = \Delta\phi \times R / \Delta t$

Sol. (a) $\because Q = I\Delta t = \frac{\varepsilon}{R}\Delta t = \frac{1}{R}\frac{\Delta\phi}{\Delta t}\Delta t$ $\left[\because \varepsilon = \frac{\Delta\phi}{\Delta t}\right]$

$$Q = \frac{\Delta\phi}{R}$$

Q.7 A graph between induced current and time is shown below, for a coil of resistance 50 Ω, when it is kept in a changing magnetic flux. The magnitude of change in flux through the coil (in weber) is

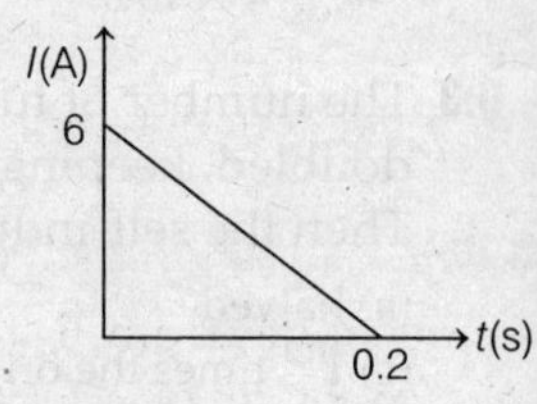

(a) 6 Wb (b) 30 Wb (c) 4 Wb (d) 2 Wb

Sol. (b) Area of induced current-time graph = induced charge

i.e., Area of triangle $= \frac{1}{2} \times 0.2 \times 6 = Q$

$$Q = 0.6\text{ C}$$

$$\because \quad Q = \frac{\Delta\phi}{R}$$

$$0.6 = \frac{\Delta\phi}{50}$$

$$\Rightarrow \quad \Delta\phi = 50 \times 0.6 = 30\text{ Wb}$$

Q.8 An aeroplane having a wing span of 35 m flies due north with the speed of 90 m/s. If the magnetic field $B = 4 \times 10^{-5}$ T then, the potential difference developed between the tip of the wings is

(a) 1.26 V (b) 1.03 V
(c) 12.6 V (d) 0.126 V

Sol. (d) $\varepsilon = Bvl = 4 \times 10^{-5} \times 90 \times 35$

$$= 12600 \times 10^{-5} = 0.126 \text{ Volt}$$

Q.9 A conducting square loop of side L and resistance R moves out of a uniform magnetic field B with a uniform velocity v as shown in the figure. The induced current in the loop is

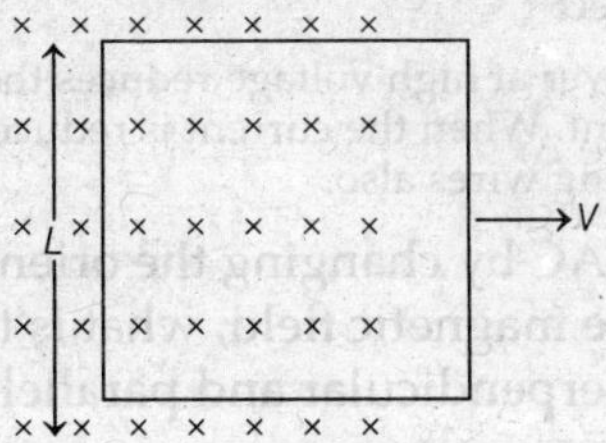

(a) zero (b) BRv
(c) BvL/R (d) BvL

Sol. (c) $\because \varepsilon = BvL$

Induced current $I = \dfrac{\varepsilon}{R} = \dfrac{BvL}{R}$

Q.10 A coil having an area A_0 is placed in a magnetic field, which changes from B_0 to $3B_0$ in time interval t. The magnitude.

(a) $3A_0\ B_0/t$ (b) $A_0\ B_0/t$
(c) $2A_0\ B_0/t$ (d) $4A_0\ B_0/t$

Sol. (c) Magnitude of emf $\varepsilon = d\phi/dt$ and $\phi = BA$

$$= A_0 d(3B_0 - B_0)/dt = 2A_0B_0/t$$

Q.11 A rectangular loop of area 20cm×30cm is placed in a magnetic field of 0.3 T, with its plane normal to the field. The magnetic flux linked with the coil is.

(a) 0.009 Wb (b) 0.018 Wb
(c) zero (d) 0.06 Wb

Sol. (b) $\phi = BA\cos 0 = 0.3 \times 20 \times 30 \times 10^{-4} \times 1 = 0.018$ Wb

☐ Short Answer Type

Q.1 Calculate the mutual inductance between two coils when a current of 2 A changes to 6 A in 2 s and induces an emf of 20 mV in the secondary coil.

Sol. $I_1 = 2\text{ A},\ I_2 = 6\text{ A},\ \Delta t = 2\text{ s},\ \varepsilon = 20\text{ mV} = 20 \times 10^{-3}\text{ V}$

$\because$
$$\varepsilon = -M\frac{\Delta I}{\Delta t}$$

$$|20 \times 10^{-3}| = \left|\frac{-M(6-2)}{2}\right| = \left|-M \times \frac{4}{2}\right|$$

$\Rightarrow$
$$M = 10 \times 10^{-3}\text{ H} \Rightarrow M = 10^{-2}\text{ H}$$

Q.2 For transmitting the power to a long distance why high voltage is preferred ?

Sol. Transmitting the power at high voltage reduces the power loss (I^2R) by decreasing the current. When the current is reduced we can reduce the size of the transmitting wires also.

Q.3 In producing the AC by changing the orientation of the coil with respect to the magnetic field, what is the induced emf when the coil is perpendicular and parallel with respect to the magnetic field ?

Sol. When the coil is perpendicular to the magnetic field the emf produced will be zero as angle between magnetic field and area vector is $\theta = 0°$, $e = e_0 \sin\theta$, $e = e_0 \sin 0 = 0$ and when parallel the emf induced will be maximum as angle between magnetic field and area vector is $\theta = 90°$, $e = e_0 \sin\theta = e_0 \sin 90°$, $e = e_0$ = maximum.

Q.4 What are the methods of producing induced emf ?

Sol. By changing

(i) the magnetic field (ii) the area of the coil

(iii) the relative orientation of the coil w.r.t magnetic field.

Q.5 What are the factors affect mutual inductance between the two coils ?

Sol.
- Number of turns
- Area
- Length of the coils
- Medium
- Coupling between the two coils

06 Mass is a measure of inertia in motion similarly how inductance acts in electric circuits ?

Sol. When a circuit is switched on, the increasing current induces an emf which opposes the growth of the current. Likewise, when the circuit is broken the decreasing current induces *i.e.*, an emf in the reverse direction. *i.e.*, electrical inertia. This emf now opposes the decay of current. Thus, inductance acts similar to mass.

Alternating Current

CHAPTER 07

Important Points

01 Instantaneous value of alternating voltage $V = V_0 \sin \omega t$,
V_0 = voltage amplitude or peak voltage, $\omega = 2\pi f$ rad/s
Instantaneous value of alternating current
$I = I_0 \sin \omega t$, I_0 = current amplitude or peak current $\omega = 2\pi f$ rad/s

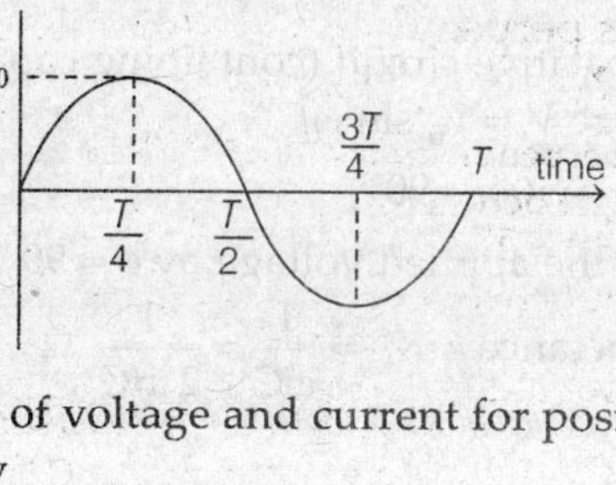

02 The mean value of voltage and current for positive positive half cycle is given by

$$V_m = \frac{2V_0}{\pi} = 0.637\, V_0$$

$$I_m = \frac{2I_0}{\pi} = 0.637\, I_0$$

03 The mean value of voltage and current for complete cycle is zero.

04 The virtual value or rms value of voltage and current flowing in the circuit is given by (for complete cycle)

$$V_{rms} = \frac{V_0}{\sqrt{2}} = 0.707\, V_0$$

$$I_{rms} = \frac{I_0}{\sqrt{2}} = 0.707\, I_0$$

05 For a pure resistance AC circuit-the applied voltage $V = V_0 \sin \omega t$ and Current $I = I_0 \sin \omega t$

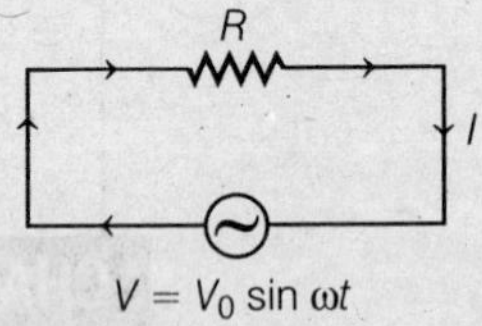

Circuit diagram

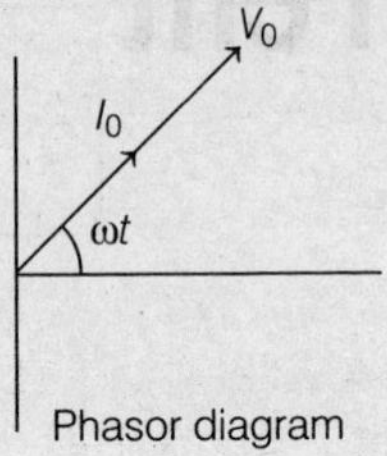

Phasor diagram

i.e., current is in phase with applied voltage ($\phi = 0$)

Resistance of AC circuit (impedance)$Z = R$

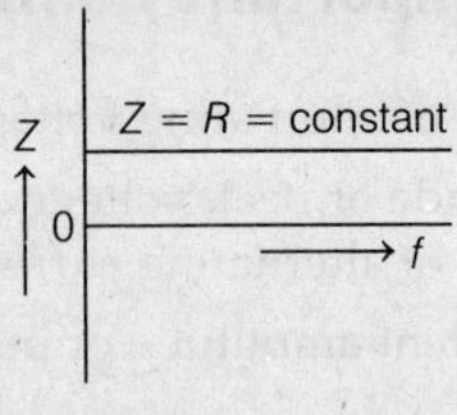

06 For a pure capacitive circuit (containing capacitor only),

Applied voltage $V = V_0 \sin \omega t$

Current $I = I_0 \sin (\omega t + 90°)$

Current leads the applied voltage by $\phi = 90°$

Capacitive reactance $= X_C = \dfrac{1}{\omega C} = \dfrac{1}{2\pi f C}\ \Omega$

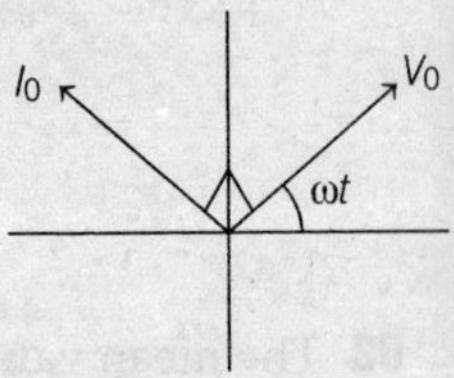

Phasor diagram

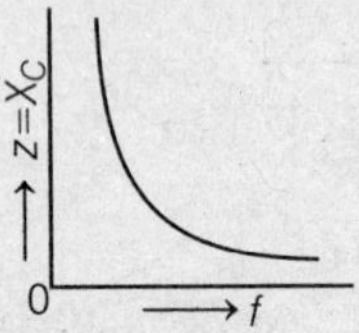

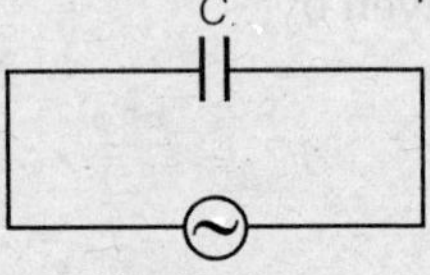

$$I_{rms} = \frac{E_{rms}}{X_C}$$

Average power consumed $= E_{rms} \cdot I_{rms} \cos 90° = 0$, therefore current in it is wattless current

07 For a pure inductive circuit,

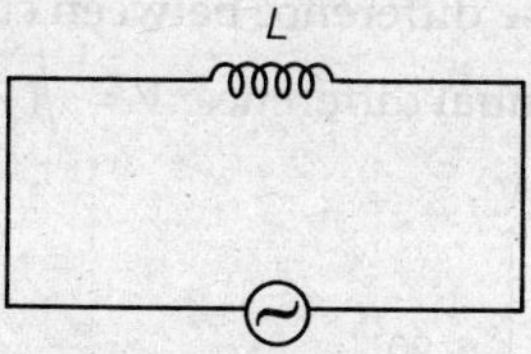

$V = V_0 \sin \omega t$

Applied voltage $V = V_0 \sin \omega t$

Current $I = I_0 \sin(\omega t - 90°)$

Current lags behind the applied voltage by 90°.

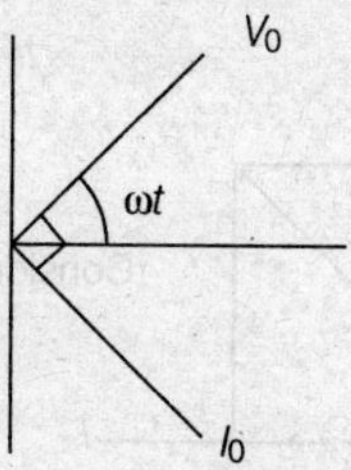

Phasor diagram

Inductive reactance $X_L = \omega L = 2\pi f L\,\Omega$

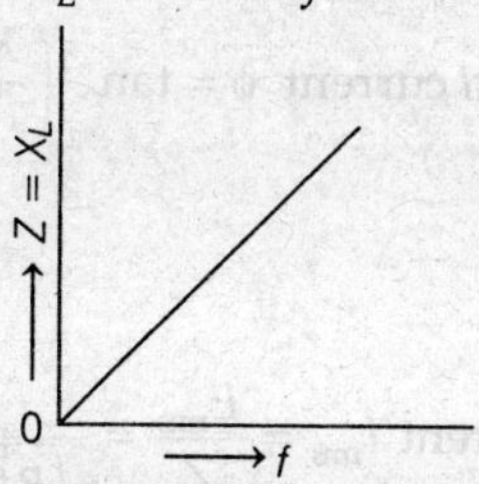

$$I_{\text{rms}} = \frac{E_{\text{rms}}}{X_L}$$

Average power consumed $= E_{\text{rms}} . I_{\text{rms}} \cos 90° = 0$, therefore current in it is called wattless current.

08 For a series *LCR* circuit,

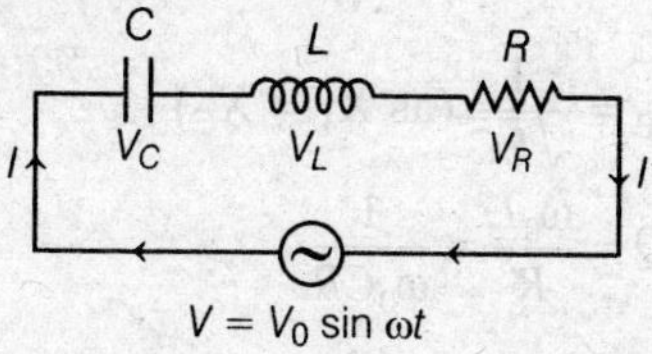

$V = V_0 \sin \omega t$

Applied voltage $V = V_0 \sin \omega t$

Current $I = I_0 \sin(\omega t - \phi)$
where, ϕ is the phase difference between current and voltage.
Resulting rms potential difference $V = \sqrt{(V_L - V_C)^2 + V_R^2}$

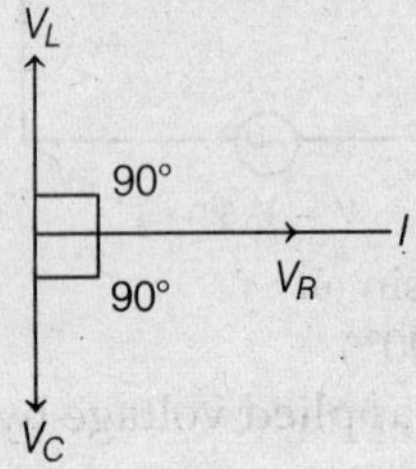

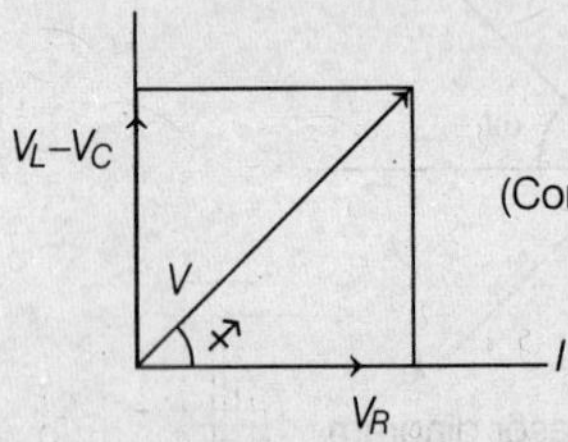

(Considering $V_L > V_C$)

Impedance of circuit $Z = \sqrt{R^2 + (X_L - X_C)^2}$

Phase angle between current $\phi = \tan^{-1}\left(\frac{X_L - X_C}{R}\right)$

$$\left[\begin{aligned} X_L &= \omega L \\ X_C &= \frac{1}{\omega C} \end{aligned}\right]$$

and r_{rms} value of current $I_{rms} = \frac{E_{rms}}{Z} = \frac{E_{rms}}{\sqrt{R^2 + (X_L - X_C)^2}}$

Average power consumed $P = I_{rms} V_{rms} \cos\phi$

[$\cos\phi = \frac{R}{Z}$ known as power factor]

09 In the condition of resonance in *LCR* circuit, the resonant frequency

$$\omega_0 = \frac{1}{\sqrt{LC}} \text{ (as } X_L = X_C)$$

Quality factor $Q = \frac{\omega_0 L}{R} = \frac{1}{\omega_0 CR}$

10 In case of transformer, if there is no energy loss

$$\frac{e_S}{e_P} = \frac{V_S}{V_P} = \frac{I_P}{I_S} = \frac{N_S}{N_P} = K \text{ (transformation ratio)}$$

e_S = EME induced in secondary

e_P = EMF induced in primary

V_S = voltage across secondary coil

V_P = voltage across primary coil

N_S = number of turns in secondary coil

N_P = number of turns in primary coil

I_S = Current in secondary coil

I_P = Current in primary coil

Types of Transformer

(i) Step up transformer $V_S > V_P$, $N_S > N_P$

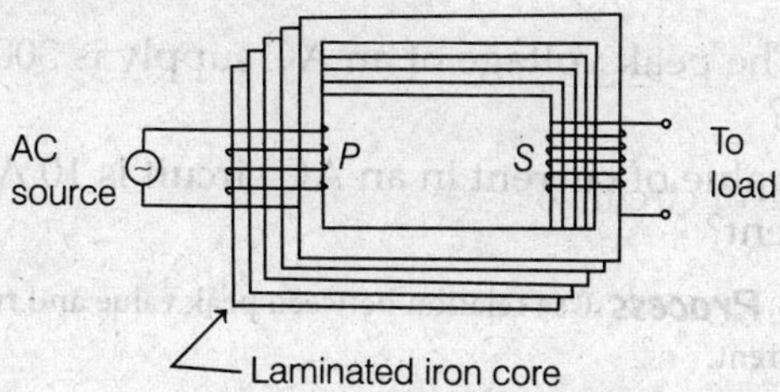

(ii) Step down transformer $V_S < V_P$, $N_S < N_P$

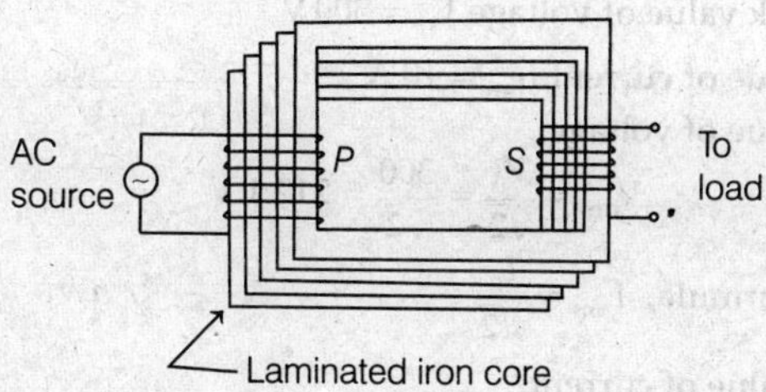

Efficiency of a transformer is given by $\eta = \dfrac{V_S \times I_S}{V_P I_P} = \dfrac{\text{Output Power}}{\text{Input Power}}$

Exercises

Question 1 A 100 Ω resistor is connected to a 220 V, 50 Hz AC supply.

(a) What is the rms value of current in the circuit?

(b) What is the net power consumed over a full cycle?

Sol. Given, resistance $R = 100\ \Omega$

$$V_{rms} = 220\ \text{V}$$

(whenever a supply value is given, it means it is rms value)

Frequency $f = 50$ Hz

(a) Current in the circuit $I_{rms} = \dfrac{V_{rms}}{R} = \dfrac{220}{100} = 2.2$ A

(b) Net power consumed in full cycle $P = V_{rms} \times I_{rms}$
$$= 220 \times 2.2 = 484\ \text{W}$$

Question 2 (a) The peak voltage of an AC supply is 300 V. What is the rms voltage?

(b) The rms value of current in an AC circuit is 10 A. What is the peak current?

◎ ***Thinking Process*** Use relation between peak value and rms value of voltage/current.

$$V_{rms} = \frac{V_0}{\sqrt{2}} \text{ and } I_{rms} = \frac{I_0}{\sqrt{2}}$$

Sol. (a) Given, peak value of voltage $V_0 = 300$ V

The rms value of current $I_{rms} = 10$ A

The rms value of voltage

$$V_{rms} = \frac{V_0}{\sqrt{2}} = \frac{300}{\sqrt{2}} = 212.1\ \text{V}$$

(b) Using the formula, $I_{rms} = \dfrac{I_0}{\sqrt{2}}$

The peak value of current

$$I_0 = \sqrt{2}\, I_{rms} = \sqrt{2} \times 10 = 14.14\ \text{A}$$

Question 3 A 44 mH inductor is connected to 220 V, 50 Hz AC supply. Determine the rms value of the current in the circuit.

Sol. Given, inductance $L = 44\ \text{mH} = 44 \times 10^{-3}$ H

$$V_{rms} = 220\ \text{V}$$

Frequency of inductor $f = 50$ Hz

Inductive reactance $X_L = 2\pi f L$

$$= 2 \times 3.14 \times 50 \times 44 \times 10^{-3} = 13.82\ \Omega$$

The rms value of current in the circuit

$$I_{rms} = \frac{V_{rms}}{X_L} = \frac{220}{13.82} = 15.92\ \text{A}$$

Mistake Alert In this type of problem, if you calculate the impedence Z incorrectly, the value of the current would also be wrong.
Remember that for an inductive circuit, the impedence is purely inductive reactance and you should not use the resistive formula.

Question 4 A 60 μF capacitor is connected to a 110 V, 60 Hz AC supply. Determine the rms value of the current in the circuit.

Sol. Given, capacitance of the capacitor $C = 60\ \mu\text{F} = 60 \times 10^{-6}$ F

$$V_{rms} = 110\ \text{V}$$

Frequency of AC supply $f = 60$ Hz

Capacitive reactance $X_C = \frac{1}{2\pi f C} = \frac{1}{2 \times 3.14 \times 60 \times 60 \times 10^{-6}} = 44.23\ \Omega$

The rms value of the current in the circuit

$$I_{rms} = \frac{V_{rms}}{X_C} = \frac{110}{44.23} = 2.49\ \text{A}$$

Question 5 In Questions 3 and 4 above, what is the net power absorbed by each circuit over a complete cycle? Explain your answer.

Sol. Average power consumed in an ac circuit $P = V_{rms}\, I_{rms} \cos\phi$

As we know that the phase difference between current and voltage in case of inductor is $\phi = 90°$.

$$P = V_{rms}\, I_{rms} \cos 90° = 0$$

We know that the phase difference between current and voltage in case of capacitor is $\phi = -90°$.

$$P = V_{rms} I_{rms} \cos(-90°) = 0$$

Hence, the net power, $P = 0$

Note Over a complete cycle, in resistive circuits, energy is continuously absorbed as heat and the net power is non-zero. In inductive and capacitive circuits, energy is stored and released without net consumption.

Question 6 A charged 30 μF capacitor is connected to a 27 mH inductor. What is the angular frequency of free oscillations of the circuit?

Sol. Capacitance of capacitor $C = 30\ \mu\text{F} = 30 \times 10^{-6}$ F

Inductance $L = 27\ \text{mH} = 27 \times 10^{-3}$ H

For free oscillations, the angular frequency should be resonant frequency.
Resonant angular frequency of oscillation of the circuit is

$$\omega_r = \frac{1}{\sqrt{LC}}$$
$$= \frac{1}{\sqrt{27 \times 10^{-3} \times 30 \times 10^{-6}}}$$
$$= 1.1 \times 10^3 \text{ rad/s}$$

Question 7 A series LCR circuit with $R = 20\ \Omega$, $L = 1.5$ H and $C = 35\ \mu$F is connected to a variable frequency 200 V AC supply. When the frequency of the supply equals the natural frequency of the circuit, what is the average power transferred to the circuit in one complete cycle?

Sol. Given, resistance $R = 20\ \Omega$, inductance L = 1.5 H, capacitance $C = 35\ \mu F = 35 \times 10^{-6}$ F and voltage $V_{rms} = 200$ V

When the frequency of the supply equal to the natural frequency of the circuit, this is the condition of resonance. At the condition of resonance,

Impedance $Z = R = 20\ \Omega$

The rms value of current in the circuit

$$I_{rms} = \frac{V_{rms}}{Z} = \frac{200}{20} = 10 \text{ A}$$

$$\phi = 0° \quad \text{(for resonance)}$$

Power transferred to the circuit in one complete cycle

$$P = I_{rms} \cdot V_{rms} \cos\phi = 10 \times 200 \times \cos 0° = 2000 \text{ W} = 2 \text{ kW}$$

Mistake Alert At resonance, the current is determined by the total impedence $Z = R$, not by the reactance values.
At resonance, the current is in phase with the voltage, So $\cos\phi = 1$.

Question 8 Figure shows a series LCR circuit connected to a variable frequency 230 V source. $L = 5.0$ H, $C = 80\ \mu$F, $R = 40\ \Omega$

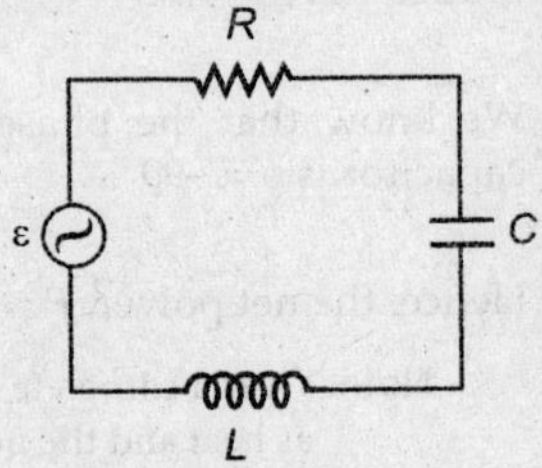

(a) Determine the source frequency which drives the circuit in resonance.

(b) Obtain the impedance of the circuit and the amplitude of current at the resonating frequency.

(c) Determine the rms potential drops across the three elements of the circuit. Show that the potential drop across the LC combination is zero at the resonating frequency.

◎ *Thinking Process* Use ohm's law for current and voltage calculations. At resonance, the potential drops across the inductor and capacitor cancel out, leaving only the voltage across the resistor.

Sol. Given, the rms value of voltage $V_{rms} = 230$ V

Inductance $L = 5$ H

Capacitance $C = 80\ \mu F = 80 \times 10^{-6}$ F

Resistance $R = 40\ \Omega$

(a) For resonance frequency of circuit

$$\omega_r = \frac{1}{\sqrt{LC}} = \frac{1}{\sqrt{5 \times 80 \times 10^{-6}}} = 50 \text{ rad/s}$$

Source frequency at resonance, then

$$\nu_0 = \frac{\omega_0}{2\pi} = \frac{50}{2 \times 3.14}$$
$$= 7.96 \text{ Hz}$$

(b) At the resonant frequency, $X_L = X_C$

So, impedance of the circuit $Z = R$

$\therefore$ Impedance $Z = 40\ \Omega$

The rms value of current in the circuit

$$I_{rms} = \frac{V_{rms}}{Z} = \frac{230}{40} = 5.75 \text{ A}$$

Amplitude of current $I_0 = I_{rms}\sqrt{2}$

$$= 5.75 \times \sqrt{2} = 8.13 \text{ A}$$

(c) The rms potential drop across L,

$$V_L = I_{rms} \times X_L = I_{rms} \times \omega_r L$$
$$= 5.75 \times 50 \times 5 = 1437.5 \text{ V}$$

The rms potential drop across R

$$V_R = I_{rms} R = 5.75 \times 40 = 230 \text{ V}$$

The rms potential drop across C,

$$V_C = I_{rms} \times X_C = I_{rms} \times \frac{1}{\omega_r C}$$
$$= 5.75 \times \frac{1}{50 \times 80 \times 10^{-6}} = 1437.5 \text{ V}$$

Potential drop across LC combinations

$$V_{rms} = I_{rms}(X_L - X_C)$$
$$= I_{rms}(X_L - X_L) = 0 \qquad (\because X_L = X_C \text{ in resonance})$$

DIKSHA APP Questions

Multiple Choice Questions

Q.1 The peak value of domestic AC supply voltage is 325 V. What is the rms value ?

(a) 325 V (b) 230 V
(c) 200 V (d) 325 V

Sol. (b) $\because V_{rms} = \frac{V_0}{\sqrt{2}} = \frac{325}{\sqrt{2}} = \frac{325}{1.414} = 230 \text{ V}$

Q.2 The equation of AC is given by $i = 100 \sin 314\, t$. What is the frequency ?

(a) 314 Hz (b) 100 Hz
(c) 50 Hz (d) 1000 Hz

Sol. (c) $\because i = i_0 \sin \omega t$

$$i = 100 \sin 314t$$
$$\omega = 314 = 2\pi f$$
$$f = \frac{314}{2\pi} = \frac{314}{2 \times 3.14} = \frac{100}{2} = 50 \text{ Hz}$$

Q.3 A transformer with primary and secondary winding as 2000 and 200 respectively. It is connected to a leclanche cell of 1.5 V. What is the output voltage of the transformer ?

(a) 0.15 V (b) 1.5 V
(c) 0.1 V (d) 0 V

Sol. (d) Transformer never works in direct current as it is based on phenomena of mutual induction hence output voltage = 0.

Q.4 What is the resistance offered by a pure inductor for DC ?

(a) Zero
(b) Infinity
(c) One
(d) Depends on the material

Sol. (a) Inductive reactance offered by inductor is $X_L = 2\pi f L \Omega$
for DC, $f = 0, X_L = 0$

Q.5 Which cannot allow DC to pass through ?

(a) Resistor (b) Inductor
(c) Capacitor (d) Transistor

Sol. (c) Resistance offered by capacitor capacitive reactance $X_C = \frac{1}{2\pi fC}\Omega$

for DC, $f = 0, X_C = \infty$, therefore capacitor blocks DC.

Q.6 When an AC is connected to a resistor what is the phase difference between the current and voltage ?

(a) 90° (b) 180° (c) 0° (d) 60°

Sol. (c) $\because V_R = V_0 \sin \omega t$

$$I_R = I_0 \sin \omega t$$

Therefore, phase difference between current and voltage $\phi = 0°$

Q.7 What happens when an AC is connected to a capacitor?

(a) Voltage is leading the current by 90°
(b) Voltage and current are in phase with each other
(c) Voltage and current are out of phase
(d) Current leads the voltage by 90°

Sol. (d) $\because V_C = V_0 \sin \omega t$

$$I_C = I_0 \sin(\omega t + 90°)$$

Current leads voltage by phase angle

$$\phi = 90°$$

Q.8 At resonance in *LCR* circuit what happens to the impedance ?

(a) Becomes zero (b) Becomes ohmic resistance
(c) Becomes high (d) Becomes infinity

Sol. (b) $\because$ impedance of $L-C-R$ circuit is

$$Z = \sqrt{(X_L - X_C)^2 + R^2}$$

at resonance $X_L = X_C$

so, $Z = R$

Q.9 If the power factor of *LCR* circuit is one then the circuit is purely

(a) inductive (b) capacitive
(c) either capacitive or inductive (d) resistive

Sol. (d) $\because$ power factor $\cos\phi = 1$

$$\phi = 0°$$

Hence, the circuit is pure resistive.

Q.10 In a LCR circuit the net reactance is equal to ohmic resistance. What is the phase difference between current and voltage.

(a) 0° (b) 45°

(c) 90° (d) 30°

Sol. (b) When the net reactance (X) in an LCR circuit equals the resistance (R), the phase difference ϕ is given by:

$$\tan\phi = \frac{X}{R} = 1 \Rightarrow \phi = 45°$$

Thus, the phase difference between current and voltage is 45°.

☐ Short Answer Type

Q.1 How inductor offers zero resistance to DC ?

Sol. The inductive reactance $X_L = L\omega$. For DC the frequency f is zero and $\omega = 2\pi f = 0$ therefore, $X_L = L\omega = 0$. The resistance offered by the inductor for DC is zero.

Q.2 Why capacitor allows AC and blocks DC ?

Sol. The capacitive reactance $X_C = 1/C\omega$. For DC, the frequency $\nu = 0$, so $\omega = 2\pi\nu = 0$. Therefore the resistance offered by capacitor X_C for DC is infinity. So, it blocks DC and allows only AC to pass.

Q.3 What happens to the impedance, current and phase difference between the voltage and current at resonant frequency in a series resonance *LCR* circuit ?

Sol. At resonant frequency the capacitive reactance is equal to the inductive reactance *i.e.* $X_C = X_L$ therefore the impedance of the circuit is

$$Z = \sqrt{(X_L - X_C)^2 + R^2}$$

reduced and it becomes ohmic resistance *i.e.* $Z = R$

When the impedance is reduced the current becomes maximum $I = \frac{V}{Z}$.

The circuit now behaves as purely ohmic. Therefore the phase difference between the voltage and current is zero. That is the voltage is in phase with the current.

Q.4 How the power factor of a circuit with capacitor only and inductor only is zero ?

Sol. The phase difference between the voltage and current in both the circuits is 90°. Therefore the power factor for purely capacitive and inductive circuits is zero. *i.e.* $\cos\phi = \cos 90° = 0$.

Q.5 The primary of a transformer has 400 turns and the secondary has 2000 turns. If the power output from the secondary at 1000V is 8kW, calculate

(i) the primary voltage

(ii) the heat loss in the primary coil if the resistance of primary is 0.1 Ω and the efficiency of the transformer is 80%.

Sol. (i) $E_1 = N_1 E_2 / N_2$

$= 400 \times 1000 / 2000$

$= 200 \text{ V}$

(ii) Output power × 100/Input power = 80

$$8000 \times 100/\text{Input power} = 80$$

$$\text{Input power} = 10{,}000 \text{ W}$$

$$\text{Also, Input power} = E_1 I_1 = 10000$$

$$200 \times I_1 = 10000$$

$$I_1 = 50 A$$

Heat loss in the primary coil $= I_1^2 R_1 = 50 \times 50 \times 0.1 = 250\text{W}$

Electromagnetic Waves

CHAPTER 08

Important Points

01 Maxwell found an inconsistency in the Ampere's circuital law and suggested the existence of an additional current that exist in vacuum called displacement current. This displacement current is due to time varying electric field and given by

$$I_d = \varepsilon_0 \frac{d\phi_E}{dt}$$

It acts as a source of magnetic field, in the same way as conduction current, so it is equal to conduction current.

02 Maxwell's equations

(i) $\oint \mathbf{E} \cdot d\mathbf{A} = \frac{q_{\text{net}}}{\varepsilon_0}$ (Gauss's law for electrostatics)

(ii) $\oint \mathbf{B} \cdot d\mathbf{A} = 0$ (Gauss's law for magnetism)

(iii) $\oint \mathbf{E} \cdot d\mathbf{l} = -\frac{d\phi_B}{dt}$ (Faraday' law of EMI)

(iv) $\oint \mathbf{B} \cdot d\mathbf{l} = \mu_0 I_C + \mu_0 \varepsilon_0 \frac{d\phi_E}{dt}$

(Maxwell modified Ampere's circuital law)

03 The ratio of amplitude of electric field to the amplitude of magnetic field in electromagnetic waves gives the speed of light in vacuum.

i.e. $$\frac{E_0}{B_0} = c$$

04 The speed of electromagnetic waves in vacuum $c = \frac{1}{\sqrt{\mu_0 \varepsilon_0}}$, where μ_0 is the absolute permeability of space and ε_0 be the absolute permittivity of space.

05 The speed of electromagnetic waves in a material medium is given by $v = \frac{1}{\sqrt{\mu\varepsilon}}$, where μ is the permeability of the medium and ε is its permittivity.

06 Electromagnetic waves carry energy as they travel through space and this energy is shared equally by the electric and magnetic fields i.e. $u_E = u_B$

07 The energy density of electric field in electromagnetic waves is given by

$$u_E = \frac{1}{2}\varepsilon_0 E^2 = u_B$$

08 The energy density of magnetic field in electromagnetic waves is given by

$$u_B = \frac{B^2}{2\mu_0} = u_E$$

09 Total average energy density in electromagnetic waves is

$$u = u_E + u_B = 2u_E = 2u_B = \frac{1}{2}\varepsilon_0 E_0^2 = \frac{B_0^2}{2\mu_0}$$

10 Electric and magnetic fields oscillate sinusoidally in space and time in an electromagnetic wave. The oscillating electric and magnetic fields, **E** and **B** are perpendicular to each other as well as perpendicular to the direction of propagation of the electromagnetic wave.

11 In electromagnetic wave, the variation of electric field vector can be given by the equation $E_y = E_0 \sin(kz - \omega t)$ and of magnetic field vector by the equation $B_x = B_0 \sin(kz - \omega t)$
Direction of wave propagation.

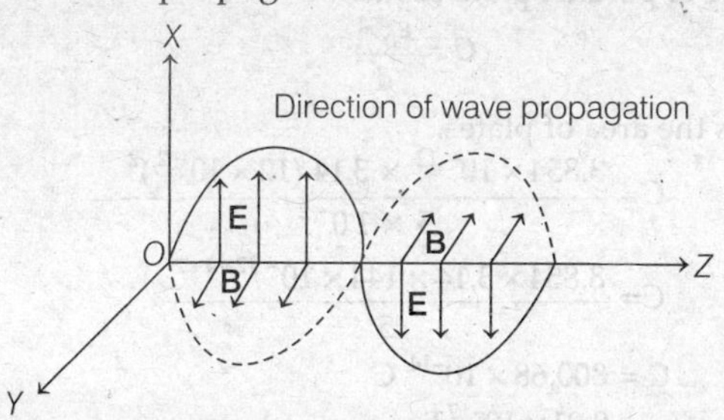

12 The electromagnetic spectrum has infinite range of wavelengths, such as γ-rays, X-rays, UV rays, visible rays, infrared rays, micro and radio waves.

Exercises

Question 1 Figure shows a capacitor made of two circular plates each of radius 12 cm and separated by 5.0 cm. The capacitor is being charged by an external source (not shown in the figure). The charging current is constant and equal to 0.15 A.

(a) Calculate the capacitance and the rate of change of potential difference between the plates.

(b) Obtain the displacement current across the plates.

(c) Is Kirchhoff's first rule (junction rule) valid at each plate of the capacitor? Explain.

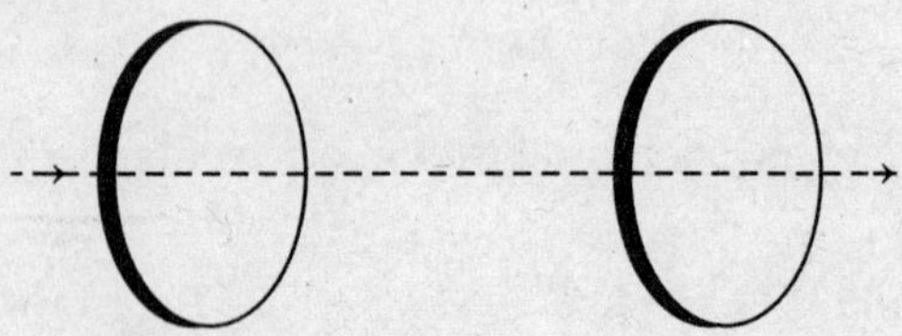

◎ ***Thinking Process*** Use the concept of parallel plate capacitor and capacitance of the capacitor $C = \frac{A\varepsilon_0}{d}$.

Sol. Given, radius of plates $r = 12 \text{ cm} = 12 \times 10^{-2}$ m

Separation between two circular plates

$d = 5 \text{ cm} = 5 \times 10^{-2}$ m

Current $I = 0.15$ A

(a) Capacitance of parallel plate capacitor

$$C = \frac{\varepsilon_0 A}{d}$$

Where, A is the area of plates.

$$C = \frac{8.854 \times 10^{-12} \times 3.14\,(12 \times 10^{-2})^2}{5 \times 10^{-2}}$$

$$C = \frac{8.854 \times 3.14 \times 144 \times 10^{-12-4+2}}{5}$$

$$C = 800.68 \times 10^{-14} \text{ C}$$

$$= 8.01 \times 10^{-12} \text{ F}$$

$$\therefore \quad C = 8.01 \text{pF}$$

Charge on the plates of the capacitor

$$q = CV$$

$$\because \quad I = \frac{dq}{dt} = C \cdot \frac{dV}{dt}$$

$$I = C \cdot \frac{dV}{dt} \qquad \left[\because \frac{dq}{dt} = I\right]$$

$$\therefore \quad \frac{dV}{dt} = \frac{I}{C} = \frac{0.15}{8.01 \times 10^{-12}} = 18.7 \times 10^{9} \text{ V/s}$$

Thus, the rate of change of potential is 1.87×10^{10} V/s.

(b) The displacement current is equal to the conduction current $I_d = 0.15$ A.

(c) Yes, Kirchhoff's first rule is valid because we take the current to be the sum of conduction currents and the displacement currents.

Question 2 A parallel plate capacitor (shown in figure) made of circular plates each of radius $R = 6.0$ cm has a capacitance $C = 100$ pF. The capacitor is connected to a 230 V AC supply with a (angular) frequency of 300 rad/s.

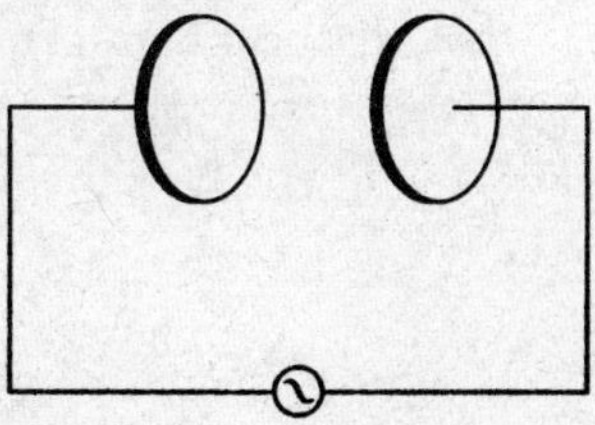

(a) What is the rms value of the conduction current?

(b) Is the conduction current equal to the displacement current?

(c) Determine the amplitude of B at a point 3.0 cm from the axis between the plates.

Thinking Process In a capacitor connected to an Ac circuit, the conduction current is equal to the displacement current, which is due to the changing electric field between the plates. Thus, the conduction current is equal to displacement current because, in an ideal capacitor, there is no actual current flowing through the capacitor itself. It is just the displacement current.

Sol. Given radius of plates $R = 6 \text{ cm} = 6 \times 10^{-2}$ m

Capacitance of capacitor

$$C = 100 \text{ pF} = 100 \times 10^{-12} \text{ F} = 10^{-10} \text{ F}$$

Voltage of capacitor $V = 230$ V

Frequency of AC source $\omega = 300$ rad/s

(a) The rms value of current $I_{rms} = \dfrac{V_{rms}}{X_C}$

$$\because \quad X_C = \frac{1}{\omega C} = \frac{1}{300 \times 10^{-10}} = \frac{10^{10}}{300}\ \Omega$$

$$\therefore \quad I_{rms} = \frac{230 \times 300}{10^{10}} = 3 \times 23 \times 1000 \times 10^{-10}$$

$$= 69 \times 10^{-7} = 6.9 \times 10^{-6} \text{ A}$$

$$I_{rms} = 6.9\ \mu\text{A}$$

(b) Yes, the conduction current is equal to displacement current

$$I_d = \varepsilon_0 \frac{d\phi_E}{dt} \quad \text{(By the definition of displacement current)}$$

$$I_d = \varepsilon_0 \frac{d}{dt}(EA) \quad (\because \phi_E = EA)$$

$$I_d = \varepsilon_0 A \frac{dE}{dt} \quad \left(\because E = \frac{\sigma}{\varepsilon_0} = \frac{Q}{\varepsilon_0 A}\right)$$

$$I_d = \varepsilon_0 A \frac{d}{dt}\left(\frac{Q}{\varepsilon_0 A}\right)$$

$$I_d = \varepsilon_0 A \cdot \frac{1}{\varepsilon_0 A} \cdot \frac{dQ}{dt} = \frac{dQ}{dt} = I_C$$

$$I_d = I_C$$

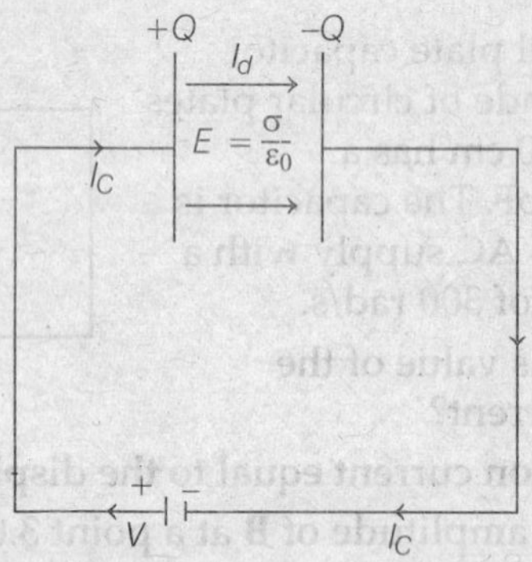

Note In a capacitor connected to an AC source, conduction current equals displacement current, ensuring continuity of current.

(c) Given, the distance of point from the axis between the plates

$r = 3 \text{ cm} = 3 \times 10^{-2}$ m

Radius of plates $R = 6 \text{ cm} = 6 \times 10^{-2}$ m

The magnetic field at a point between the plates

$$B = \frac{\mu_0}{2\pi R^2} \cdot r \cdot I_d$$

$$B = \frac{\mu_0 r}{2\pi R^2} I_C \quad (I_d = I_C)$$

If $I = I_0$, maximum value of current then $I_C = \sqrt{2}\, I_{\text{rms}}$.

$$B = \frac{\mu_0 r}{2\pi R^2} \sqrt{2} I_{\text{rms}}$$

$$B = \frac{4\pi \times 10^{-7} \times 0.03 \times \sqrt{2} \times 6.9 \times 10^{-6}}{2\pi \times 0.06 \times 0.06}$$

$$B = 1.63 \times 10^{-11} \text{ T}$$

Mistake Alert In this problem, use $r = 3\text{cm}$, not the plate radius (6 cm) and remember $V_{\max} = \sqrt{2}.\, V_{rms}$ instead of using the RMS voltage directly.

Question 3 What physical quantity is the same for X-rays of wavelength 10^{-10} m, red light of wavelength 6800 Å and radiowaves of wavelength 500 m?

Sol. Here, X-rays, red light and radiowaves all are the electromagnetic waves. As we know that all the electromagnetic waves travel with the same speed c that is speed of light in vacuum . Thus, the speed is same for X-rays, red light and radiowaves but wavelength differs.

Question 4 A plane electromagnetic wave travels in vacuum along Z-direction. What can you say about the directions of its electric and magnetic field vectors? If the frequency of the wave is 30 MHz, what is its wavelength?

Sol. As we know that the direction of electromagnetic wave is perpendicular to both electric and magnetic fields. Here, electromagnetic wave is travelling in Z-direction, then electric and magnetic fields are in X and Y direction or Y and X direction and are perpendicular to each other.

Frequency of waves $f = 30\text{ MHz} = 30 \times 10^6$ Hz

Speed $c = 3 \times 10^8$ m/s

Using the formula, $c = f\lambda$

Wavelength of electromagnetic waves

$$\lambda = \frac{c}{f} = \frac{3 \times 10^8}{30 \times 10^6} = \frac{300}{30} = 10\text{ m}$$

Thus, the wavelength of electromagnetic waves is 10 m.

Question 5 A radio can tune into any station in the 7.5 MHz to 12 MHz band. What is the corresponding wavelength band?

Sol. Given, frequency $f_1 = 7.5$ MHz

Frequency $f_2 = 12$ MHz

Speed of EM wave $c = 3 \times 10^8$ m/s

Wavelength corresponding to frequency f_1

$$\lambda_1 = \frac{c}{f_1} = \frac{3 \times 10^8}{7.5 \times 10^6} = \frac{3000}{7.5} = 40\text{ m}$$

Wavelength corresponding to frequency f_2

$$\lambda_2 = \frac{c}{f_2} = \frac{3 \times 10^8}{12 \times 10^6} = \frac{300}{12} = 25\text{ m}$$

Thus, the corresponding wavelength band is 40 m to 25 m.

Question 6 A charged particle oscillates about its mean equilibrium position with a frequency of 10^9 Hz. What is the frequency of the electromagnetic waves produced by the oscillator?

Sol. According to the question,

Frequency of the electromagnetic waves = 10^9 Hz

The frequency of electromagnetic waves produced by the oscillator is same as that of the oscillating charged particle about its equilibrium position, *i.e.*, 10^9 Hz.

Question 7 The amplitude of the magnetic field part of a harmonic electromagnetic wave in vacuum is $B_0 = 510$ nT. What is the amplitude of the electric field part of the wave?

Sol. Given, amplitude of the magnetic field part of harmonic electromagnetic wave

$$B_0 = 510\,\text{nT} = 510 \times 10^{-9}\,\text{T}$$

Speed of electromagnetic wave in vacuum $c = \dfrac{E_0}{B_0}$

where, E_0 is the amplitude of electric field part of the wave

$$3 \times 10^8 = \frac{E_0}{510 \times 10^{-9}}$$

or $$E_0 = 153\,\text{N/C}$$

Thus, the amplitude of the electric field part of wave is 153 N/C.

Question 8 Suppose that the electric field amplitude of an electromagnetic wave is $E_0 = 120$ N/C and that its frequency is $\nu = 50.0$ MHz. (a) Determine, B_0, ω, k and λ. (b) Find expressions for **E** and **B**.

Sol. Given, electric field amplitude of an electromagnetic wave, $E_0 = 120$ N/C

Frequency of wave $\nu = 50\,\text{MHz} = 50 \times 10^6$ Hz

(a) Speed of electromagnetic wave in vacuum

$$c = \frac{E_0}{B_0}$$

$$B_0 = \frac{E_0}{c} = \frac{120}{3 \times 10^8} = 40 \times 10^{-8}$$

or $$B_0 = 400 \times 10^{-9}\,\text{T} = 400\,\text{nT}$$

Angular frequency of electromagnetic wave,

$$\omega = 2\pi v = 2 \times 3.14 \times 50 \times 10^6$$

$$\omega = 3.14 \times 10^8\ \text{rad/s}$$

Wave number of electromagnetic waves

$$k = \frac{\omega}{c} = \frac{3.14 \times 10^8}{3 \times 10^8} = 1.05\,\text{m}^{-1}$$

Wavelength of electromagnetic wave

$$\lambda = \frac{c}{v} = \frac{3 \times 10^8}{50 \times 10^6} = 6.00\,\text{m}$$

(b) Expression of electric field $E = E_0 \sin(kx - \omega t)$

$$E = 120 \sin(1.05x - 3.14 \times 10^8 t)$$

Expression of magnetic field B

$$B = B_0 \sin(kx - \omega t)$$

$$B = 4 \times 10^{-7} \sin(1.05x - 3.14 \times 10^8 t)$$

Question 9 The terminology of different parts of the electromagnetic spectrum is given in the text. Use the formula $E = h\nu$ (for energy of a quantum of radiation : photon) and obtain the photon energy in units of eV for different parts of the electromagnetic spectrum. In what way are the different scales of photon energies that you obtain related to the sources of electromagnetic radiation?

◎ ***Thinking Process*** The energy of a photo is directly proportional to its frequency, means that higher-frequency radiation (e.g., gamma rays) has more energy per photon than lower-frequency radiation (e.g., radio waves). Also, to calculate the frequencies, we can use the formula $\nu = \frac{c}{\lambda}$ or we can also use $E = \frac{hc}{\lambda}$.

Sol. Given, energy of photon $E = h\nu$

For γ-rays

Wavelength of γ-rays $= 10^{-15}$ m

$$\text{Energy of γ-rays } E = h\nu = \frac{hc}{\lambda} = 6.6 \times 10^{-34} \times \frac{3 \times 10^8}{10^{-15}} = 1.98 \times 10^{-10} \text{ J}$$

or $$E = \frac{1.98 \times 10^{-10}}{1.6 \times 10^{-19}} = 1.24 \times 10^9 \text{ eV}$$

The source of γ-rays is nuclear origin.

For X-rays

Wavelength of X-rays $\lambda = 10^{-12}$ m

$$\text{Energy of X-rays } E = h\nu = \frac{hc}{\lambda} = 6.6 \times 10^{-34} \times \frac{3 \times 10^8}{10^{-12}} = 1.98 \times 10^{-13} \text{ J}$$

or $$E = \frac{1.98 \times 10^{-13}}{1.6 \times 10^{-19}} = 1.24 \times 10^6 \text{ eV}$$

The retardation of high energy electron produces X-rays.

For ultraviolet rays

Wavelength of rays $\lambda = 10^{-9}$ m

$$\text{Energy of ultraviolet rays } E = h\nu = \frac{hc}{\lambda} = 6.6 \times 10^{-34} \times \frac{3 \times 10^8}{10^{-9}} = 1.98 \times 10^{-16} \text{ J}$$

or $$E = \frac{6.6 \times 10^{-16}}{1.6 \times 10^{-19}} = 1.24 \times 10^3 \text{ eV}$$

It originates by the excitation of atoms.

For visible rays

Wavelength of visible rays $\lambda = 5 \times 10^{-7}$ m

$$\text{Energy of visible rays } E = h\nu = \frac{hc}{\lambda} = 6.6 \times 10^{-34} \times \frac{3 \times 10^8}{5 \times 10^{-7}} = 3.96 \times 10^{-19} \text{ J}$$

or $$E = \frac{3.96 \times 10^{-19}}{1.6 \times 10^{-19}} = 2.475 \text{ eV}$$

They produce by the excitation of valance electrons.

For infrared rays

Wavelength of infrared rays $\lambda = 10^{-3}$ m

Energy of infrared rays $E = h\nu = \frac{hc}{\lambda} = 6.6 \times 10^{-34} \times \frac{3 \times 10^8}{10^{-3}}$

$= 19.8 \times 10^{-23}$ J

or $E = \frac{19.8 \times 10^{-23}}{1.6 \times 10^{-19}} = 1.24 \times 10^{-3}$ eV

They originate by the excitation of atoms and molecules.

For microwaves

Wavelength of microwaves $\lambda = 0.1$ m

Energy of microwaves $E = h\nu = \frac{hc}{\lambda} = 6.6 \times 10^{-34} \times \frac{3 \times 10^8}{0.1} = 1.98 \times 10^{-24}$ J

or $E = \frac{1.98 \times 10^{-24}}{1.6 \times 10^{-19}} = 1.24 \times 10^{-5}$ eV

They originate by the oscillating current in vacuum tubes.

For radiowaves

Wavelength of radio waves $\lambda = 10^3$ m

Energy of radiowaves $E = h\nu = \frac{hc}{\lambda} = 6.6 \times 10^{-34} \times \frac{3 \times 10^8}{10^3}$

$= 1.98 \times 10^{-28}$ J

or $E = \frac{1.98 \times 10^{-28}}{1.6 \times 10^{-19}} = 1.24 \times 10^{-9}$ eV

They originate by oscillating current.

Type of radiation	Photon energy
γ-rays	1.24×10^9 eV
X-rays	1.24×10^6 eV
Ultraviolet rays	1.24×10^3 eV
Visible waves	2.475 eV
Infrared waves	1.24×10^{-3} eV
Microwaves	1.24×10^{-5} eV
Radiowaves	1.24×10^{-9} eV

Mistake Alert Ensure you use the correct value for planck's constant ($h = 6.626 \times 10^{-34}$ Js) and the speed of light ($c = 3 \times 10^8$ m/s) when calculating photon energies. Also, remember to convert the energy from joules to electron volts (1 eV $= 1.6 \times 10^{-19}$ J)

Question 10 In a plane electromagnetic wave, the electric field oscillates sinusoidally at a frequency of 2.0×10^{10} Hz and amplitude 48 V/m.

(a) What is the wavelength of the wave?

(b) What is the amplitude of the oscillating magnetic field?

(c) Show that the average energy density of the **E** field equals the average energy density of the **B** field. [$c = 3 \times 10^8$ m/s.]

◎ *Thinking Process* In this problem, the energy density of the electric field is proportional to the square of the electric field amplitude, while the energy density of the magnetic field is proportional to the square of the magnetic field amplitude. In an electromagnetic waves, the average densities of the electric and magnetic fields are equal.

Sol. Frequency of oscillation $= 2 \times 10^{10}$ Hz

Given, $c = 3 \times 10^8$ m/s

Electric field amplitude $E_0 = 48$ V/m

(a) Wavelength of waves $\lambda = \dfrac{c}{f} = \dfrac{3 \times 10^8}{2 \times 10^{10}} = 1.5 \times 10^{-2}$ m

(b) Using the formula, $c = \dfrac{E_0}{B_0}$

The amplitude of the oscillating magnetic field

$$B_0 = \frac{E_0}{c} = \frac{48}{3 \times 10^8} = 1.6 \times 10^{-7} \text{ T}$$

(c) The average energy density of electric field

$$u_E = \frac{1}{4}\varepsilon_0 E_0^2 \quad \ldots\text{(i)}$$

We know that, $E_0 = cB_0$

Putting in Eq. (i),

$$\therefore \quad u_E = \frac{1}{4}\varepsilon_0 . c^2 B_0^2 \quad \ldots\text{(ii)}$$

Speed of electromagnetic waves, $c = \dfrac{1}{\sqrt{\mu_0 \varepsilon_0}}$

Putting the value of c in Eq. (ii), we get

$$u_E = \frac{1}{4}\varepsilon_0 B_0^2 \cdot \frac{1}{\mu_0 \varepsilon_0}$$

$$u_E = \frac{1}{4} \cdot \frac{B_0^2}{\mu_0} = \frac{B_0^2}{4\mu_0} = \mu_B.$$

Thus, the average energy density of the **E** field equals the average energy density of **B** field.

DIKSHA APP Questions

Multiple Choice Questions

Q.1 The unit of 1/ permittivity × permeability is

(a) ms^{-1} (b) no unit (c) m^2 (d) m^2s^{-2}

Sol. (d) $c = \frac{1}{\sqrt{\mu_0 \varepsilon_0}}$

$$c^2 = \frac{1}{\mu_0 \varepsilon_0}$$

$$\frac{1}{\mu_0 \varepsilon_0} = c^2 = (ms^{-1})^2 = m^2s^{-2}$$

Q.2 The angle between electric and magnetic field vectors in an electromagnetic waves is

(a) 0° (b) 90° (c) 180° (d) 60°

Sol. (b) ∵ Electric and magnetic field vectors are perpendicular to each other. so, the angle between electric and magnetic field vectors in an electromagnetic waves is 90°.

Q.3 The phase difference between the electric and magnetic fields in an electromagnetic wave is

(a) 0° (b) 90° (c) 180° (d) 45°

Sol. (a) 0°

In an electromagnetic wave, the electric field (E) and magnetic field (B) oscillate in phase means they reach their maximum and zero values simultaneously. Therefore, the phase difference between them is 0°.

As $$E_y = E_0 \sin(kz - wt)$$
$$B_x = B_0 \sin(kz - wt)$$

Q.4 The relative permeability and permittivity of the medium are 4 and 16 respectively. What is the refractive index of the medium?

(a) 64 (b) 4 (c) 16 (d) 8

Sol. (d) 8

We use the relationship between the relative permittivity (ε_r) and relative permeability (μ_r)

$$n = \sqrt{\varepsilon_r \times \mu_r}$$

Given, $$\varepsilon_r = 16$$
$$\mu_r = 4$$
$$n = \sqrt{16 \times 4} = \sqrt{64} = 8$$

Q.5 The electromagnetic wave which is used to study the molecular structure is

(a) visible light (b) ultra violet radiation
(c) infrared radiation (d) gamma radiation

Sol. (c) Infrared radiation is used to study the molecular structure.

Ray Optics and Optical Instruments

CHAPTER 09

Important Points

01 According to laws of reflection, angle of incidence $\angle i$ is equal to angle of reflection $\angle r$. *i.e.* $\angle i = \angle r$. Relation between focal length and radius of curvature of mirror

$$f = \frac{R}{2}$$

02 Mirror formula, $\frac{1}{f} = \frac{1}{v} + \frac{1}{u}$, u = object distance from pole

v = image distance from pole

f = focal length of mirror

magnification by mirror $m = \frac{-v}{u} = \frac{h_i}{h_0}$

03 Snell's law, $\frac{\sin i}{\sin r} = \mu = \frac{\text{Velocity of light in vacuum } (c)}{\text{Velocity of light in medium } (v)}$

04 Refractive index of medium a w.r.t. medium b is given by

$${}^a\mu_b = \frac{\mu_b}{\mu_a} = \frac{\frac{c}{v_b}}{\frac{c}{v_a}} = \frac{v_a}{v_b}$$

05 Principle of reversibility

$$^{a}\mu_{b} = \frac{1}{^{b}\mu_{a}}$$

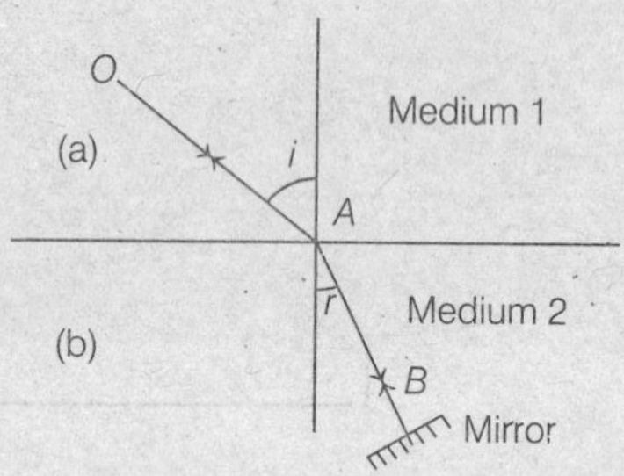

06 Multiple Refraction

$$^{a}\mu_{b} \times {}^{b}\mu_{c} \times {}^{c}\mu_{a} = 1$$

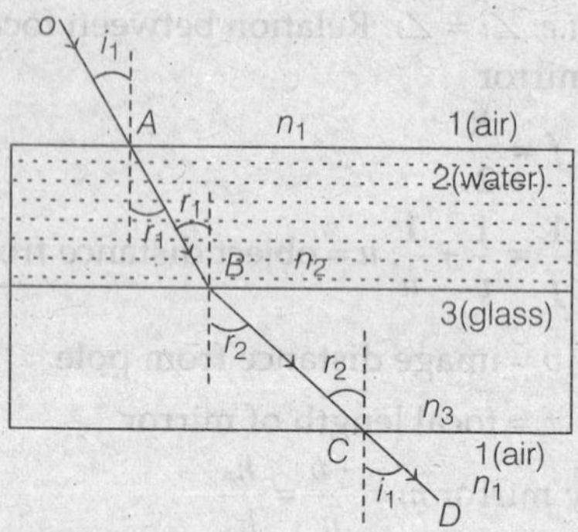

07 $\mu = \frac{\text{Real depth}}{\text{Apparent depth}}$

$BO =$ Real depth

$BI =$ Apparent depth

$OI =$ Normal shift

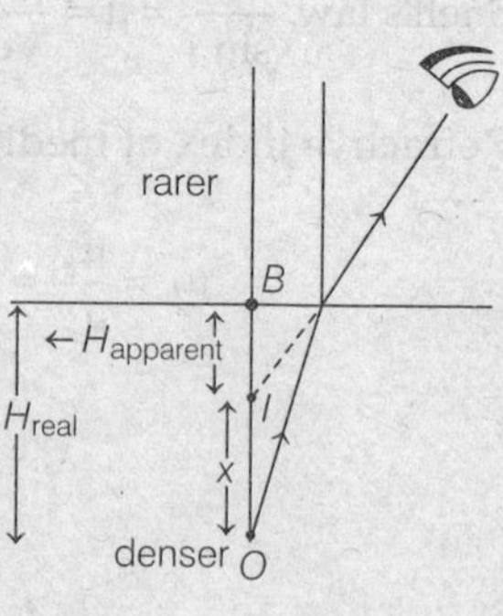

08 Lateral shift $= \dfrac{t[\sin(i-r)]}{\cos r}$

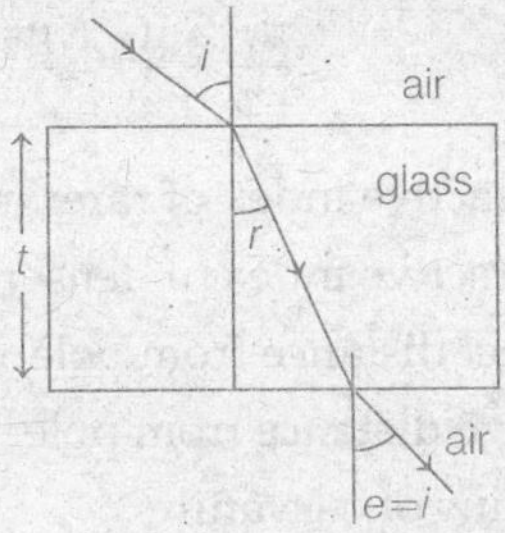

09 Normal shift $= t\left(1 - \dfrac{1}{^{a}\mu_n}\right)$

10 Critical angle $\sin i_C = \dfrac{1}{\mu}$

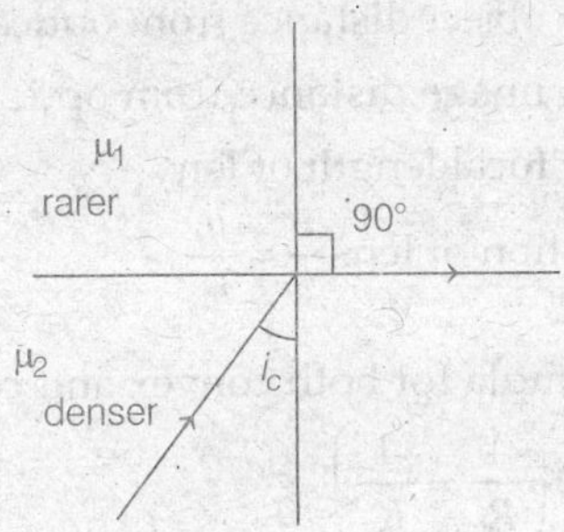

11 The necessary conditions for total internal reflection are

(i) refraction takes place from denser medium to rarer medium.

(ii) the angle of incidence must be greater than the critical angle for the pair of media in contact.

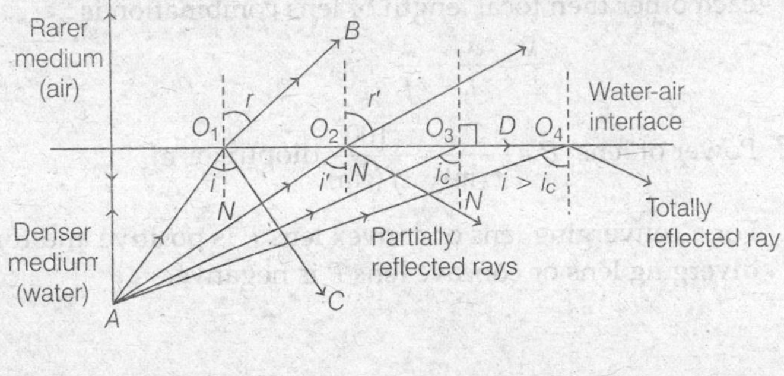

12 For refraction through spherical surfaces

(i) When refraction occurs from rarer to denser medium.

$$\frac{\mu_1}{-u}+\frac{\mu_2}{v}=\frac{\mu_2-\mu_1}{R}$$

μ_1 = Refractive index of rarer medium

μ_2 = Refractive index of denser medium

u = object distance from pole

v = image distance from pole

R = Radius of curvature

(ii) When refraction occurs from denser to rarer medium

$$-\frac{\mu_2}{u}+\frac{\mu_1}{v}=\frac{\mu_1-\mu_2}{R}$$

13 The Lens Formula $\frac{1}{v}-\frac{1}{u}=\frac{1}{f}$, where

u = object distance from optical centre

v = image distance from optical centre

f = focal length of lens.

14 Linear magnification of lens $\frac{v}{u}=\frac{h_i}{h_0}$

15 Lens maker's formula for both convex and concave lenses

$$\frac{1}{f}=(\mu-1)\left(\frac{1}{R_1}-\frac{1}{R_2}\right),$$

μ = Refractive index of material of lens

R_1 = Radius of curvature of first surface

R_2 = Radius of curvature of second surface

16 If thin lenses of focal length f_1, f_2 ...... are placed in contact to each other then focal length of lens combination is

$$\frac{1}{F}=\frac{1}{f_1}+\frac{1}{f_2}+\ldots.$$

17 Power of lens $P=\frac{1}{f(\text{m})}=\frac{100}{f(\text{cm})}$ dioptre or m^{-1}

For a converging lens or convex lens P is positive and for a diverging lens or concave lens P is negative.

18 For combination of lenses, the power is given by

$$P = P_1 + P_2 + P_3 + \ldots$$

19 For a prism of angle A and of refractive index μ is given by

$$\mu = \frac{\sin\left(\frac{A+\delta_m}{2}\right)}{\sin\frac{A}{2}}$$

δ_m is the angle of minimum deviation

20 In refraction through a prism

(i) $A + \delta = i + e$

i.e., sum of prism angle and deviation angle is equal to sum of incident angle and emergent angle.

(ii) $r_1 + r_2 = A$ *i.e.* sum of refraction angle at two refracting surfaces is equal to prism angle.

(iii) When $\delta = \delta_m \Rightarrow i_1 = e$ and $r_1 = r_2$.

21 Magnifying power of simple microscope,

$m = 1 + \frac{D}{f}$ when final image is formed at least distance of distinct vision $m = \frac{D}{f}$ when final image is formed at infinity *i.e.* in normal adjustment.

where, D is least distant of distinct vision.

22 Magnifying power of a compound microscope

(i) When final image formed at least distance of distinct vision or angular magnification

$$m = +\frac{v_0}{u_o}\left(1 + \frac{D}{f_e}\right) = \frac{-L}{f_0}\left(1 + \frac{D}{f_e}\right)$$

where, $L = |v_0| + |u_e|$, length of the tube.

(ii) When final image is formed at infinity

$$m = +\frac{v_0}{u_0} \times \frac{D}{f_e} = \frac{-L}{f_0} \times \frac{D}{f_e}$$

23 Magnifying power of an astronomical telescope

(i) In normal adjustment $m = -\frac{f_o}{f_e}$

f_0 = focal length of objective lens, f_e = focal length of eye lens

(ii) When image formed at least distance of distinct vision

$$m = -\frac{f_o}{f_e}\left(1 + \frac{f_e}{D}\right)$$

length of tube $L = |f_0| + |u_e|$

where, D is the least distance of distinct vision.

24 Length of astronomical telescope tube for normal adjustment is given by

$$L = |f_o| + |f_e|$$

Exercises

Question 1 A small candle, 2.5 cm in size is placed at 27 cm in front of a concave mirror of radius of curvature 36 cm. At what distance from the mirror should a screen be placed in order to obtain a sharp image? Describe the nature and size of the image. If the candle is moved closer to the mirror, how would the screen have to be moved?

Sol. Given, radius of curvature of concave mirror, $R = -36$ cm

[$\because R$ is negative for a concave mirror]

(For concave mirror radius of curvature is taken as negative)

$\therefore$ Focal length $f = \frac{R}{2} = -\frac{36}{2} = -18$ cm

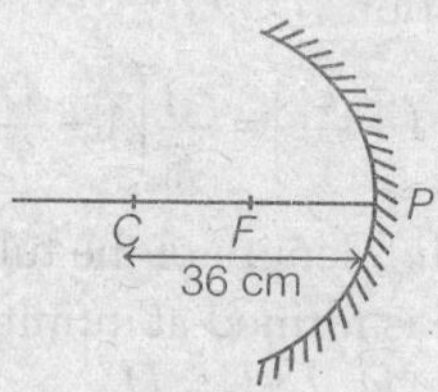

Distance of object $u = -27$ cm (Object distance is always taken as negative)

Height of object $O = 2.5$ cm

Use the mirror formula

$$\frac{1}{f} = \frac{1}{v} + \frac{1}{u} \Rightarrow -\frac{1}{18} = \frac{1}{v} - \frac{1}{27}$$

$$\frac{1}{v} = -\frac{1}{18} + \frac{1}{27} = \frac{-3+2}{54} = -\frac{1}{54}$$

Distance of screen from mirror $v = -54$ cm

Let the size of image be I. By using the formula of magnification for mirror

$$m = -\frac{v}{u} = \frac{I}{O}$$

$$\frac{-(-54)}{-27} = \frac{I}{2.5}$$

$$I = -5 \text{ cm}$$

The negative sign shows that the image is real and inverted.

If we move the object closer to the mirror (as $u \to f, v \to \infty$), the screen should be moved away from mirror. If the distance of object is less than focal length ($u < f$), no screen is required, because the image formed is virtual.

Question 2 A 4.5 cm needle is placed 12 cm away from a convex mirror of focal length 15 cm. Give the location of the image and the magnification. Describe what happens as the needle is moved farther from the mirror?

Sol. Given, focal length of convex mirror $f = +15$ cm (Focal length of convex mirror is taken as positive)

Distance of object $u = -12$ cm

Size of object $O = 4.5$ cm

Using the mirror formula,

$$\frac{1}{f} = \frac{1}{v} + \frac{1}{u}$$

$$\frac{1}{15} = \frac{1}{v} - \frac{1}{12} \Rightarrow \frac{1}{v} = \frac{1}{15} + \frac{1}{12} = \frac{4+5}{60} = \frac{9}{60}$$

Distance of image from the mirror $v = +6.67$ cm

The positive sign shows that the image is formed behind the mirror.

Using the formula of magnification,

$$m = -\frac{v}{u} = \frac{I}{O}$$

$$\frac{-6.7}{-12} = \frac{I}{4.5}$$

Size of image $I = 2.5$ cm

As I is positive, so image is erect and virtual.

Magnification m is given by

$$m = \frac{I}{O} = \frac{2.5}{4.5} = \frac{25}{45} = \frac{5}{9} = 0.555$$

As the needle moves away from the mirror, the image shift towards the focus (but never beyond f) and goes on decreasing in size.

Question 3 A tank is filled with water to a height of 12.5 cm. The apparent depth of a needle lying at the bottom of the tank is measured by a microscope to be 9.4 cm. What is the refractive index of water? If water is replaced by a liquid of refractive index 1.63 up to the same height, by what distance would the microscope have to be moved to focus on the needle again?

Sol. **Case I** When tank is filled with water

Given, the apparent depth = 9.4 cm

Height of water = 12.5 cm

$\therefore$ Real depth = 12.5 cm

Refractive index of water

$$\mu_w = \frac{\text{Real depth}}{\text{Apparent depth}} = \frac{12.5}{9.4} = 1.33$$

Case II When tank is filled with the liquid

Refractive index of liquid $\mu = 1.63$,

$$\text{Again, } \mu = \frac{\text{Real depth}}{\text{Apparent depth}}$$

$$\therefore \quad 1.63 = \frac{12.5}{\text{Apparent depth}}$$

$$\text{Apparent depth} = \frac{12.5}{1.63} = 7.67 \text{ cm}$$

$\therefore$ The microscope is shifted by = 9.4 − 7.67 = 1.73 cm

Question 4 Figures (a) and (b) show refraction of a ray in air incident at 60° with the normal to a glass-air and water-air interface, respectively. Predict the angle of refraction in glass when the angle of incidence in water is 45° with the normal to a water-glass interface [Fig.(c)].

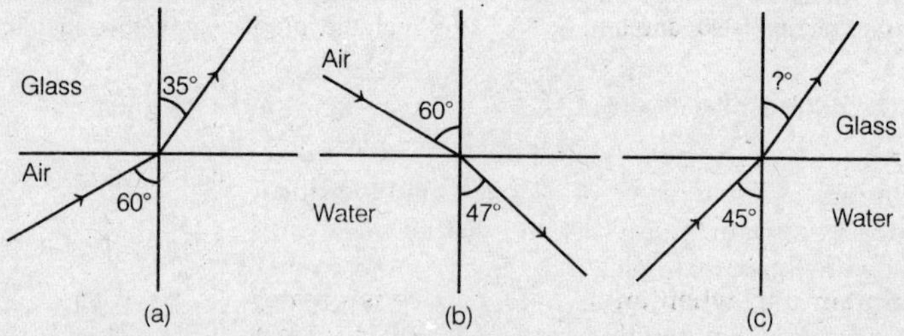

Sol. Given, From Fig. (a)

Angle of incidence $\quad i = 60°$

Angle of refraction $\quad r = 35°$

Refractive index of glass w.r.t. air, $${}^a\mu_g = \frac{\sin 60°}{\sin 35°} = 1.51 \quad \text{...(i)}$$

From Fig. (b)

Angle of incidence $i = 60°$, angle of refraction $r = 47°$

Refractive index of water w.r.t. air

$$^{a}\mu_{w} = \frac{\sin 60°}{\sin 47°} = 1.184 \qquad ...(ii)$$

From Fig. (c)

Angle of incidence $i = 45°$, let r be the angle of refraction

Refractive index of glass w.r.t. to water

$$^{w}\mu_{g} = \frac{\sin 45°}{\sin r} \qquad ...(iii)$$

As, we know that $^{w}\mu_{g} = \frac{^{a}\mu_{g}}{^{a}\mu_{w}}$ (formula for multiple refraction)

$$^{w}\mu_{g} = \frac{1.51}{1.184} = 1.275$$

From equation (iii) and (iv), we get

$$\frac{\sin 45°}{\sin r} = 1.275$$

$$\sin r = \frac{\sin 45°}{1.275} = 0.5545$$

$\therefore$ $$r = \sin^{-1}(0.5545) = 33.68°$$

Hence, the Angle of refraction at the water - glass interface is 33.68°.

Question 5 A small bulb is placed at the bottom of a tank containing water to a depth of 80 cm. What is the area of the surface of water through which light from the bulb can emerge out? Refractive index of water is 1.33. (Consider the bulb to be a point source.)

◎ *Thinking Process* Use relation between critical angle and refractive index. When light is incident at an angle of incidence equal to the critical angle, the angle of refraction is 90° and light will pass through the interface of the two media.

Sol. Let the bulb is placed at point O

$$AB = AC = r$$

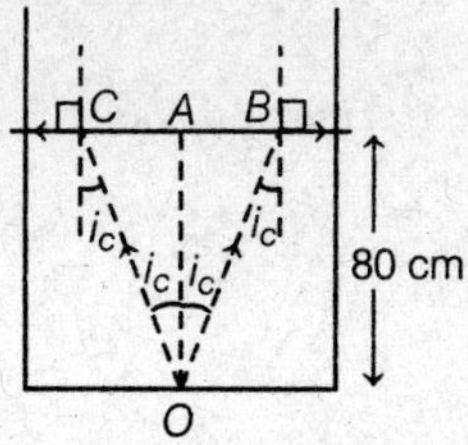

If the light falls at an angle of incidence equal to critical angle i_c, then only a circular area is formed because if angle of incidence is less than the critical angle it will refract into air and when angle of incidence is greater than critical angle then it will be reflected back in water)

The source of light is 80 cm below the surface of water *i.e.* $AO = 80$ cm, $\mu_w = 1.33$

Using the formula for critical angle,

$$\sin i_c = \frac{1}{\mu_w}$$

$$\sin i_c = \frac{1}{1.33} = 0.75$$

$$i_c = 48.6°$$

In ΔOAB

$$\tan i_c = \frac{AB}{AO} \text{ or } \tan i_c = \frac{r}{AO}$$

$$r = AO \tan i_c = 80 \tan 48.6$$

$$r = 80 \times 1.1345 = 90.7 \text{ cm}$$

Area of circular surface of water, through which light will emerge

$$A = \pi r^2$$

$$A = 3.14 \times (90.7)^2 = 25831.17 \text{ cm}^2, A = 2.58 \text{ m}^2$$

Question 6 A prism is made of glass of unknown refractive index. A parallel beam of light is incident on a face of the prism. The angle of minimum deviation is measured to be 40°. What is the refractive index of the material of the prism? The refracting angle of the prism is 60°. If the prism is placed in water (refractive index 1.33), predict the new angle of minimum deviation of a parallel beam of light.

Sol. Given, angle of minimum deviation $\delta_m = 40°$

The refracting angle of the prism $A = 60°$

Refractive index of glass w.r.t. air

$$^a\mu_g = \frac{\sin\left(\frac{A+\delta_m}{2}\right)}{\sin\frac{A}{2}} = \frac{\sin\left(\frac{60° + 40°}{2}\right)}{\sin\frac{60°}{2}} = \frac{\sin 50°}{\sin 30°}$$

$$^a\mu_g = \frac{0.766}{0.5} = 1.532$$

When prism is placed in water

The refractive index of water w.r.t. air

$$^a\mu_w = 1.33$$

Refractive index of glass with respect to water

$$^w\mu_g = \frac{\sin\left(\frac{A+\delta'_m}{2}\right)}{\sin\frac{A}{2}}$$

(where the new angle of deviation is δ'_m)

$$\therefore \quad \frac{^a\mu_g}{^a\mu_w} = \frac{\sin\left(\frac{A+\delta'_m}{2}\right)}{\sin\frac{60°}{2}} \quad \left[\because {^w\mu_g} = \frac{^a\mu_g}{^a\mu_w}\right]$$

$$\sin\left(\frac{A+\delta'_m}{2}\right) = \frac{{}^a\mu_g}{{}^a\mu_w} \times \sin 30° = \frac{1.532 \times \sin 30°}{1.33}$$

or $$\sin\left(\frac{A+\delta'_m}{2}\right) = \frac{0.5 \times 1.532}{1.33} = 0.5759$$

or $$\sin\left(\frac{A+\delta'_m}{2}\right) = \sin 35°10'$$

$$\frac{A+\delta'_m}{2} = 35°10'$$

$$A+\delta'_m = 70°20'$$

$$60° + \delta'_m = 70°20'$$

$$\delta'_m = 70°20' - 60°$$

$$\delta'_m = 10°20'$$

Thus, the new angle of minimum deviation is 10° 20′.

Question 7 Double-convex lenses are to be manufactured from a glass of refractive index 1.55, with both faces of the same radius of curvature. What is the radius of curvature required if the focal length is to be 20 cm?

Sol. Given, the refractive index of glass with respect to air

$${}^a\mu_g = 1.55$$

Focal length of the double convex lens, $f = 20$ cm

Radius of curvature of one face of the lens = R_1

Radius of curvature of the other face of the lens = R_2

Radius of curvature of double convex lens = R

If $R_1 = R$ then, $R_2 = -R$

Using the Lens maker's formula

$$\frac{1}{f} = ({}^a\mu_g - 1)\left(\frac{1}{R_1} - \frac{1}{R_2}\right)$$

$$\frac{1}{20} = (1.55 - 1)\left(\frac{1}{R} + \frac{1}{R}\right)$$

$$\frac{1}{20} = 0.55 \times \frac{2}{R}$$

$$R = 0.55 \times 2 \times 20 = 22 \text{ cm}$$

Thus, the required radius of curvature is 22 cm.

Question 8 A beam of light converges at a point P. Now a lens is placed in the path of the convergent beam 12 cm from P. At what point does the beam converge if the lens is (a) a convex lens of focal length 20 cm and (b) a concave lens of focal length 16 cm?

Sol. Here, the point P is on the right side of lens acts as virtual object.

(a) Given, distance of object from the lens $u = 12$ cm

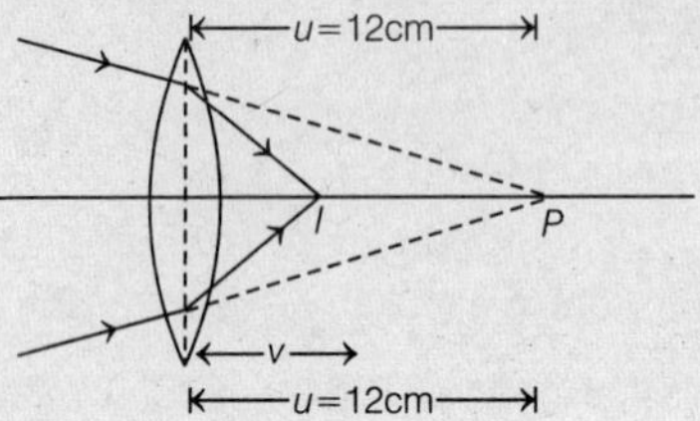

Focal length of convex lens $f = + 20$ cm

Using Lens formula, $\frac{1}{v} - \frac{1}{u} = \frac{1}{f}$

$$\frac{1}{v} - \frac{1}{12} = \frac{1}{20}$$

$$\frac{1}{v} = \frac{1}{20} + \frac{1}{12} = \frac{3+5}{60} = \frac{8}{60}$$

$$v = 7.5 \text{ cm}$$

Thus, the beam converges on the right side of lens at a distance of 7.5 cm.

(b) Distance of object from the lens $u = 12$ cm

Focal length of concave lens $f = - 16$ cm

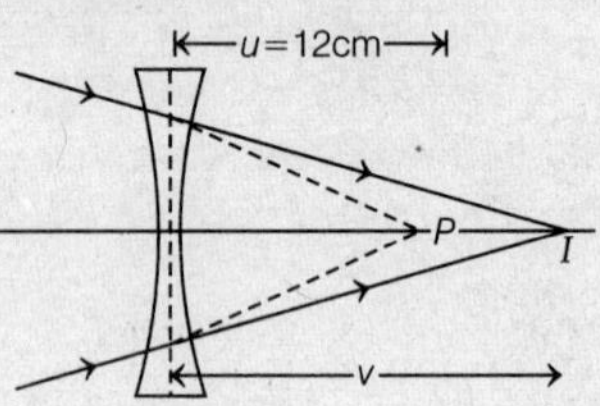

Using Lens formula,

$$\frac{1}{v} - \frac{1}{u} = \frac{1}{f}$$

$$\frac{1}{v} - \frac{1}{12} = -\frac{1}{16}$$

$$\Rightarrow \quad \frac{1}{v} = \frac{1}{12} - \frac{1}{16} = \frac{4-3}{48}$$

$$v = 48 \text{ cm}$$

Thus, the beam converges on the right side of lens at a distance of 48 cm.

Question 9 An object of size 3.0 cm is placed 14 cm in front of a concave lens of focal length 21 cm. Describe the image produced by the lens. What happens if the object is moved further away from the lens?

Sol. Size of object, $O = 3$ cm

Focal length of lens $f = -21$ cm

($\because$ Focal length of concave lens is taken as negative.)

Distance of object from the concave lens $u = -14$ cm

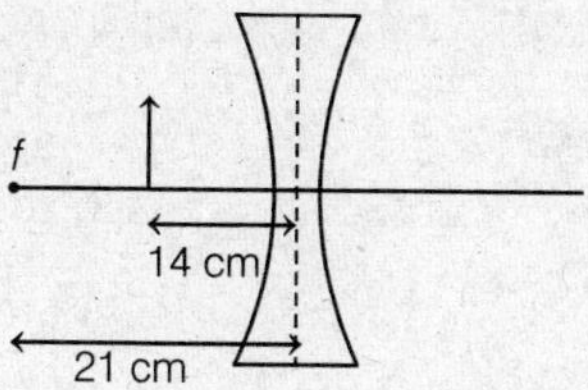

Using lens formula,

$$\frac{1}{v} - \frac{1}{u} = \frac{1}{f}$$

$$\frac{1}{v} + \frac{1}{14} = -\frac{1}{12}$$

$$\Rightarrow \quad \frac{1}{v} = -\frac{1}{21} - \frac{1}{14} = \frac{-2-3}{42} = -\frac{5}{42} \Rightarrow v = -8.4 \text{ cm}$$

Negative sign of v indicates that the image is virtual, erect and formed on the same side as the object.

Using the formula of magnification

$$m = \frac{v}{u} = \frac{I}{O}$$

where, I = height of image and O = height of object

$$\frac{(-8.4)}{-14} = \frac{I}{3}$$

$$I = 1.8 \text{ cm}$$

i.e. the image is diminised in size.

If the object moves further away from the lens, the image moves towards the lens (never beyond focus). The size of image decreases gradually.

Question 10 What is the focal length of a convex lens of focal length 30 cm in contact with a concave lens of focal length 20 cm? Is the system a converging or a diverging lens? Ignore thickness of the lenses.

Sol. Given, focal length of convex lens $f_1 = 30$ cm,

Focal length of concave lens $f_2 = -20$ cm

Using the formula of combination of lenses

$$\frac{1}{f} = \frac{1}{f_1} + \frac{1}{f_2} = \frac{1}{30} + \frac{1}{-20} = \frac{2-3}{60} = -\frac{1}{60}$$

$$f = -60 \text{ cm}$$

Since, the focal length of combination is negative in nature. So the combination behaves like a diverging lens *i.e.* as a concave lens.

Question 11 A compound microscope consists of an objective lens of focal length 2.0 cm and an eye-piece of focal length 6.25 cm separated by a distance of 15 cm. How far from the objective should an object be placed in order to obtain the final image at (a) the least distance of distinct vision (25 cm) and (b) at infinity? What is the magnifying power of the microscope in each case?

Sol. Given, focal length of objective lens, $f_o = 2$ cm

Focal length of eye-piece $f_e = 6.25$ cm

Distance between both lenses $L = 15$ cm

(a) Distance of final image from eye-piece $v_e = -25$ cm

Using the lens formula for eye-piece

$$\frac{1}{v_e} - \frac{1}{u_e} = \frac{1}{f_e}$$

$$\frac{1}{u_e} = \frac{1}{v_e} - \frac{1}{f_e}$$

$$= \frac{1}{-25} - \frac{1}{6.25} = \frac{-1-4}{25} = \frac{-5}{25}$$

$$u_e = -5 \text{ cm}$$

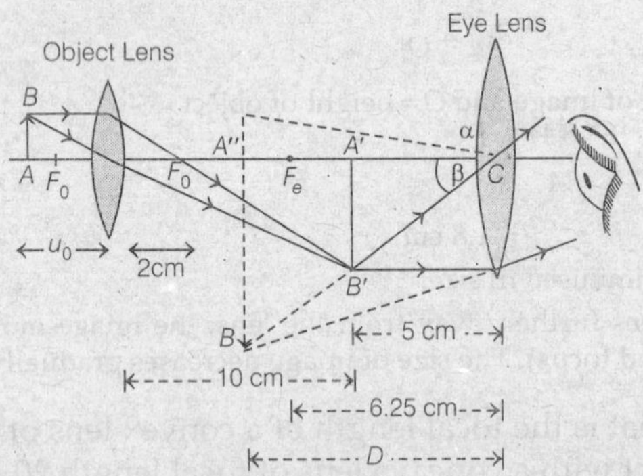

As the distance between objective and eye-piece $(|v_o| + |u_e|) = 15$ cm

$$L = |v_o| + |u_e|$$

Distance of image formed by object lens

$$v_o = L - |u_e| = 15 - 5 = 10 \text{ cm}$$

Using the lens equation for objective lens

$$\frac{1}{v_o} - \frac{1}{u_o} = \frac{1}{f_o}$$

$$\frac{1}{u_o} = \frac{1}{v_o} - \frac{1}{f_o} = \frac{1}{10} - \frac{1}{2} = \frac{1-5}{10} = -\frac{4}{10} \Rightarrow u_o = -2.5 \text{ cm}$$

So, the object should be placed 2.5 cm in front of the convex lens.

Magnifying power of compound microscope

$$m = \frac{-v_o}{u_o}\left(1 + \frac{D}{f_e}\right) = \frac{-10}{-2.5}\left(1 + \frac{25}{6.25}\right) \qquad (\because D = 25 \text{ cm})$$

$$m = 20$$

(b) The final image will be formed at infinity *i.e.* normal adjustment only if the image formed by the objective is in the focal plane of the eye-piece *i.e.*, at principal focus of the eye-piece.

Thus, here $\quad v_e = -\infty,\ f_e = 6.25 \text{ cm}$

Using the lens formula for eye- piece

$$\frac{1}{v_e} - \frac{1}{u_e} = \frac{1}{f_e}$$

$$\frac{1}{u_e} = \frac{1}{v_e} - \frac{1}{f_e} \Rightarrow \frac{1}{u_e} = \frac{1}{\infty} - \frac{1}{6.25} \Rightarrow u_e = 0\ 6.25 \text{ cm.}$$

Image distance of objective lens

$$v_o = L - |u_e| = 15\,|-6.25| = 8.75 \text{ cm} \qquad [\because L = |v_0| + |u_e|]$$

Using lens formula,

$$\frac{1}{v_o} - \frac{1}{u_o} = \frac{1}{f_o}$$

$$\frac{1}{u_o} = \frac{1}{v_o} - \frac{1}{f_o} = \frac{1}{8.75} - \frac{1}{2} = \frac{2-8.75}{17.5}$$

$$u_o = -\frac{17.5}{6.75} = -2.59 \text{ cm}$$

$\therefore$ The distance of object from objective = 2.59 cm

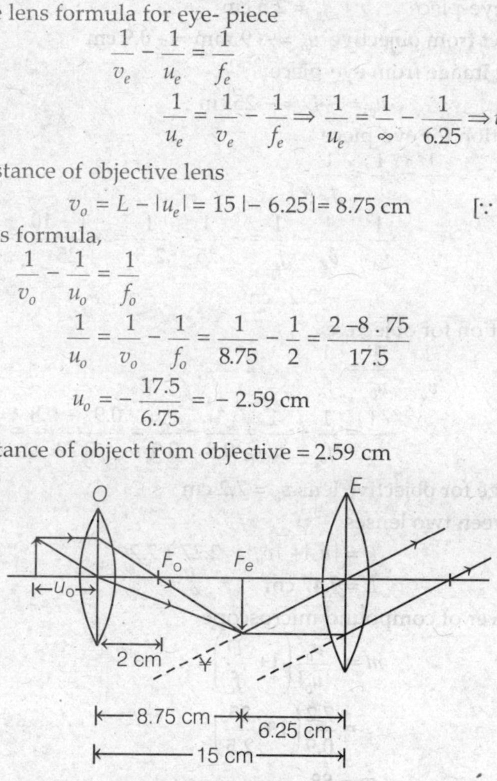

Magnifying power of the microscope

$$m = \frac{-v_o}{u_o}\left(\frac{D}{f_e}\right) = \frac{-8.75}{-2.59}\left(\frac{25}{6.25}\right) \Rightarrow m = 13.5$$

Question 12 A person with a normal near point (25 cm) using a compound microscope with objective of focal length 8.0 mm and an eye-piece of fochal length 2.5 cm can bring an object placed at 9.0 mm from the objective in sharp focus. What is the separation between the two lenses? Calculate the magnifying power of the microscope.

◎ ***Thinking Process*** We are dealing with a compound microscope, which consists of two lenses: an objective lens (close to the object) and an eye piece lens (close to the observer's eye)
Calculate v_e distance of the intermediate image from the eye piece using the known focal length (f_e) and the condition that the final image is at the near point (25 cm.)

Sol. Given, focal length of objective $f_o = 8 \text{ mm} = 0.8 \text{ cm}$

Focal length of eye-piece $f_e = 2.5 \text{ cm}$

Distance of object from objective $u_o = -9 \text{ mm} = -0.9 \text{ cm}$

Distance of final image from eye-piece

$$v_e = -D = -25 \text{ cm}$$

Using lens equation for eye-piece

$$\frac{1}{v_e} - \frac{1}{u_e} = \frac{1}{f_e}$$

or

$$\frac{1}{u_e} = \frac{1}{v_e} - \frac{1}{f_e} = -\frac{1}{25} - \frac{1}{2.5} = \frac{-1-10}{25} = -\frac{11}{25}$$

$$u_e = -2.27 \text{ cm}$$

Using lens equation for objective

$$\frac{1}{v_o} - \frac{1}{u_o} = \frac{1}{f_o}$$

or

$$\frac{1}{v_o} = \frac{1}{f_o} + \frac{1}{u_o} = \frac{1}{0.8} - \frac{1}{0.9} = \frac{0.9 - 0.8}{0.72} = \frac{0.1}{0.72}$$

Distance of image for objective lens $v_o = 7.2 \text{ cm}$

Separation between two lenses

$$L = |u_e| + |v_o| = 2.27 + 7.2$$

$$L = 9.47 \text{ cm}$$

Magnifying power of compound microscope

$$m = \frac{v_o}{|u_o|}\left(1 + \frac{D}{f_e}\right)$$

$$= \frac{7.2}{0.9}\left(1 + \frac{25}{2.5}\right)$$

$$m = 88$$

Question 13 A small telescope has an objective lens of focal length 144 cm and an eye-piece of focal length 6.0 cm. What is the magnifying power of the telescope? What is the separation between the objective and the eye piece?

Sol. Given, focal length of objective lens $f_o = 144$ cm

Focal length of eye-piece $f_e = 6$ cm

Magnifying power of the telescope in normal adjustment

(i.e., when the final image is formed at infinity)

$$m = \frac{f_o}{f_e} = \frac{144}{6} = 24$$

$\therefore$ Separation between lenses $L = f_o + f_e = 144 + 6 = 150$ cm

Question 14

(a) A giant refracting telescope at an observatory has an objective lens of focal length 15 m. If an eye-piece of focal length 1.0 cm is used, what is the angular magnification of the telescope?

(b) If this telescope is used to view the moon, what is the diameter of the image of the moon formed by the objective lens? The diameter of the moon is 3.48×10^6 m and the radius of lunar orbit is 3.8×10^8 m.

Sol. Given, focal length of objective lens, $f_o = 15$ m

Focal length of eye-piece $f_e = 1$ cm $= 0.01$ m

(a) Angular magnification by the telescope in normal adjustment

$$m = \frac{f_o}{f_e} = \frac{15}{0.01} = 1500$$

(b) Let d be the diameter of the image of the moon formed by the objective lens.

$\therefore$ Angle subtended by the image, $\tan\alpha = \frac{d}{f_o} = \frac{d}{15}$

Diameter of object $d_o = 3.48 \times 10^6$ m

Radius of orbit $r = 3.8 \times 10^8$ m

The angle subtended by the diameter of the moon at objective lens

$$\tan\alpha = \frac{\text{Diameter of moon}}{\text{Radius of lunar orbit}} = \frac{3.48 \times 10^6}{3.8 \times 10^8}$$

The angle subtended by the image is equal to the angle subtended by the object.

$$\therefore \quad \frac{d}{15} = \frac{3.48 \times 10^6}{3.8 \times 10^8}$$

or

$$d = \frac{3.48 \times 15 \times 10^{-2}}{3.8} = 13.73 \times 10^{-2} \text{ m}$$

or

$$d = 13.73 \text{ cm}$$

Thus, the diameter of the image of moon is 13.73 cm.

Question 15 Use the mirror equation to deduce that

(a) an object placed between f and $2f$ of a concave mirror produces a real image beyond $2f$.

(b) a convex mirror always produces a virtual image independent of the location of the object.

(c) the virtual image produced by a convex mirror is always diminished in size and is located between the focus and the pole.

(d) an object placed between the pole and focus of a concave mirror produces a virtual and enlarged image.

Note This exercise helps you deduce algebraically properties of images that one obtains from explicit ray diagrams.

Sol. (a) The mirror equation formula $\frac{1}{v}+\frac{1}{u}=\frac{1}{f}$

For concave mirror $f<0$. As object always placed on the left side of mirror, so $u<0$. According to question, $2f<u<f$

(Object lies between f and $2f$)

$$\frac{1}{2f}>\frac{1}{u}>\frac{1}{f} \text{ or } -\frac{1}{2f}<-\frac{1}{u}<-\frac{1}{f}$$

Add $\frac{1}{f}$ on both sides, we get

$$\frac{1}{f}-\frac{1}{2f}<\frac{1}{f}-\frac{1}{u}<0 \quad \ldots\text{(i)}$$

From mirror formula, $\frac{1}{f}-\frac{1}{u}=\frac{1}{v}$ so from Eq. (i), we get

$$\frac{1}{f}-\frac{1}{2f}<\frac{1}{v}<0$$

i.e., $\frac{1}{v}$ is negative.

It implies that v is negative and greater than $2f$.

So, the image formed is real and image lies beyond $2f$.

(b) For convex mirror f is always positive $f>0$. As object always placed on left side of mirror $u<0$.

Using mirror formula $\frac{1}{f}=\frac{1}{v}+\frac{1}{u}$

$$\frac{1}{v}=\frac{1}{f}-\frac{1}{u}$$

As $f>0$ and $u<0$ the value of $\frac{1}{v}>0$ or $v>0$ or v is always positive. The image formed is virtual. It does not depends on the location of object.

(c) For convex mirror, focal length is positive *i.e.* $f > 0$ and object distance is negative *i.e.* $u < 0$

Using mirror formula $\frac{1}{f} = \frac{1}{v} + \frac{1}{u}$

$$\frac{1}{v} = \frac{1}{f} - \frac{1}{u} \text{ so } \frac{1}{v} > \frac{1}{f} \text{ or } v < f$$

Thus, image always located between pole and focus of the mirror.

Magnification

$$m = \frac{-v}{u} = \frac{-v}{-u}$$

$$m < 1 \qquad [\because v < |u|]$$

m is positive and less than 1 so image is virtual and diminished.

(d) For concave mirror $f < 0$.

As object is placed between pole and focus of concave mirror

$$\therefore \quad f < u < 0$$

$$\frac{1}{f} > \frac{1}{u}$$

$$\therefore \quad \frac{1}{f} - \frac{1}{u} > 0$$

Using mirror formula $\frac{1}{f} = \frac{1}{v} + \frac{1}{u}$

$$\frac{1}{f} - \frac{1}{u} = \frac{1}{v} > 0 \Rightarrow v > 0$$

It means that v is positive, image is formed on right and virtual.

Magnification $m = \frac{-v}{u}$

$$\frac{1}{v} < \frac{1}{|u|}$$

i.e. $v > |u|$ so, $m > 1$ hence, the image is enlarged.

Mistake Alert Forgetting that $u - f$ is negative when $u < f$, leading to incorrect sign for v.

Always apply the correct sign for f and ensure that f is positive in convex mirrors.

Question 16 A small pin fixed on a table top is viewed from above from a distance of 50 cm. By what distance would the pin appear to be raised if it is viewed from the same point through a 15 cm thick glass slab held parallel to the table? Refractive index of glass = 1.5. Does the answer depend on the location of the slab?

Sol. Given, thickness of glass slab (real depth) = 15 cm

Refractive index of glass with respect to air ${}^a\mu_g = 1.5$

Using the formula $^{a}\mu_{g} = \frac{\text{Real depth}}{\text{Apparent depth}} = 1.5$

Apparent depth of pin $y = 15/1.5 = 10$ cm

Distance by which the pin appears to be raised

$$= \text{Real depth} - \text{Apparent depth} = 15 - 10 = 5 \text{ cm}$$

The answer does not depend on the location of the slab.

Quick Solution

Given thickness of glass slab $t = 15$ cm

Refractive index of glass $\mu = 1.5$

The normal shift in the position of the pin

$$d = t\left(1 - \frac{1}{\mu}\right) = 15\left(1 - \frac{1}{1.5}\right)$$

$$= 15 \times \frac{1}{3} = 5 \text{ cm}$$

The pin appears raised by 5 cm.

Question 17

(a) Figure shows a cross-section of a 'light pipe' made of a glass fibre of refractive index 1.68. The outer covering of the pipe is made of a material of refractive index 1.44. What is the range of the angles of the incident rays with the axis of the pipe for which total reflections inside the pipe take place, as shown in the figure.

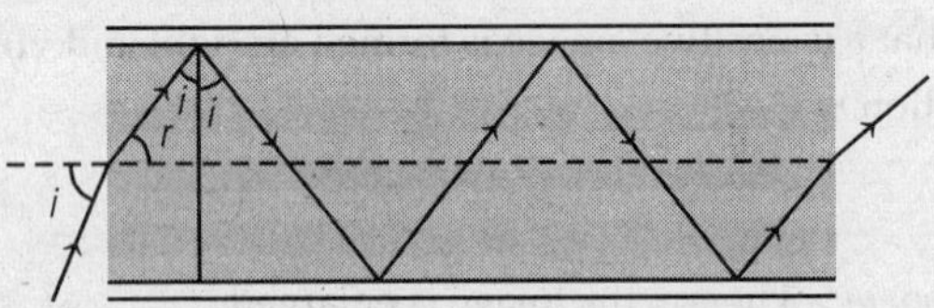

(b) What is the answer if there is no outer covering of the pipe?

◎ **Thinking Process** The working of an optical fibre is based on the phenomena of total internal reflection. Therefore use condition for total internal reflection.

Sol.

(a) Given, refractive index of the glass fibre with respect to air

$$\mu_2 = {}^{a}\mu_{g} = 1.68$$

Refractive index of the outer coating material cladding with respect to air

$$\mu_1 = {}^{a}\mu_{\text{outer}} = 1.44$$

Let the critical angle be i_c.

$$\mu = \frac{\mu_2}{\mu_1} = \frac{1}{\sin i_c}$$

$$\sin i_c = \frac{\mu_1}{\mu_2} = \frac{1.44}{1.68} = 0.8571$$

$$i_c = 59^\circ$$

The total internal reflection will take place when the angle of incidence i will be greater than the critical angle i_c

i.e., $i > 59^\circ$ or when angle of refraction, $r < r_{max}$

where $r_{max} = 90^\circ - i_c = 90^\circ - 59^\circ = 31^\circ$

So, $${}^a\mu_g = \frac{\sin i_{max}}{\sin r_{max}} = 1.68$$

or $$\sin i_{max} = 1.68 \sin 31^\circ = 1.68 \times 0.5150 = 0.8652$$

$$i_{max} = \sin^{-1}(0.8652) = 60^\circ$$

Thus, all the rays which are incident in the range $0 < i < 60^\circ$, will suffer total internal reflection in the pipe (but $i \neq 0$).

(b) If there is no outer covering of the pipe then reflection inside the pipe shall take place from the glass to air interface

$$\sin i'_c = \frac{\mu_1}{\mu_2} = \frac{1}{1.68} = 0.5952 \qquad [\because \mu_1 = 1 \text{ and } \mu_2 = 1.68]$$

Critical angle $i'_c = 36.5^\circ$

Now, $i = 90^\circ$, we have $r = 36.5^\circ$, $r = 1.68 = \dfrac{\sin 90^\circ}{\sin r}$

So, $i' = 90^\circ - 36.5^\circ = 53.5^\circ$

Here, i' is greater than the critical angle. Thus, all the rays incident at an angles in the range zero to 90° will suffer total internal reflection.

Question 18 The image of a small electric bulb fixed on the wall of a room is to be obtained on the opposite wall 3 m away by means of a large convex lens. What is the maximum possible focal length of the lens required for the purpose?

Sol. Suppose the object is placed at u metre in front of the lens, the image is formed at v and the distance of object from the lens is $3 - v$ m

i.e. $u = (3 - v)$ m

From lens formula,

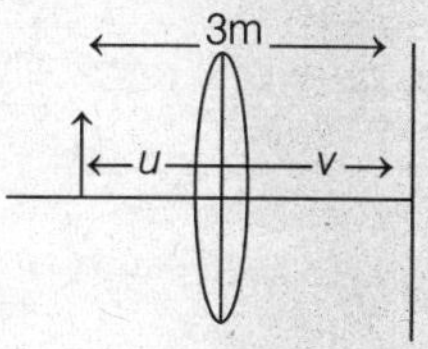

$$\frac{1}{v} - \frac{1}{u} = \frac{1}{f}$$

$$\frac{1}{v} - \frac{1}{-(3-v)} = \frac{1}{f}$$

or $$\frac{1}{v} + \frac{1}{3-v} = \frac{1}{f}$$

or $$\frac{3 - v + v}{v(3-v)} = \frac{1}{f}$$

$$3f = 3v - v^2$$

$$v^2 - 3v + 3f = 0$$

Now, $$v = \frac{-(-3) \pm \sqrt{9 - 4 \times (3f)}}{2}$$

$$v = \frac{+3 \pm \sqrt{9 - 12f}}{2}$$

Condition for image to be formed real on the screen, $v > 0$

$\therefore$ $$9 - 12\,f \geq 0$$

or $$9 \geq 12f \text{ or } f \leq 0.75\,\text{m}$$

Thus, the maximum possible focal length of the lens required for this purpose is 0.75 m.

> **Note** To achieve the maximum possible focal length, the object distance u must be chosen in a way that maximizes f.
> Image distances are negative for objects on the same side as the light source.
> Image distances are positive for real images and negative for virtual images.

Question 19 A screen is placed 90 cm from an object. The image of the object on the screen is formed by a convex lens at two different locations separated by 20 cm. Determine the focal length of the lens.

Sol. Given, distance between screen and object $a = 90$ cm

Distance between two locations of the lens $d = 20$ cm

$$u + 20 + u = 90$$

$$2u = 90 - 20 = 70$$

$$u = 35\,\text{cm}$$

again $$u + v = 90$$

$$35 + v = 90$$

$$v = 90 - 35 = 55\,\text{cm}$$

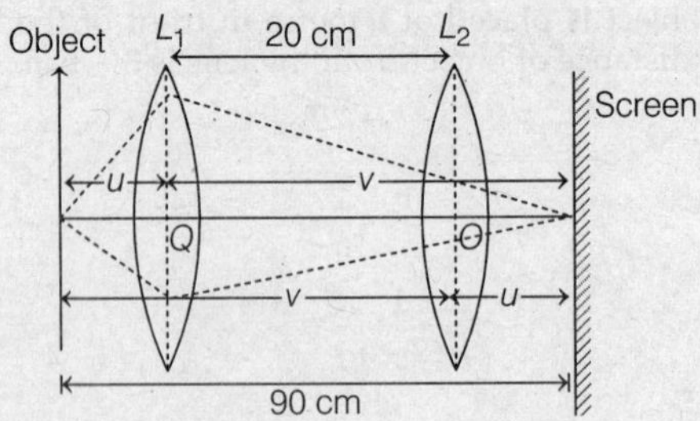

Using lens formula

$$\frac{1}{f} = \frac{1}{v} - \frac{1}{u}$$

$$\frac{1}{f} = \frac{1}{55} - \frac{1}{-35} = \frac{1}{55} + \frac{1}{35}$$

$$\frac{1}{f} = \frac{35 + 55}{35 \times 55} = \frac{1}{f} = \frac{90}{1925}$$

$$\therefore \quad f = \frac{1925}{90} = 21.38 \text{ cm}$$

Question 20

(a) Determine the 'effective focal length' of the combination of the two lenses in question 10, if they are placed 8.0 cm apart with their principal axes coincident. Does the answer depend on which side of the combination a beam of parallel light is incident? Is the notion of effective focal length of this system useful at all?

(b) An object 1.5 cm in size is placed on the side of the convex lens in the arrangement (a) above. The distance between the object and the convex lens is 40 cm. Determine the magnification produced by the two-lens system and the size of the image.

Sol. (a) Given, $f_1 = 30$ cm the focal length of convex lens.

The focal length of concave lens $f_2 = -20$ cm, $d = 8$ cm

(i) Let us take that the incident beam falls on convex lens and assume that concave lens is absent.

$$u_1 = \infty, f_1 = 30 \text{ cm}$$

Using the lens formula for for convex lens

$$\frac{1}{f_1} = \frac{1}{v_1} - \frac{1}{u_1} \Rightarrow \frac{1}{30} = \frac{1}{v_1} - \frac{1}{\infty}$$

Position of the image formed by convex lens

$$v_1 = 30 \text{ cm}$$

Now, this image acts as an object for concave lens.

Now, distance of object

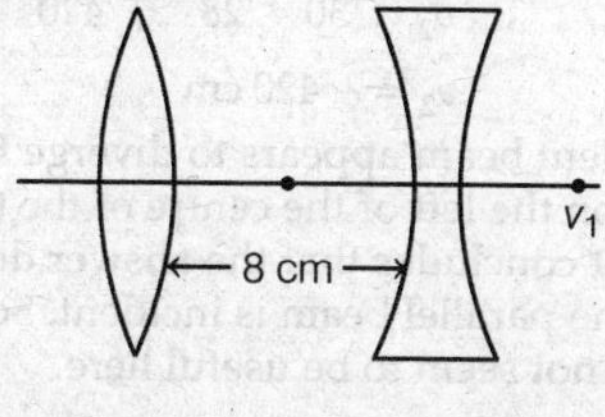

$$u_2 = +(30 - 8) = 22 \text{ cm}$$
$$f_2 = -20 \text{ cm}$$

Using lens formula for concave lens

$$\frac{1}{f_2} = \frac{1}{v_2} - \frac{1}{u_2}$$

$$\frac{1}{v_2} = -\frac{1}{20} + \frac{1}{22} = -\frac{1}{220}$$

Distance of final image $v_2 = -220$ cm.

Thus, the parallel beam would appear to diverge from a point $220 - 4 = 216$ cm from the centre of two lens system.

(ii) Let us take that the parallel beam first falls on concave lens.

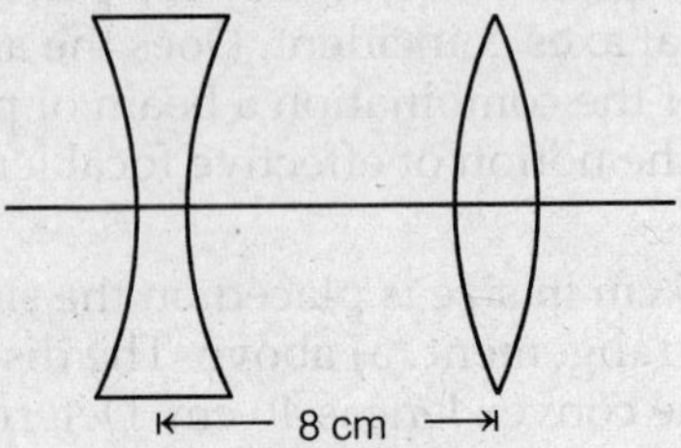

$$u_1 = -\infty,\ f_1 = -20 \text{ cm},\ v_1 = ?$$

using lens formula for concave lens $\frac{1}{f_1} = \frac{1}{v_1} - \frac{1}{u_1}$

$$\frac{1}{v_1} + \frac{1}{\infty} = \frac{1}{-20}$$

$$v_1 = -20 \text{ cm}$$

This image v_1, will acts as an object for convex lens at 28 cm.

$u_2 = -(20 + 8) = -28$ cm, $f_2 = 30$ cm, $v_2 = ?$

Using lens formula for convex lens

$$\frac{1}{f_2} = \frac{1}{v_2} - \frac{1}{u_2}$$

$$\frac{1}{v_2} + \frac{1}{28} = \frac{1}{30}$$

$$\frac{1}{v_2} = \frac{1}{30} - \frac{1}{28} = \frac{14 - 15}{420} = -\frac{1}{420}$$

$$v_2 = -420 \text{ cm}$$

The parallel incident beam appears to diverge from a point $420 - 4 = 416$ cm on the left of the centre of the two lens system. From the above two cases it concludes that the answer depends on which side of the lens system the parallel beam is incident. So, the notion of effective focal length does not seem to be useful here.

(b) Given, size of object $O_1 = 1.5$ cm

Distance from the convex lens $u_1 = -40$ cm,

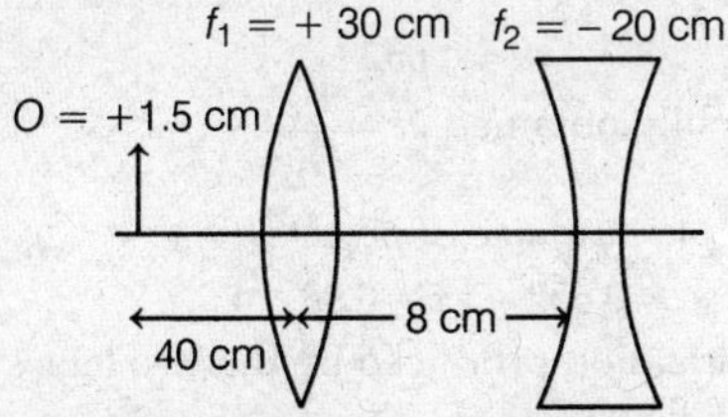

For the convex lens, $\frac{1}{v_1} - \frac{1}{u_1} = \frac{1}{f_1}$

$$\frac{1}{v_1} = \frac{1}{30} + \frac{1}{(-40)}$$

$$= \frac{4-3}{120} = \frac{1}{120}$$

$$v_1 = 120 \text{ cm}$$

Magnification produced by convex lens

$$m_1 = \frac{I_1}{O_1} = \frac{v_1}{u_1} = \frac{120}{-40} = -3$$

$$\frac{I_1}{O_1} = -3$$

$$\frac{I_1}{1.5} = -3, \; I_1 = -4.5 \text{ cm}$$

Now, this image acts as an object for concave lens.

∴ For concave lens $u_2 = 120 - 8 = 112$ cm, $f_2 = -20$ cm

Using lens formula

$$\frac{1}{f_2} = \frac{1}{v_2} - \frac{1}{u_2}$$

$$\frac{1}{v_2} = \frac{1}{f_2} + \frac{1}{u_2}$$

$$\frac{1}{v_2} = \frac{1}{-20} + \frac{1}{112} = \frac{-112+20}{112 \times 20} = \frac{-92}{112 \times 20}$$

$$v_2 = \frac{-112 \times 20}{92} \text{ cm}$$

Magnification produced by concave lens

$$m_2 = \frac{v_2}{u_2} = \frac{(-112 \times 20)}{92 \times 112} = \frac{-20}{92}$$

Magnification produced by lens combination

$$m = m_1 \times m_2 = (-3) \times \left(-\frac{20}{92}\right) = \frac{60}{92}$$

$$m = 0.652$$

Size of image finally obtained $m = \dfrac{I_2}{O_2}$

Size of image $(I_2) = m \times$ size of objects (O_2)

$$= 0.652 \times 1.5 = 0.98 \text{ cm}$$

Thus, the magnification produced by the two lens system is 0.652 and size of image is 0.98 cm.

Question 21 At what angle should a ray of light be incident on the face of a prism of refracting angle 60° so that it just suffers total internal reflection at the other face? The refractive index of the material of the prism is 1.524.

Sol. Angle of prism, $A = 60°$

Refractive index of prism $\mu = 1.524$

Let i be the angle of incidence which is equal to the critical angle i_c because it just suffers total internal reflection on surface AC.

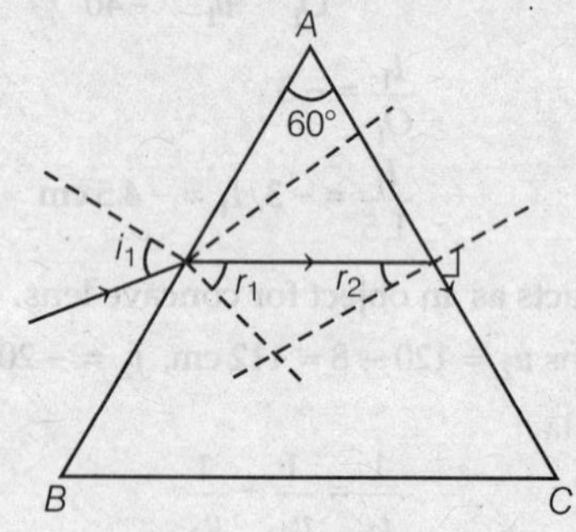

$$\sin i_c = \frac{1}{\mu} = \frac{1}{1.524} = 0.6561$$

$$i_c = 41°$$

For a prism $r_1 + r_2 = A$ here $r_2 = i_c$

$\therefore$ $$r_1 + i_c = A$$

$$r_1 + 41° = 60° \Rightarrow r_1 = 19°$$

Using the formula, $$\mu = \frac{\sin i_1}{\sin r_1}$$

$$1.524 = \frac{\sin i_1}{\sin 19°}$$

or $$\sin i_1 = 1.524 \sin 19° = 1.524 \times 0.3256$$

or $$i_1 = \sin^{-1}(0.4962) \Rightarrow i_1 = 29° \, 75'$$

Thus, the angle of incident on surface AB should be 29° 75′.

Question 22 A card sheet divided into squares each of size 1 mm^2 is being viewed at a distance of 9 cm through a magnifying glass (a converging lens of focal length 9 cm) held close to the eye.

(a) What is the magnification produced by the lens? How much is the area of each square in the virtual image?

(b) What is the angular magnification (magnifying power) of the lens?

(c) Is the magnification in (a) equal to the magnifying power in (b)? Explain.

Sol. (a) Given, focal length of converging lens $f = 9$ cm,

Distance of object from lens $u = -9$ cm

Size of object $O = 1$ mm

Using Lens formula

$$\frac{1}{f} = \frac{1}{v} - \frac{1}{u}$$

$$\frac{1}{9} = \frac{1}{v} + \frac{1}{9}$$

$$\Rightarrow \quad \frac{1}{v} = \frac{1}{9} - \frac{1}{9} = \frac{1}{\infty}$$

or $$v = \infty$$

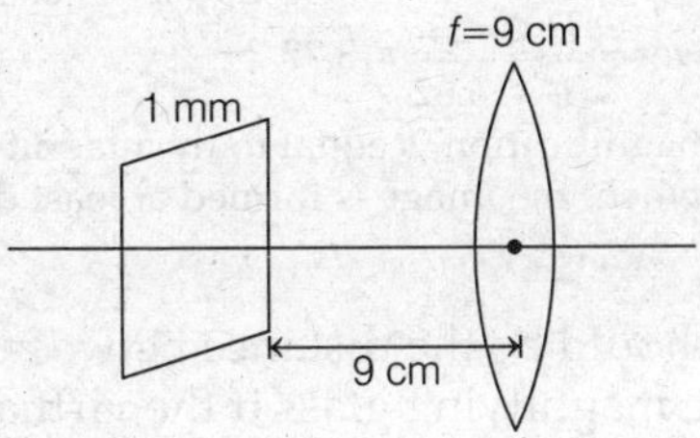

The magnification produced by the lens

$$m = \frac{I}{O} = +\frac{v}{u} = -\frac{(\infty)}{-9} = \infty$$

$$I = O \times m = 1 \times \infty = \infty$$

Area of each square in virtual image $= (\infty)^2 = \infty$

Thus, the magnification is ∞ and area of each square in the virtual image is also infinite.

(b) Angular magnification, $m = \frac{D}{|u|} = \frac{25}{9} = 2.8$

($\because$ Least distance of distinct vision $D = 25$ cm)

(c) No, the linear magnification by a lens $m = \frac{v}{u}$ and magnifying power (angular magnification) $m = \frac{D}{u}$ are not equal. They are equal if image is at least distance of distinct vision *i.e.* $v = D$ (Least distance of distinct vision).

Question 23 (a) At what distance should the lens be held from the figure in question 22 in order to view the squares distinctly with the maximum possible magnifying power?

(b) What is the magnification in this case?

(c) Is the magnification equal to the magnifying power in this case? Explain.

Sol. (a) Given, $v = -25$ cm and $f = 9$ cm.

For maximum possible magnifying power the image should be formed at least distant of distinct vision *i.e.* 25 cm.

Using lens formula

$$\frac{1}{f} = \frac{1}{v} - \frac{1}{u}$$

$$\Rightarrow \quad \frac{1}{9} = \frac{1}{-25} - \frac{1}{u}$$

$$\frac{1}{u} = \frac{1}{-25} - \frac{1}{9} = \frac{-34}{225}$$

$$u = \frac{-225}{34} = -6.62 \text{ cm}$$

(b) Linear magnification in this case $m = \frac{I}{O} = \frac{v}{u} = \frac{-25}{-6.62} = 3.77$

(c) Magnifying power $= \frac{D}{u} = \frac{25}{6.62} = 3.77$

Yes, the linear magnification is equal to the magnifying power (angular magnification) when, the image is formed at least distance of distinct vision.

Question 24 What should be the distance between the object in question 23 and the magnifying glass if the virtual image of each square in the figure is to have an area of 6.25 mm^2. Would you be able to see the squares distinctly with your eyes very close to the magnifier?

Sol. Given, area of square shaped virtual image, $A_I = 6.25 \text{ mm}^2$

Area of square shaped object, $A_O = 1 \text{ mm}^2$

Focal length of lens, $f = 9$ cm

Linear magnification, $m = \sqrt{\frac{A_I}{A_O}} = \sqrt{\frac{6.25}{1}} = 2.5$

Again, magnification, $m = \frac{v}{u}$

or $\quad v = m \times u = 2.5 \times u \quad$ ...(i)

From lens formula,

$$\frac{1}{f} = \frac{1}{v} - \frac{1}{u}$$

$$\frac{1}{9} = \frac{1}{2.5\,u} - \frac{1}{u}$$

$$u = -5.4 \text{ cm}$$

$$v = 2.5u = 2.5 \times (-5.4) \quad \text{[From Eq. (i)]}$$

$$v = -13.5 \text{ cm}$$

Thus, the virtual image is formed at a distance of 13.5 cm which is less than the near point (25 cm) of a normal human eye. So, it cannot be seen by the eyes distinctly.

Question 25 Answer the following questions.

(a) The angle subtended at the eye by an object is equal to the angle subtended at the eye by the virtual image produced by a magnifying glass. In what sense then does a magnifying glass provide angular magnification?

(b) In viewing through a magnifying glass, one usually positions one's eyes very close to the lens. Does angular magnification change if the eye is moved back?

(c) Magnifying power of a simple microscope is inversely proportional to the focal length of the lens. What then stops us from using a convex lens of smaller and smaller focal length and achieving greater and greater magnifying power?

(d) Why must both the objective and the eye-piece of a compound microscope have short focal lengths?

(e) When viewing through a compound microscope, our eyes should be positioned not on the eye-piece but a short distance away from it for best viewing. Why? How much should be that short distance between the eye and eye-piece?

Sol.

(a) As the size of image is much bigger than the size of object and, angular size of image is equal to angular size of object. A magnifying glass helps to see the objects placed closer than the least distance of distinct vision (*i.e.* 25 cm), as an object gets closer, its angular size increases.

(b) Yes, the angular magnification changes. As the distance between eye and magnifying glass is increased, the angular magnification decreases.

(c) If focal length of lens decreases, radius of curvature also decreases. Hence, lens become thick and chromatic and spherical aberrations become significant. Grinding for small focal length lens is very difficult practically a convex lens of magnifying power 3 can be made easily. We cannot make the lenses having very small focal length very easily.

(d) As the angular magnification produced by the eye-piece of a compound microscope is $\left(1 + \frac{D}{f_e}\right)$.

As f_e is small, the angular magnification will be large.

Further, magnification of objective lens is $\frac{v}{u}$. As object lies close to focus of objective lens $u \approx f_o$. To increase this magnification $\left(\frac{v}{f_o}\right)$, f_o should be smaller.

Thus, f_o and f_e both are small.

(e) When we place our eyes too much close to the eye-piece of a compound microscope, we are unable to collect the refracted light in large amount because the field of view will be reduced. So, the clarity of image is blurred.

The best position of the eye for viewing through a compound microscope is at the eye ring attached to the eye-piece.

Question 26 An angular magnification (magnifying power) of 30 X is desired using an objective of focal length 1.25 cm and an eye-piece of focal length 5 cm. How will you set up the compound microscope?

Sol. We assume the microscope in common usage, i.e., the final image is formed at the least distance of distinct vision.

Given, focal length of objective, $f_o = 1.25$ cm

Focal length of eye-piece, $f_e = 5$ cm

Least distance of distinct vision, $D = 25$ cm

Angular magnification of lens, $m = 30$

The magnification produced by eye-piece, $m_e = 1 + \frac{D}{f_e} = 1 + \frac{25}{5} = 6$

The magnification produced by microscope

$$m = m_o \times m_e$$

$$30 = m_o \times 6$$

where, m_o is the magnification produced by objective lens.

$$m_o = 5$$

Again, we know that magnification of objective lens

$$m_o = \frac{v_o}{-u_o}$$

$$5 = \frac{v_o}{-u_o}$$

or $$v_o = -5\,u_o \qquad \text{...(i)}$$

Using lens formula for objective lens,

$$\frac{1}{f_o} = \frac{1}{v_o} - \frac{1}{u_o}$$

$$\frac{1}{1.25} = \frac{1}{-5u_o} - \frac{1}{u_o} = -\frac{6}{5u_o}$$

$$u_o = -\frac{6}{5} \times 1.25 = -1.5 \text{ cm}$$

From Eq. (i), we get

$$v_o = -5u_o = -5(-1.5) = 7.5 \text{ cm}$$

Thus, the object should placed at a distance of 1.5 cm from the objective lens to get the desired magnification.

Now, using the lens formula for eye-piece

$$\frac{1}{f_e} = \frac{1}{v_e} - \frac{1}{u_e}$$

$$\frac{1}{u_e} = \frac{1}{v_e} - \frac{1}{f_e}$$

$$= -\frac{1}{25} - \frac{1}{5} = -\frac{6}{25} \qquad (\because v_e = -25 \text{ cm})$$

$$u_e = -4.17 \text{ cm}$$

The separation between objective and eye-piece

$$|v_o| + |u_e| = 4.17 + 7.5$$

$$= 11.67 \text{ cm}$$

Thus, the microscope is settled as the distance between eye-piece and objective is 11.67 cm.

Question 27 A small telescope has an objective lens of focal length 140 cm and an eye-piece of focal length 5.0 cm. What is the magnifying power of the telescope for viewing distant objects, when

(a) the telescope is in normal adjustment (*i.e.*, when the final image is at infinity)?

(b) the final image is formed at the least distance of distinct vision (25 cm)?

Sol. Given, focal length of objective lens $f_o = 140$ cm and focal length of eye lens $f_e = 5$ cm

(a) For normal adjustment, the magnification

$$m = +\frac{f_o}{f_e} = +\frac{140}{5} = +28$$

(b) For least distance of distinct vision, the magnification

$$m = \frac{f_o}{f_e}\left(1 + \frac{f_e}{D}\right) = \frac{140}{5}\left(1 + \frac{5}{25}\right)$$

$$m = 28(1 + 0.2) = 33.6$$

Question 28 (a) For the telescope described in Q. 27 (a), what is the separation between the objective lens and the eye-piece?

(b) If this telescope is used to view a 100 m tall tower 3 km away, what is the height of the image of the tower formed by the objective lens?

(c) What is the height of the final image of the tower if it is formed at 25 m?

Sol. Given, $f_o = 140$ cm, $f_e = 5$ cm and $D = 25$ cm

(a) (i) In normal adjustment, the separation between eye-piece and objective

$$= f_o + f_e = 140 + 5 = 145 \text{ cm}$$

(ii) When final image is formed at least distance of distinct vision

i.e. $$v_e = D = 25 \text{ cm}$$

$\because$ $$\frac{1}{f_e} = \frac{1}{v_e} - \frac{1}{u_e}$$

$$\frac{1}{5} = \frac{1}{-25} - \frac{1}{u_e} \Rightarrow \frac{1}{-u_e} = \frac{6}{25}$$

$\Rightarrow$ $$u_e = \frac{-25}{6} = -4.16 \text{ cm}$$

Separation between objective and eye-piece

$$L = f_0 + |u_e| = 140 + 4.16 = 144.16 \text{ cm}$$

(b) Height of tower, $h_0 = 100$ m

Distance of tower, $u = 3$ km $= 3000$ m

The angle subtended by the object

$$\theta_O = \frac{h_0}{u} = \frac{100}{3000} = \frac{1}{30} \text{ rad} \quad \text{...(i)}$$

The angle subtended by the image.

$$\theta_I = \frac{h_i}{f_o} = \frac{h_i}{140} \quad \text{...(ii)}$$

($\because h_i$ = height of image tower)

As $$\theta_O = \theta_I$$

$$\frac{1}{30} = \frac{h_i}{140}$$

$$h_i = \frac{14}{3} = 4.67 \text{ cm}$$

Thus, the height of image of tower is 4.67 cm.

(c) Image formed at distance, $D = 25$ cm, then magnification produced by eye-piece

$$m = 1 + \frac{D}{f_e} = 1 + \frac{25}{5} = 6$$

Let I be the height of the final image of the tower, so size of the image formed by objective

$$O = \frac{14}{3} \text{ cm} = 4.67 \text{ cm} \quad \because \quad m = \frac{I}{O}$$

$\therefore$ Height of final image $I = m \times O = 6 \times 4.67 = 28$ cm

Thus, the height of final image of tower is 28 cm.

Question 29 A Cassegrain telescope uses two mirrors as shown in figure. Such a telescope is built with the mirrors 20 mm apart. If the radius of curvature of the large mirror is 220 mm and the small mirror is 140 mm, where will the final image of an object at infinity be?

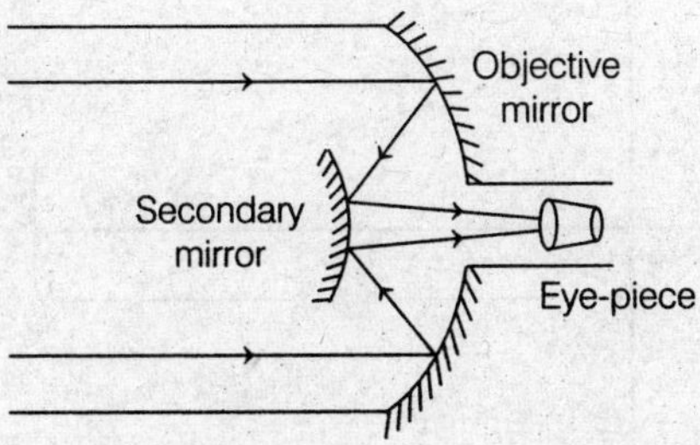

Sol. Given, distance between objective mirror and another mirror $d = 20$ mm

Radius of curvature of objective mirror $= R_1 = 220$ mm

$\therefore$ Focal length of objective mirror, $f_1 = \dfrac{220}{2} = 110$ mm

Radius of curvature of small mirror $R_2 = 140$ mm

$\therefore$ Focal length of small mirror, $f_2 = \dfrac{140}{2} = 70$ mm

Since the secondary mirror is convex, $f_2 = -70$ mm

The image of an object placed at infinity, formed by the objective concave mirror, will act as a virtual object for small convex mirror.

So, the object distance for small convex mirror $u = -(f_1 - d)$

i.e.,

$$u = -(110 - 20) = -90 \text{ mm}$$

Using mirror formula, $\dfrac{1}{v} + \dfrac{1}{u} = \dfrac{1}{f_2}$

$$\frac{1}{v} = \frac{1}{f_2} - \frac{1}{u}$$

$$= \frac{1}{-70} - \frac{1}{(-90)} = \frac{7-9}{630} = \frac{-2}{630}$$

$$v = -315 \text{ mm}$$

or $$v = -31.5 \text{ cm}$$

Thus, the final image is formed at 315 mm away from small mirror.

Mistake Alert Misinterpreting the sign conventions or confusing the distances with mirror placements can mislead conclusions.

Question 30 Light incident normally on a plane mirror attached to a galvanometer coil retraces backwards as shown in figure.
A current in the coil produces a deflection of 3.5° of the mirror. What is the displacement of the reflected spot of light on a screen placed 1.5 m away?

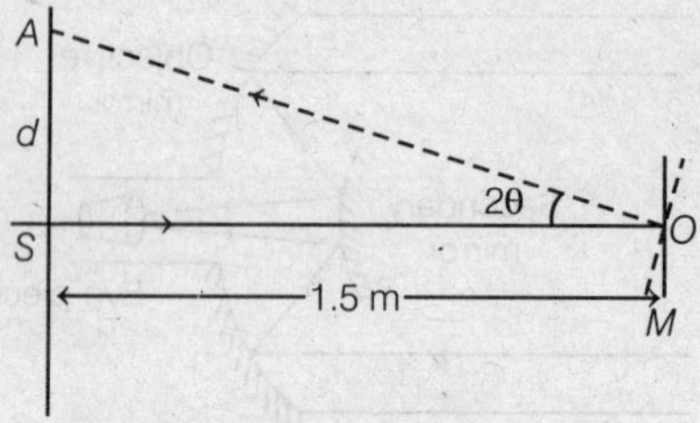

Sol. Given, deflection of the mirror, $\theta = 3.5°$
Distance between screen and mirror, $x = 1.5$ m
As, we know that when mirror turns by angle θ, the reflected ray turned by 2θ.

$$\therefore \quad 2\theta = 2 \times 3.5 = 7° = \frac{7\pi}{180} \text{ rad}$$

Again, in ΔAOS

$$\tan 2\theta = \frac{AS}{SO}$$

$$\tan\left(\frac{7\pi}{180}\right) = \frac{AS}{1.5} = \frac{d}{1.5} \text{ or } d = 1.5 \tan\left(\frac{7\pi}{180}\right)$$

For small angle,

$$\tan \frac{7\pi}{180} \approx \frac{7\pi}{180}$$

$$d = 1.5 \times \frac{7\pi}{180} = 0.18 \text{ m}$$

Question 31 Figure shows an equiconvex lens (of refractive index 1.50) in contact with a liquid layer on top of a plane mirror. A small needle with its tip on the principal axis is moved along the axis until its inverted image is found at the position of the needle. The distance of the needle from the lens is measured to be 45.0 cm. The liquid is removed and the experiment is repeated. The new distance is measured to be 30.0 cm. What is the refractive index of the liquid?

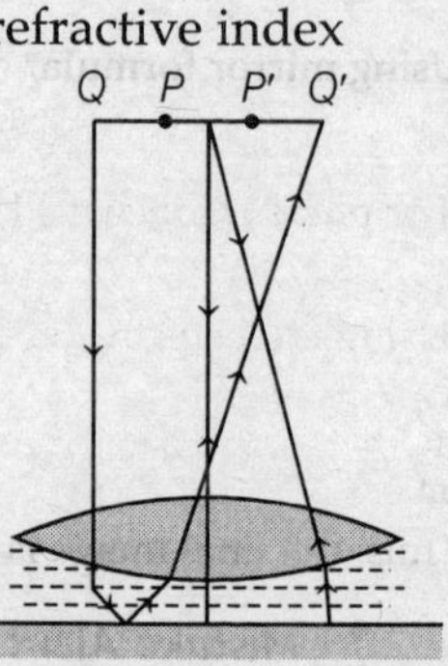

◎ *Thinking Process* The system with the liquid layer acts as a combination of two lenses (the convex lens and the liquid). Use the lens combination formula:

$$\frac{1}{f'} = \frac{1}{f_{\text{lens}}} + \frac{1}{f_{\text{liquid}}}$$

When there is a liquid layer, the effective focal length of the system (f') changes due to the combined effect of the lens and liquid.

Sol. Given, focal length of double convex lens of glass, $f_1 = 30$ cm.

When liquid is filled between lens and plane mirror the image is formed at position of object at 45 cm hence the object must be placed at focus of equivalent lens of equiconvex lens and plano concave lens of liquid.

Focal length of combination of double convex lens and plano concave liquid lens

$$f = 45 \text{ cm}$$

Refractive index of lens, $\mu_g = 1.5$

Let f_2 be the focal length of the plano concave lens made of liquid between the convex lens and plane mirror.

For combination of lenses

$$\frac{1}{f_1} + \frac{1}{f_2} = \frac{1}{f}$$

$$\frac{1}{30} + \frac{1}{f_2} = \frac{1}{45}$$

$$\Rightarrow \quad \frac{1}{f_2} = \frac{1}{45} - \frac{1}{30} = -\frac{1}{90}$$

$$f_2 = -90 \text{ cm}$$

For the convex lens of glass, $R_1 = R$, $R_2 = -R$

Using lens maker's formula

$$\frac{1}{f_1} = (\mu - 1)\left(\frac{1}{R_1} - \frac{1}{R_2}\right) = \left(\frac{3}{2} - 1\right)\left(\frac{1}{R} + \frac{1}{R}\right)$$

$$\frac{1}{30} = \frac{1}{2} \times \frac{2}{R} \Rightarrow R = 30 \text{ cm}$$

For plano – concoave lens, $f = -90$ cm

$$R_1 = -R = -30 \text{ cm}, R_2 = \infty$$

Using the Lens maker's formula

$$\frac{1}{f_2} = (\mu_l - 1)\left(\frac{1}{R_1} - \frac{1}{R_2}\right)$$

$$-\frac{1}{90} = (\mu_l - 1)\left(\frac{1}{-30} - \frac{1}{\infty}\right) \Rightarrow \frac{1}{90} = \frac{1}{30}(\mu_l - 1)$$

$$\mu_l = 1 + \frac{1}{3} = \frac{4}{3} = 1.33$$

Thus, the refractive index of liquid is $\frac{4}{3}$ or 1.33.

Mistake Alert Always ensure consistent sign conventions for object and image distance.
Combining focal lengths of lenses requires careful attention to positive/negative contributions.

Note The focal length of a lens is related to its refractive index (μ) and radius of curvature (R) via:

$$\frac{1}{f} = (\mu - 1)\left(\frac{1}{R_1} - \frac{1}{R_2}\right)$$

you will use this relationship to determine the refractive index of the liquid once f_{liquid} is calculated.
When combining lenses, remember that each lens (or medium) contributes to the overall focal length according to the formula:

$$\frac{1}{f} = \frac{1}{f_1} + \frac{1}{f_2}$$

DIKSHA APP Questions

Multiple Choice Questions

Q.1 The objective lens of an astronomical telescope must be of

(a) high power (b) large focal length
(c) high refractive index (d) low refractive index

Sol. (b) $\because m = \frac{-f_0}{f_e}$, $f_0 >> f_e$, so that astronomical telescope, have large magnifying power.

Q.2 When length of compound microscope increases, its magnifying power

(a) decreases (b) increases
(c) does not change (d) may increases or decreases

Sol. (b) We know that $m = \frac{-L}{f_0}\left(1 + \frac{D}{f_e}\right)$ [When final image is at D]

$\therefore$ $m \propto L$

Thus, length of compound microscope increases, its magnifying power also increases.

Q.3 The focal length of an equiconvex lens is equal to the radius of curvature of either face. What is the refractive index of the lens material

(a) 1.5 (b) 1.6
(c) 2 (d) 1.42

Sol. (a) $\frac{1}{f} = (\mu - 1)\left[\frac{1}{R_1} - \frac{1}{R_2}\right]$

$$\frac{1}{x} = (\mu - 1)\left[\frac{1}{x} - \frac{1}{-x}\right] \qquad [\because R_1 = x]\,[R_2 = -x]$$

$$\frac{1}{x} = (\mu - 1)\frac{2}{x} \Rightarrow \mu - 1 = \frac{1}{2} \Rightarrow \mu = 1 + \frac{1}{2} = \frac{3}{2} = 1.5$$

Q.4 Which of the following relation is false, for a prism placed in position of minimum deviation ?

(a) $i_1 = i_2$ (b) $r_1 = r_2$ (c) $r_2 \neq r_1$ (d) None of these

Sol. (c) For minimum deviation in prism

$$i_1 = i_2$$
$$r_1 = r_2$$

Q.5 Optical fibres are based on the phenomena of

(a) reflection (b) refraction
(c) dispersion (d) total internal reflection

Sol. (d) In an optical fibre, total internal reflection occurs from medium where the entire incident light (100%) is reflected back into the denser medium.

Q.6 For which of the following pair is the critical angle smallest ?

(a) water-air (b) glass-water
(c) glass-air (d) glass-glass

Sol. (c) $\because \mu = \frac{1}{\sin C}$

Since, the refractive index (μ) is highest for the glass-air pair, the critical angle is minimum.

Q.7 A beam of monochromatic light of wavelength 4200 Å (in air) travels in water. Its wavelength in water will be

(a) 2800Å (b) 5010Å (c) 3150Å (d) 4200Å

Sol. (c) $\lambda_a = 4200$ Å, $\mu_w = \frac{4}{3}$

$$\lambda_w = \frac{\lambda_a}{\mu_w} = \frac{4200}{\frac{4}{3}} = 1050 \times 3 = 3150\text{ Å}$$

Q.8 When light enters from air to glass, its wavelength

(a) increases (b) decreases
(c) remain unchanged (d) data is insufficient

Sol. (b) $\because \lambda_w = \dfrac{\lambda_a}{\mu}$

When light enters from air to glass, its wavelength decreases. This is because light travels slower in glass than in air. To maintain a constant frequency the wavelength of light decreases.

Q.9 A convex lens of glass, of focal length 10 cm is immersed in water. The new focal length is

(a) 27 cm (b) 40 cm
(c) 48 cm (d) 12 cm

Sol. (b) $f_w = \dfrac{{}_a\mu_g - 1}{{}_w\mu_g - 1} \times f_a = \dfrac{{}_a\mu_g - 1}{\dfrac{\mu_g}{\mu_w} - 1} \times f_a$ (from lens makers' formula)

$$f_w = \frac{1.5 - 1}{\dfrac{1.5}{1.33} - 1} \times 10 = 39.3 \text{ cm}$$

Therefore, the new focal length is nearly 40 cm.

Q.10 The Sky would appear red instead of blue if

(a) atmospheric particles scattered blue light
(b) atmospheric particles scattered all colour equally
(c) atmospheric particles scattered red light more than blue light
(d) the sun was much hotter

Sol. (c) The sky would appear red instead of blue if atmospheric particle scattered red light more then blue light.

□ Short Answer Type

Q.1 A converging and diverging lens of equal focal length are placed coaxially in contact. Find the power and focal length of the combination.

Sol. As power of converging lens $P_1 = 1/f$

power of diverging lens $P_2 = -1/f$

So $P = P_1 + P_2 = 0$

Now focal length of combination $f = 1/P = \dfrac{1}{0}$ = infinite

Q.2 An astronomical telescope has an angular magnification of magnitude 5 for a distant object. The separation between the objective and eye-piece is 36 cm and the final image is formed at infinity. Calculate the focal length of objective and eye-piece.

Sol. As $m = f_0 / f_e = 5$

$\Rightarrow \quad f_0 = 5 f_e \quad \ldots(i)$

Length of tube, $L = f_0 + f_e$

$36 = 6 f_e \Rightarrow f_e = 6$ cm

$f_e = 6$ cm putting f_e in Eq. (i) we get $f_0 = 30$ cm

Q.3 A ray of light incident normally on one face of a right isosceles prism is totally reflected as shown in the figure. What must be the minimum value of refractive index of glass ?

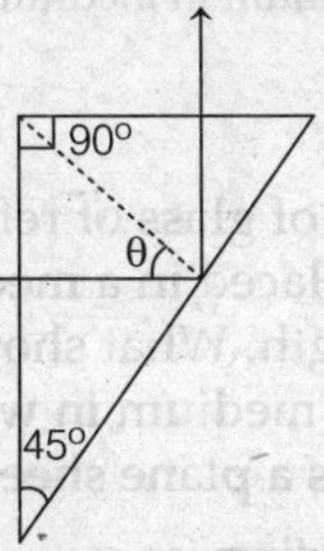

Sol. A ray is totally internally reflected when $i > i_c$

Here $\quad \theta = 45° > i_c$ or $i_c < 45°$

or $\quad \sin i_c < \sin 45°$

$\sin i_c < 1/\sqrt{2}$

$1/\sin i_c > \sqrt{2} \quad \ldots(i)$

we know $\quad \mu = 1/\sin i_c \quad \ldots(ii)$

From Eq. (i) and (ii)

$\mu > \sqrt{2}$

Minimum value of refractive index of glass = $\sqrt{2}$

Q.4 A lens having different radii of curvature for its two faces, forms an image of the object placed on its axis. If the lens is now placed with its faces reversed, will the position of the image change ?

Sol. No, the image will be formed at the same position. From lens maker's formula

$$\frac{1}{F} = (\mu - 1)\left(\frac{1}{R_1} - \frac{1}{R_2}\right)$$

It is clear that when we interchange R_1 and R_2, the magnitude of F remain the same.

Q.5 For the same value of angle of incidence, the angles of refraction in three media *A*, *B* and *C* are 15°, 25° and 35° respectively. In which medium would the velocity of light be minimum ?

Sol. As $\mu = \dfrac{\sin i}{\sin r} = \dfrac{c}{v}$

or
$$v = \frac{\sin r}{\sin i} \times c$$

For a given angle of incidence, $v \propto \sin r$

∴ Velocity of light is minimum in medium A.

□ Long Answer Type

Q.1 A biconvex lens made of glass of refractive index 1.5, having focal length 20 cm is placed in a medium of refractive index 1.65. Find its focal length. What should be the value of the refractive index of the medium in which the lens should be placed so that it acts as a plane sheet of glass ?

Sol. Focal length of lens in medium is

$$\because \quad f_m = \frac{{}_a\mu_g - 1}{{}_m\mu_g - 1} \times f_a$$

$$= \frac{{}_a\mu_g - 1}{\dfrac{\mu_g}{\mu_m} - 1} \times f_a = \frac{1\cdot 5 - 1}{\dfrac{1.5}{1.65} - 1} \times 20$$

$$= \frac{0.5 \times 1.65}{-0.15} \times 20 = -110 \text{ cm}$$

To make the glass lens act like a plane sheet of glass in a medium, the refractive index of medium must be same as that of glass.

$$\therefore \quad \eta_m = \eta_g = 1.5$$

Q.2 You are given two converging lenses of focal length 1.25 cm and 5 cm, to design a compound microscope. If it is desired to have a magnification of 30, find the separation between the objective and the eyepiece.

Sol. The magnification due to the objective lens

$$m_0 = v_0 / -u_0$$

If the object is close to focus of the objective lens then

$$\mu_0 = f_0 \text{ and } v_0 = L \qquad (L = \text{distance between two lenses})$$

$$m_0 = L / f_0$$

If the final image is at the near point, then magnification due to eye lens is

$$m_e = (1 + D / f_e)$$

$$\because \quad M = m_0 \times m_e = (L / f_0)(1 + D / f_e)$$

Use $f_0 = 1.25$ cm and $f_e = 5$ cm

$$L = (30 \times 1.25) / 6 = 6.25 \text{ cm}$$

Separation between two lenses is 6.25 cm

Q.3 Explain the following with reasons

(i) When monochromatic light is incident on a surface separating two media, the reflected and refracted light both have the same frequency as the incident frequency.

(ii) When light travels from a rarer to a denser medium, the speed decreases. Does this decrease in speed imply a reduction in the energy carried by the wave ?

(iii) For which colour the refractive index of prism material is (i) maximum and (ii) minimum ?

Sol. (i) Reflection and refraction arise through interaction of incident light with atomic constituents of matter which vibrate with the same frequency as that of the incident light. Hence, frequency of reflected and refracted light both have the same frequency as the incident frequency.

(ii) No, the energy of the wave depends only on its frequency. Since, the frequency does not change as the wave travels from one medium to another, there will be no reduction in the energy carried by the wave.

(iii) Refractive index of prism material is maximum for violet colour and refractive index of prism material is minimum for red colour.

We know refractive index,

$$\mu = \frac{c}{v}$$

where c is the velocity of light in vacuum.

v is the velocity of light in the medium.

$\because v = f\lambda$ where f is the frequency, λ is the wavelength.

substituting these values in the refractive index equation

$$\mu = \frac{c}{f\lambda}$$

Refractive index is inversely proportional to wavelength.

Hence, light with the least wavelength is refracted the most (violet-maximum refractive index), while the light with the maximum wavelength is refracted the least (red-least refractive index).

Wave Optics

CHAPTER 10

Important Points

01 $\frac{w_1}{w_2} = \frac{a^2}{b^2} = \frac{I_1}{I_2}$

where, w_1, w_2 are the slit widths, a, b are the amplitudes of waves and I_1, I_2 are intensities of waves, respectively.

02 When the two sources are coherent and there is interference, then

$$\frac{I_{max}}{I_{min}} = \frac{(a+b)^2}{(a-b)^2} = \left(\frac{\frac{a}{b}+1}{\frac{a}{b}-1}\right)^2$$

03 The resultant intensity at any point, due to superposition of cohrent waves of intensity I_1 and I_2 is

$$I = [I_1 + I_2 + 2\sqrt{I_1 \cdot I_2}\cos\phi]$$

where ϕ is phase difference.

04 In the Young's double- sl it experiment; the position

(i) of nth bright fringe is given by $x_n = n\frac{D\lambda}{d}$,

where $n = 0, \pm 1, \pm 2, \pm 3, ...$

(ii) of nth dark fringe is given by $x_n = (2n-1)\frac{D\lambda}{2d}$,

where, $n = \pm 1, \pm 2, \pm 3, ...$

D is distance between screen and slit,

d is distance between two slits,

λ is wavelength of light.

05 Fringe width for interference is given by $\beta = \dfrac{\lambda D}{d}$.

06 When the apparatus is immersed in a transparent medium of refractive index (μ), the fringe width will given by

$$\beta' = \frac{\beta}{\mu} = \frac{\lambda D}{\mu d} \qquad (\lambda' = \lambda/\mu)$$

07 Angular fringe width is given by $\theta = \dfrac{\beta}{D} = \dfrac{\lambda}{d}$ independent of screen distance (D)

08 Condition for diffraction due to single slit

(i) For secondary minima, $a \sin\theta = n\lambda$, where $n = 1, 2, 3, \ldots$

(ii) For secondary maxima, $a \sin\theta = (2n+1)\dfrac{\lambda}{2}$, where $n = 1, 2, 3, \ldots$

09 Width of central maximum in diffraction due to single slit is given by $2x = \dfrac{2D\lambda}{a}$; where x is the distance between centre of the screen and height of central maximum in $+y$ direction.

10 Angular width of central maxima in diffraction due to single slit is given by $2\theta = \dfrac{2\lambda}{a}$.

11 Fresnel distance is the distance of screen from slit up to which diffraction is not significant. Fresnel's distance is given by $Z_f \le \dfrac{a^2}{\lambda}$ where a is aperture and λ is wavelength.

Exercises

Question 1 Monochromatic light of wavelength 589 nm is incident from air on a water surface. What are the wavelength, frequency and speed of (a) reflected and (b) refracted light? Refractive index of water is 1.33.

Sol. Given, wavelength of monochromatic light, $\lambda = 589 \text{ nm} = 589 \times 10^{-9}$ m

Refractive index of water $\mu_w = 1.33$, Speed of light in air $c = 3 \times 10^8$ m/s

(a) **For reflected light**

(i) Wavelength of reflected light $\lambda = 589 \times 10^{-9}$ m

(ii) Frequency of reflected light $\nu = \dfrac{c}{\lambda} = \dfrac{3 \times 10^8}{589 \times 10^{-9}}$, $\nu = 5.09 \times 10^{14}$ Hz

(iii) As the reflection takes place in the same medium so

Speed of reflected light $c = 3 \times 10^8$ m/s

(b) **For refracted light**

(i) Wavelength of refracted light $\lambda' = \frac{\lambda}{\mu} = \frac{589 \times 10^{-9}}{1.33} = 4.42 \times 10^{-7}$ m

(ii) Frequency of light does not change on refraction.

$\therefore$ Frequency of refracted light will remain same *i.e.*, 5.09×10^{14} Hz.

(iii) Velocity of refracted light $v = \frac{c}{\mu} = \frac{3 \times 10^8}{1.33} = 2.25 \times 10^8$ m/s

Mistake Alert Students generally make mistakes they calculate frequency for the both medium, but in such case frequency of light does not depend on nature of medium.

Question 2 What is the shape of the wavefront in each of the following cases?

(a) Light diverging from a point source.

(b) Light emerging out of a convex lens when a point source is placed at its focus.

(c) The portion of the wavefront of light from a distant star intercepted by the earth.

Sol.

(a) When the light diverging from a point source, then the shape of wavefront is diverging spherical as shown in diagram (*a*).

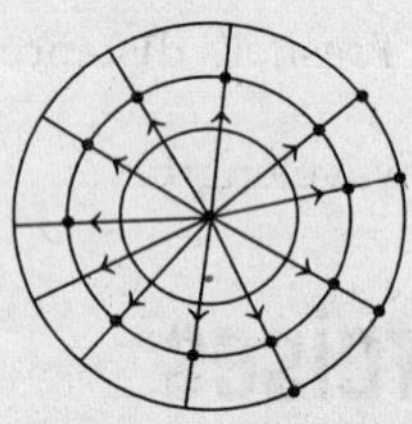

(a)

(b) As the rays of light becomes parallel after refraction from convex lens. So the wavefront is plane as shown in diagram (*b*).

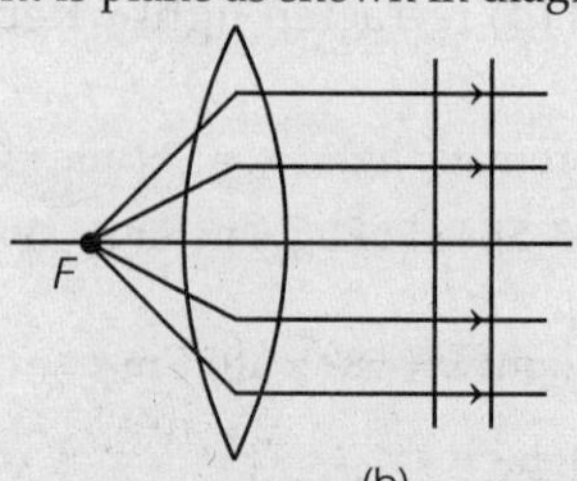

(b)

(c) The light rays which are coming from a distant star are almost parallel to each other because star is at infinity. Thus, the wavefront is plane as shown in diagram (c).

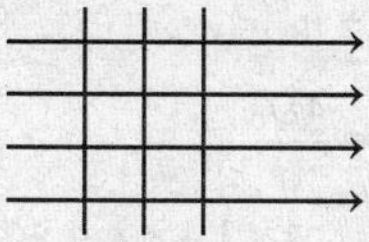

(c)

Question 3 (a) The refractive index of glass is 1.5. What is the speed of light in glass? (Speed of light in vacuum is 3.0×10^8 m/s)

(b) Is the speed of light in glass independent of the colour of light? If not, which of the two colours red and violet travels slower in a glass prism?

Sol. (a) Given, refractive index of glass $\mu_{glass} = 1.5$

Speed of light in vacuum $c = 3 \times 10^8$ m/s

Speed of light in glass $v = \frac{c}{\mu} = \frac{3 \times 10^8}{1.5}$

$$v = 2 \times 10^8 \text{ m/s}$$

(b) No, the speed of light in glass is not independent of colour of light. As we know that the refractive index of violet is greater than red,

$$\mu_V > \mu_R$$

So, velocity of violet is less than the velocity of red. Therefore, violet colour travels slower in glass prism, then the red colour

$$v_V < v_R \qquad \left[\because \mu = \frac{c}{v}\right]$$

Question 4 In a Young's double-slit experiment, the slits are separated by 0.28 mm and the screen is placed 1.4 m away. The distance between the central bright fringe and the fourth bright fringe is measured to be 1.2 cm. Determine the wavelength of light used in the experiment.

Thinking Process Recognize that the distance given (1.2cm) is the distance between the central and the 4th bright fringe. This corresponds to x_4, *i.e.*, the distance for $n = 4$.

When solving for the wavelength, substitute the known values into the formula carefully. Watch out for the correct order of operations and handle small numbers accurately.

Sol. Given, separation between slits $d = 0.28$ mm $= 0.28 \times 10^{-3}$ m.

Distance between screen and slit $D = 1.4$ m,

Distance between central bright and fourth bright fringe

$$x_4 = 1.2\,\text{cm} = 1.2 \times 10^{-2}\ \text{m}$$

Number of fringes $n = 4$

For constructive interference $x_n = n\dfrac{D\lambda}{d}$

$$x_4 = \frac{4D\lambda}{d}$$

$$1.2 \times 10^{-2} = \frac{4 \times 1.4 \times \lambda}{0.28 \times 10^{-3}}$$

Wavelength, $$\lambda = \frac{1.2 \times 10^{-2} \times 0.28 \times 10^{-3}}{4 \times 1.4}$$

$$\lambda = 6 \times 10^{-7}\ \text{m}$$

or $$\lambda = 600 \times 10^{-9}\ \text{m}$$

$$= 600\ \text{nm} \qquad [\because 1\ \text{nm} = 10^{-9}\ \text{m}]$$

Hence, the wavelength of light is 6×10^{-7} m.

Question 5 In Young's double-slit experiment using monochromatic light of wavelength λ, the intensity of light at a point on the screen where path difference is λ is K units. What is the intensity of light at a point where path difference is $\lambda/3$?

Sol. Given, wavelength of light = λ

When the path difference is λ, the phase difference

$$\phi = \frac{2\pi}{\lambda} \cdot x = \frac{2\pi}{\lambda} \cdot \lambda = 2\pi$$

Resultant intensity $I_R = I_1 + I_2 + 2\sqrt{I_1 I_2} \cos \phi$,

where, ϕ = phase difference between two waves

$$I_R = I + I + 2\sqrt{I^2} \cos 2\pi = 2I + 2I = 4I = K \qquad \text{...(i)}$$

(For monochromatic light wave, $I_1 = I_2 = I$)

When path difference is $\lambda/3$, then

Phase difference $= \dfrac{2\pi}{\lambda} \cdot \dfrac{\lambda}{3} = \dfrac{2\pi}{3}$

In this condition, resultant intensity

$$I'_R = I + I + 2\sqrt{I^2} \cos\left(\frac{2\pi}{3}\right) = 2I + 2I\left(-\frac{1}{2}\right) \qquad \left[\because \cos\left(\frac{2\pi}{3}\right) = -\frac{1}{2}\right]$$

$$I'_R = I = \frac{K}{4} \qquad \text{[From Eq. (i)]}$$

Thus, the intensity of light at a point of path difference $\dfrac{\lambda}{3}$ is $\dfrac{K}{4}$ units.

Mistake Alert Ensure that you correctly differentiate between path difference and wavelength. The path difference determines constructive or destructive interference. Intensity does not remain constant at all points, it varies with the path difference.

Question 6 A beam of light consisting of two wavelengths 650 nm and 520 nm is used to obtain interference fringes in a Young's double-slit experiment.

(a) Find the distance of the third bright fringe on the screen from the central maximum for wavelength 650 nm.

(b) What is the least distance from the central maximum where the bright fringes due to both the wavelengths coincide?

Sol. Given, wavelength $\lambda_1 = 650\,\text{nm} = 650 \times 10^{-9}$ m

and $\lambda_2 = 520\,\text{nm} = 520 \times 10^{-9}$ m

(a) For third bright fringe, $n = 3$

The distance of third bright fringe from central maximum.

$$x_3 = \frac{n\lambda D}{d} = 3 \times 650 \times 10^{-9} \times \left(\frac{D}{d}\right) \text{m}$$

$$1.95 \times 10^{-6} \left(\frac{D}{d}\right) \text{m}$$

(b) Let nth bright fringe due to wavelength $\lambda_2 = 520$ nm, coincide with $(n-1)$th bright fringe due to wavelength $\lambda_1 = 650$ nm.

i.e., $$n\lambda_2 \frac{D}{d} = (n-1)\,\lambda_1 \frac{D}{d}$$

$$n \times 520 \times 10^{-9} = (n-1)\, 650 \times 10^{-9}$$

or $$4n = 5n - 5 \text{ or } n = 5$$

Thus, the least distance $$x = n\lambda_2 \frac{D}{d} = 5 \times 520 \times 10^{-9} \frac{D}{d}$$

$$x = 2600 \frac{D}{d} \times 10^{-9} \text{ m} = 2.6 \times 10^{-6} \frac{D}{d} \text{ m}$$

Note The interference fringes arise due to the constructive and destructive interference of light passing through two slits.

DIKSHA APP Questions

☐ Multiple Choice Questions

Q.1 Two waves having the intensities in the ratio of 9 : 1, produce interference. The ratio of maximum to minimum intensity is

(a) 10 : 8 (b) 9 : 1 (c) 4 : 1 (d) 2 : 1

Sol. (c) $\because \frac{I_1}{I_2} = \frac{a^2}{b^2} = \frac{9}{1} \Rightarrow \frac{a}{b} = \frac{3}{1}$

$$\frac{I_{max}}{I_{min}} = \left(\frac{\frac{a}{b}+1}{\frac{a}{b}-1}\right)^2 = \left(\frac{\frac{3}{1}+1}{\frac{3}{1}-1}\right)^2 = \left(\frac{4}{2}\right)^2 = (2)^2 = \frac{4}{1}$$

Q.2 The wavefront due to an unknown source at an infinite distance from the source is

(a) spherical (b) cylindrical (c) plane (d) circular

Sol. (c) Plane wavefront

Q.3 The phase difference between two light waves reaching at a point is $\pi / 2$. What is the resultant amplitude, if the individual amplitudes are 3 mm and 4 mm ?

(a) 4 mm (b) 3 mm (c) 5 mm (d) 8 mm

Sol. (c) $a_1 = 3\text{ mm}, b = 4\text{ mm}, \phi = \dfrac{\pi}{2}$

$$R = \sqrt{a^2 + b^2 + 2ab\cos\phi} = \sqrt{3^2 + 4^2 + 2 \times 3 \times 4\cos\frac{\pi}{2}}$$

$$= \sqrt{9 + 16} = \sqrt{25} = 5\text{ mm}$$

Q.4 Find the maximum intensity in a case of interference of n identical waves each of intensity I_0, if the interference is incoherent.

(a) nI_0 (b) n / I_0 (c) n^2 / I_0 (d) $n^2 I_0$

Sol. (a) For incoherent sources, $< \cos\phi > = 0$

Hence, resultant intensity

$$I = I_1 + I_2 + 2\sqrt{I_1 I_2}\cos\phi$$

$$I = I_1 + I_2$$

For n identical waves

$$I = I_0 + I_0 + \dots n \text{ times}$$

$$I = nI_0$$

Q.5 On a hot summer night, the refractive index of air is least near the ground and increases with height from the ground. When a light beam is directed horizontally, the Huygen principle lead us to conclude that, as it travels, the light beam

(a) becomes narrower (b) goes horizontally without any deflection
(c) bends downward (d) bends upward

Sol. (d) On a hot summer night, the air near the ground has a lower refractive index, and it increases with height. According to Huygen's principle, light bends towards the medium with a higher refractive index. Therefore, the light beam bends upward as it travels horizontally.

Q.6 In Young's double slit experiment, the fringe pattern as seen on the screen is

(a) parabola (b) hyperbola (c) ellipse (d) spiral

Sol. (b) Hyperbola

Q.7 Diffraction pattern is obtained by using a beam of red light. What happens when the red light replaced by the blue light ?

(a) There is no change
(b) The bands disappear
(c) The diffraction band becomes narrow and crowded
(d) The bands become broader and space between then increases answer is C.

Sol. (c) As width of central maxima is $\beta = \frac{2\lambda D}{a}$

$\because \quad \lambda_R > \lambda_B$

$\therefore \quad \beta_R > \beta_B$

So, if the red light replaced by the blue light, the diffraction band becomes narrow and crowded.

Q.8 The first minimum due to single slit diffraction is at $\theta = 30°$ for light of wavelength 5000 Å. The width of the slit is

(a) 5×10^{-5} cm (b) 10×10^{-5} cm
(c) 2.5×10^{-5} cm (d) 1.25×10^{5} cm

Sol. (b) $\theta = 30°$, $\lambda = 5000$ Å $= 5000 \times 10^{-10}$ m $= 5 \times 10^{-7}$ m

$\because$ Angular position of first minimum due to single slit

$$\sin\theta = \frac{\lambda}{a}$$

$$\sin 30° = \frac{5 \times 10^{-7}}{a} \Rightarrow \frac{1}{2} = \frac{5 \times 10^{-7}}{a}$$

$$a = 10 \times 10^{-7} \text{ m} = 10 \times 10^{-5} \text{ cm} = 10^{-4} \text{ cm.}$$

Q.9 In the propagation of electromagnetic waves, the angle between the direction of propagation and plane of Polarisation is

(a) 0° (b) 45° (c) 90° (d) 180°

Sol. (a) Plane of vibration is perpendicular to direction of propagation and also perpendicular to plane of polarisation. Therefore, angle of polarisation and direction of propagation is 0°.

Q.10 In the Young's double slit experiment, when we place a converging lens after the slits and place the screen, at the focus of the lens, it

(a) introduces an extra path difference in the parallel beam.
(b) introduces no path difference in the parallel beam.
(c) introduces an extra phase difference in the parallel beam.
(d) introduces an extra fringe in the interference pattern.

Sol. (b) Introducing a converging lens in the path of parallel beam does not introduce any extra path differences in a parallel beam. Rather it gives a more intense pattern on the screen.

Q.11 When exposed to sunlight, thin films of oil on water, often exhibit brilliant colours due to the phenomenon of

(a) interference (b) diffraction
(c) dispersion (d) polarization

Sol. (a) When exposed to sunlight, thin films of oil on water often exhibit brilliant colors due to the phenomenon of interference. These colours arise due to interference of sunlight reflected from the upper and lower surfaces of the film.

□ Short Answer Type

Q.1 What is the effect on the interference pattern in Young's double slit experiment when

(a) the screen is moved closer to the slit ?
(b) the separation between slits is increased ?

Sol. (a) In Young's double slit experiment, the fringe width is given by $\beta = \lambda D / d$

When D is decreased then β also decreases.

(b) When d increases then β decreases.

Q.2 How does the fringe width of interference fringes change, when the whole apparatus of Young's experiment is kept in a liquid of refractive index 1.3 ?

Sol. On immersing the apparatus in water, the speed of wave travelling in water decreases and hence its wavelength decreases as $v \propto \lambda$.

Thus, the new wavelength is $\lambda' = \dfrac{\lambda}{n}$

Where n is refractive index of medium.
The fringe width originally is given by

$$\beta_1 = \frac{\lambda D}{d}$$

The new fringe width within water will be given by

$$\beta_2 = \lambda' \frac{D}{d} = \frac{\lambda D}{n d} = \frac{\beta_1}{n} = \frac{\beta_1}{1.3}$$

When light enters a denser medium, its wavelength decreases by a factor 1.3 and hence the fringe width also decreases by a factor of 1.3.

Q.3 What changes in the interference pattern in Young's double slit experiment will be observed when (i) light of smaller frequency is used ? (ii) the two coherent sources are far apart?

Sol. In Young's double slit experiment, the fringe width is given by

$$\beta = D\lambda / d = \frac{Dc}{\nu d} \qquad [\because \text{Frequency } \nu = \frac{c}{\lambda}]$$

(i) When light of smaller frequency is used, fringe width increases as $\beta \propto \frac{1}{\nu}$

(ii) No pattern will be detected as fringe width becomes too small to be detected as $\beta \propto \frac{1}{d}$

□ Long Answer Type

Q.1 (a) Write the necessary conditions to obtain sustained interference fringes. Also write the expression for the fringe width.

(b) In Young's double slit experiment, what is the shape of graph showing the variation of fringe width *versus* the distance of the screen from the plane of the slits, keeping other parameters same. What information can one obtain from the slope of the curve?

(c) What is the effect on the fringe width if the distance between the slits is reduced keeping other parameters same?

Sol.

(a) Conditions for sustained interference :

(i) The interfering sources must be coherent.

(ii) Interfering waves must have same or nearly same amplitude, so that there may be contrast between maxima and minima.

(b) Shape of graph is linear as $\beta = \frac{D\lambda}{d}$; $\beta \propto D$. Information, from the slope :

Slope $= \frac{\beta}{D} = \frac{\lambda}{d}$

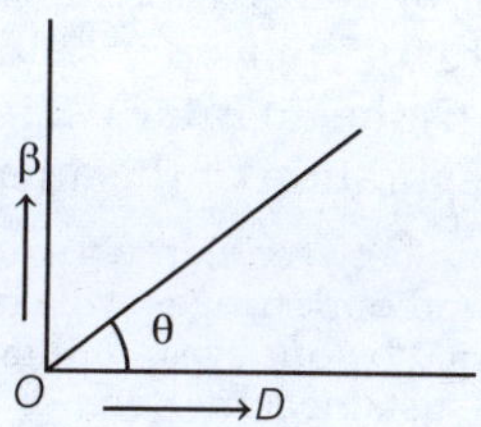

(c) **Effect** : From relation,

$$\beta = D\lambda / d$$

Fringe width $\beta \propto 1/d$

If distance d between the slits is reduced, the fringe width will increase.

Q.2 In the experiment on diffraction due to a single slit, show that

(i) the intensity of diffraction fringes decreases as the order (n) increases.

(ii) angular width of the central maximum is twice that of the first order secondary maximum.

Sol.

(i) The intensity of central maximum is due to constructive interference of wavelets from all parts of slit, the first secondary maximum is due to contribution of wavelets from one third part of slit (wavelets from remaining two parts interfere destructively) the second secondary maximum is due to contribution of wavelets from one fifth part only and so on.

(ii) For 1st secondary minima $a\sin\theta = \lambda$ or $a\theta = \lambda$

[as angle θ is small hence $\sin\theta \approx \theta$, $\tan\theta \approx \theta$]

$$\tan\theta = y / D \text{ or } \theta = y_1 / D$$

$$ay_1 / D = \lambda \text{ or } y_1 = \lambda D / a = y_2$$

Here y_1 and y_2 are distances of 1st minima on both sides of central maxima

Hence the angular width of central maximum $= 2\lambda D / a$

Width of secondary maximum = Separation between nth and $(n+1)$th minima

For minima $\theta_n = n\lambda / a$ and $\theta_{n+1} = (n+1)\lambda / a$

Angular width of secondary maximum $= \theta_{n+1} - \theta_n = \lambda / a$

Hence β = Angular width $\times D = \lambda D / a$

Thus, central maximum has twice the angular width of secondary maximum.

Q.3 (a) What happens to the interference pattern if the phase difference between the two sources varies continuously ?

(b) A double slit is illuminated by light of wavelength 600 nm. The slits are 0.1 cm as part and the screen is placed 1 m away. Calculate (i) the angular position of 10th maximum in radian and (ii) separation of the adjacent minima.

Sol. (a) If the phase difference between the two sources varies continuously, the positions of bright and dark fringes will change rapidly. Such rapid change cannot be detected by our eyes. A uniform illumination is seen on the screen therefore no sustained interference is observed.

(b) (i) $n = 10$, $d = 0.1\,\text{cm} = 0.001\,\text{m}$, $\lambda = 600\,\text{nm} = 6 \times 10^{-7}$ m

The angular position of nth maximum is

$$\theta_n = \frac{n\lambda}{d}$$

$$\theta_{10} = \frac{10 \times 6 \times 10^{-7}}{0.001} = 0.006\,\text{rad.}$$

(ii) Separation of the adjacent minima = fringe width

$$\beta = D\lambda / d = \frac{1 \times 600 \times 10^{-9}}{0.1 \times 10^{-2}} = 0.6\,\text{mm}$$

Dual Nature of Radiation and Matter

CHAPTER 11

Important Points

01 Energy of each photon is given by $E = h\nu = \frac{hc}{\lambda}$

02 Momentum of each photon is given by $p = \frac{h}{\lambda} = \frac{h\nu}{c}$

03 Mass of photon is calculated as
Energy $E = mc^2 \Rightarrow m = \frac{E}{c^2} = \frac{h\nu}{c^2} = \frac{h}{c\lambda}$

04 Work function is given by $\phi_0 = h\nu_0 = \frac{hc}{\lambda_0}$, where ν_0 is the threshold frequency and λ_0 is the threshold wavelength.
$h = 6.63 \times 10^{-34}$ is called Planck's constant.

05 Kinetic energy of emitted photoelectron using Einstien photoelectric equation

$$K_{max} = \frac{1}{2} mv_{max}^2 = eV_0 = h\nu - \phi_0 = \frac{hc}{\lambda} - \frac{hc}{\lambda_0}$$

where, V_0 is the stopping potential.

06 The photoelectric current depends on intensity of incident light, potential difference applied between the two electrodes and the nature of the emitter material.

07 de-Broglie wavelength of particle of mass m is given by $\lambda = \frac{h}{mv}$

where, $m = \frac{m_0}{\sqrt{1 - \frac{v^2}{c^2}}}$, m_0 being the rest mass of the particle and c is the speed of light.

08 de-Broglie wavelength of an electron, $\lambda = \frac{12.27}{\sqrt{V}}$ Å

where, V is potential difference.

09 de-Broglie wavelength of a particle is given by

$$\lambda = \frac{h}{\sqrt{2mE}} = \frac{h}{\sqrt{2meV}}$$

where, E is the kinetic energy of particle.

10 Number of photons per sec per unit area $= \frac{\phi}{E}$

$$= \frac{\text{Energy flux}}{\text{Energy of photon per second per unit area}}$$

$$= \frac{\text{Energy radiated / second}}{\text{Energy of each photon}} = \frac{P}{E}$$

Exercises

Question 1 Find the

(a) maximum frequency and

(b) minimum wavelength of X-rays produced by 30 kV electrons.

Sol. Given, voltage $V = 30\text{ kV} = 30 \times 10^3$ V and $e = 1.6 \times 10^{-19}$ C

(a) Using formula for energy

$$E = eV = h\nu_{max}$$

or $$\nu_{max} = \frac{eV}{h} = \frac{1.6 \times 10^{-19} \times 30 \times 10^3}{6.63 \times 10^{-34}} = 7.24 \times 10^{18} \text{ Hz}$$

Maximum frequency $\nu_{max} = 7.24 \times 10^{18}$ Hz

(b) Minimum wavelength of X-ray,

$$\lambda_{max} = \frac{c}{\nu_{max}} = \frac{3 \times 10^8}{7.24 \times 10^{18}}$$

where $c = 3 \times 10^8$ m/s

$$\lambda_{max} = 0.414 \times 10^{-10}$$
$$= 0.0414 \times 10^{-9} \text{ m} = 0.0414 \text{ nm}$$

Question 2 The work function of caesium metal is 2.14 eV. When light of frequency 6×10^{14} Hz is incident on the metal surface, photoemission of electrons occurs. What is the

(a) maximum kinetic energy of the emitted electrons,

(b) stopping potential and

(c) maximum speed of the emitted photoelectrons?

Sol. Given, work function of caesium metal $\phi_0 = 2.14$ eV

Frequency of light $\nu = 6 \times 10^{14}$ Hz

(a) Maximum kinetic energy of emitted electrons (Einstein's photo electric equation)

$$KE_{max} = h\nu - \phi_0 = \left(\frac{h\nu}{e} - \phi_0\right) \text{eV}$$

$$= \frac{6.63 \times 10^{-34} \times 6 \times 10^{14}}{1.6 \times 10^{-19}} - 2.14 = 0.35 \text{ eV}$$

(b) Let stopping potential be V_0.

We know that

$$KE_{max} = eV_0$$

$$0.35 \text{ eV} = eV_0$$

$$V_0 = 0.35 \text{ V}$$

(c) Maximum kinetic energy $KE_{max} = \frac{1}{2} m v_{max}^2$

$$0.35 \text{ eV} = \frac{1}{2} m v_{max}^2$$

$$v_{max}^2 = \frac{2 \times 0.35 \text{ eV}}{m}$$

(where, v_{max} is the maximum speed and m is the mass of electron)

or $$\frac{0.35 \times 2 \times 1.6 \times 10^{-19}}{9.1 \times 10^{-31}} = v_{max}^2 \qquad (\because e = 1.6 \times 10^{-19})$$

or $$v_{max}^2 = 0.123 \times 10^{12}$$

or $$v_{max} = 350713.55 \text{ m/s}$$

$$= 350.7 \text{ km/s}$$

Question 3 The photoelectric cut-off voltage in a certain experiment is 1.5 V. What is the maximum kinetic energy of photoelectrons emitted?

Sol. Given, cut-off voltage $V_0 = 1.5$ V

Maximum kinetic energy is given by,

$$KE_{max} = eV_0 = 1.5 \text{ eV}$$

$$= 1.5 \times 1.6 \times 10^{-19}$$

$$= 2.4 \times 10^{-19} \text{ J}$$

Mistake Alert In this problem the maximum kinetic energy of photo electrons is given by $KE = eV_0$. However ensure that the voltage is given in the correct units (volts) and use the value of $e = 1.6 \times 10^{-19}$ C for accuracy.

Question 4 Monochromatic light of wavelength 632.8 nm is produced by a helium-neon laser. The power emitted is 9.42 mW.

(a) Find the energy and momentum of each photon in the light beam.

(b) How many photons per second, on the average, arrive at a target irradiated by this beam? (Assume the beam to have uniform cross-section, which is less than the target area.)

(c) How fast does a hydrogen atom have to travel in order to have the same momentum as that of the photon?

Sol. Given, wavelength of monochromatic light,

$$\lambda = 632.8 \text{ nm} = 632.8 \times 10^{-9} \text{ m}$$

$$\text{Power} = 9.42 \text{ mW} = 9.42 \times 10^{-3} \text{ W}$$

(a) Energy of each photon, $E = \dfrac{hc}{\lambda}$

$$= \frac{6.63 \times 10^{-34} \times 3 \times 10^{8}}{632.8 \times 10^{-9}} = 3.14 \times 10^{-19} \text{ J}$$

We know that momentum of each photon, $p = \dfrac{h}{\lambda}$

$$p = \frac{6.63 \times 10^{-34}}{632.8 \times 10^{-9}} = 1.05 \times 10^{-27} \text{ kg-m/s}$$

(b) Let n be the number of photons per second. So,

$$n = \frac{\text{Power}}{\text{Energy of each photon}}$$

$$= \frac{9.42 \times 10^{-3}}{3.14 \times 10^{-19}} = 3 \times 10^{16} \text{ photon/s}$$

(c) Momentum $p = mv$

Velocity of hydrogen atom,

$$v = \frac{p}{m} = \frac{1.05 \times 10^{-27}}{1.66 \times 10^{-27}} = 0.63 \text{ m/s}$$

[$\because m = 1.66 \times 10^{-27}$ kg (mass of hydrogen atom)]

Question 5 In an experiment on photoelectric effect, the slope of the cut-off voltage *versus* frequency of incident light is found to be 4.12×10^{-15} V-s. Calculate the value of Planck's constant.

◎ **Thinking Process** In the photoelectric effect, the slope of the cut-off voltage (V_0) *versus* frequency (ν) graph equals $\frac{h}{e}$, where h is the planck's constant and e is the elementary charge. Thus, $h = e_X$ slope.

Sol. Given, slope of graph $\tan\theta = 4.12 \times 10^{-15}$ V-s and charge on electron $e = 1.6 \times 10^{-19}$ C

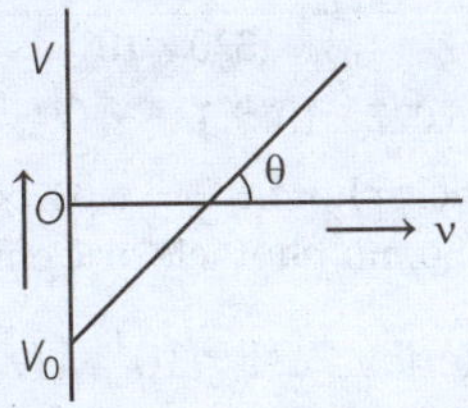

For slope of graph $\tan\theta = \frac{V}{\nu}$

We know that $h\nu = eV$

Slope $\frac{V}{\nu} = \frac{h}{e}$

$\therefore$ $\frac{h}{e} = 4.12 \times 10^{-15}$

$$h = 1.6 \times 10^{-19} \times 4.12 \times 10^{-15} = 6.592 \times 10^{-34} \text{ J-s}$$

Question 6 The threshold frequency for a certain metal is 3.3×10^{14} Hz. If light of frequency 8.2×10^{14} Hz is incident on the metal, predict the cut-off voltage for the photoelectric emission.

Sol. Given, threshold frequency for a metal, $\nu_0 = 3.3 \times 10^{14}$ Hz

Frequency of light, $\nu = 8.2 \times 10^{14}$ Hz

Let V_0 be the cut-off voltage.

Using the formula for kinetic energy,

$$KE = eV_0 = h\nu - h\nu_0$$

$$V_0 = \frac{h(\nu - \nu_0)}{e}$$

$$= \frac{6.63 \times 10^{-34}(8.2 \times 10^{14} - 3.3 \times 10^{14})}{1.6 \times 10^{-19}}$$

$$= 2.03 \text{ V}$$

Question 7 The work function for a certain metal is 4.2 eV. Will this metal give photoelectric emission for incident radiation of wavelength 330 nm?

Sol. Given, work function $\phi_0 = 4.2$ eV

$$= 4.2 \times 1.6 \times 10^{-19} \text{ J} = 6.72 \times 10^{-19} \text{ J}$$

Wavelength of radiation, $\lambda = 330 \text{ nm} = 330 \times 10^{-9}$ m

If the energy of each photon is more than the work function, then only the photoelectirc emission takes place.

Energy of each photon,

$$E = \frac{hc}{\lambda} = \frac{6.63 \times 10^{-34} \times 3 \times 10^{8}}{330 \times 10^{-9}}$$
$$= 6.027 \times 10^{-19} \text{ J}$$

As the value of energy of each photon, $E = 6.027 \times 10^{-19}$ J is less than the work function, $\phi_0 = 6.72 \times 10^{-19}$ J. So, no photoelectric emission takes place.

Question 8 Light of frequency 7.21×10^{14} Hz is incident on a metal surface. Electrons with a maximum speed of 6.0×10^{5} m/s are ejected from the surface. What is the threshold frequency for photoemission of electrons?

Sol. Given, frequency of light, $\nu = 7.21 \times 10^{14}$ Hz

Mass of electron, $m = 9.1 \times 10^{-31}$ kg

Maximum speed of electrons, $v_{max} = 6 \times 10^{5}$ m/s

Let ν_0 be the threshold frequency.

Use the formula for kinetic energy,

$$\text{KE} = \frac{1}{2} m v_{max}^2 = h\nu - h\nu_0$$

i.e.
$$= \frac{1}{2} \times 9.1 \times 10^{-31} \times (6 \times 10^{5})^2$$
$$= 6.63 \times 10^{-34} (\nu - \nu_0)$$

or
$$\nu - \nu_0 = \frac{36 \times 9.1 \times 10^{-21}}{2 \times 6.63 \times 10^{-34}} = 2.47 \times 10^{14}$$

or
$$\nu_0 = 7.21 \times 10^{14} - 2.47 \times 10^{14} \qquad (\because \nu = 7.21 \times 10^{14} \text{ Hz})$$
$$= 4.74 \times 10^{14} \text{ Hz}$$

Question 9 Light of wavelength 488 nm is produced by an argon laser, which is used in the photoelectric effect. When light from this spectral line is incident on the emitter, the stopping (cut-off) potential of photoelectrons is 0.38 V. Find the work function of the material from which the emitter is made.

Sol. Given, wavelength of light, $\lambda = 488 \text{ nm} = 488 \times 10^{-9}$ m

Cut-off potential $V_0 = 0.38$ V, $e = 1.6 \times 10^{-19}$ C

Planck constant $h = 6.62 \times 10^{-34}$ J-s

Velocity of light $c = 3 \times 10^{8}$ m/s

Let ϕ_0 be the work function.

Use the formula for kinetic energy, from Einstein photoelectric equation.

$$\text{KE} = eV_0 = \frac{hc}{\lambda} - \phi_0$$

$$1.6 \times 10^{-19} \times 0.38 = \frac{6.63 \times 10^{-34} \times 3 \times 10^{8}}{488 \times 10^{-9}} - \phi_0$$

or $$6.08 \times 10^{-20} = 40.75 \times 10^{-20} - \phi_0$$

or $$\phi_0 = (40.75 - 6.08) \times 10^{-20}$$
$$= 34.67 \times 10^{-20} \text{ J}$$

or $$= \frac{34.67 \times 10^{-20}}{1.6 \times 10^{-19}} \text{ eV} = 2.17 \text{ eV}$$

Note When light of a certain frequency shines on a metal surface, it can eject electrons.
The minimum energy required to remove an electron from the metal surface is called the work function.

Question 10 What is the de-Broglie wavelength of

(a) a bullet of mass 0.040 kg travelling at the speed of 1.0 km/s,

(b) a ball of mass 0.060 kg moving at a speed of 1.0 m/s, and

(c) a dust particle of mass 1.0×10^{-9} kg drifting with a speed of 2.2 m/s?

◎ ***Thinking Process*** According to de-Broglie's hypothesis, every moving particle exhibits wave-like properties, with a wavelength given by the equation $\lambda = \frac{h}{mv}$. This wave-like nature is significant only for very small particles, such as electrons, as their de-broglie wavelength can be comparable to their size. For macroscopic objects, like bullets and balls, the wavelength is so small that it has no observable effect.

Sol. Given, mass of bullet $m = 0.040$ kg

speed of bullet $v = 1000$ m/s

(a) de-Broglie wavelength

$$\lambda = \frac{h}{mv} = \frac{6.63 \times 10^{-34}}{0.040 \times 1 \times 10^3} \qquad \left(\because m = 0.040 \text{ kg}, \; v = 1 \text{ km/s} = 1000 \text{ m/s}\right)$$

$$= 1.66 \times 10^{-35} \text{ m}$$

(b) Mass of the ball, $m = 0.060$ kg

speed of the ball, $v = 1$ m/s

$$\lambda = \frac{h}{mv} = \frac{6.63 \times 10^{-34}}{0.060 \times 1} = 1.1 \times 10^{-32} \text{ m}$$

(c) Mass of a dust particle, $m = 1 \times 10^{-9}$ kg

speed of the dust particle, $v = 2.2$ m/s

$$\lambda = \frac{h}{mv} = \frac{6.63 \times 10^{-34}}{1 \times 10^{-9} \times 2.2}$$

$$= 3.0 \times 10^{-25} \text{ m}$$

Question 11 Show that the wavelength of electromagnetic radiation is equal to the de-Broglie wavelength of its quantum (photon).

Sol. The momentum of a photon of frequency ν, wavelength λ is given by

$$p = \frac{h\nu}{c} = \frac{h}{\lambda}$$

or $$\lambda = \frac{h}{p}$$

de-Broglie wavelength of photon,

$$\lambda = \frac{h}{p} = \frac{h}{h\nu/c} = \frac{c}{\nu}$$

Thus, the wavelength of electromagnetic radiation is equal to the de-Broglie wavelength.

DIKSHA APP Questions

Multiple Choice Questions

Q.1 The experiment which establishes the wave nature of a particle is

(a) Millikan's oil drop expriment
(b) Frank-Hertz experiment
(c) Photoelectric experiment
(d) Davisson-Germer experiment

Sol. (d) Davisson-Germer experiment

Q.2 The wavelength associated with proton and electron are λ_p and λ_e respectively. If they are given the same amount of energy, then

(a) $\lambda_p > \lambda_e$ (b) $\lambda_e > \lambda_p$
(c) $\lambda_p = \lambda_e$ (d) $\lambda_p = C\lambda_e$

Sol. (b) $\because \lambda_p = \frac{h}{\sqrt{2m_p k}}$

$$\lambda_e = \frac{h}{\sqrt{2m_e k}}$$

$$\frac{\lambda_p}{\lambda_e} = \sqrt{\frac{m_e}{m_p}}$$

$\because$ $m_e < m_p$

$\therefore$ $\lambda_e > \lambda_p$

Q.3 Which of the following represents the wavelength of a photon, if it has velocity c and frequency ν ?

(a) $h\nu$ (b) hc/E

(c) $h\nu/c^2$ (d) $h\nu/c$

Sol. (b) $\because$ Energy of photon

$$E = h\nu = \frac{hc}{\lambda}$$

$$\therefore \quad \lambda = \frac{hc}{E}$$

Q.4 What is the energy of a photon whose wavelength is 684 nm?

(a) 2.4 eV (b) 1.81 eV

(c) 11.2 eV (d) –13.6 eV

Sol. (b) $\lambda = 684\text{ nm} = 684 \times 10^{-9}\text{ m}$

$$\because \quad E = h\nu = \frac{hc}{\lambda}\text{ J} = \frac{hc}{e\lambda}\text{ eV} \qquad [\because 1\text{ eV} = 1.6 \times 10^{-19}\text{ J}]$$

$$E = \frac{6.634 \times 10^{-34} \times 3 \times 10^{8}}{1.6 \times 10^{-19} \times 684 \times 10^{-9}} = 1.81\text{ eV}$$

Q.5 Using Einstein's photoelectric equation, if a graph is a plotted between the kinetic energy of the emitted photoelectrons and the frequency of the incident radiation, a straight line is obtained. Then, the slope of the graph

(a) depends on the intensity of the radiation

(b) is the same for all metals and independent of the intensity of the radiation

(c) depends on the nature of the metal used

(d) depends both on the intensity of the radiation and nature of the metal used

Sol. (b) Since slope of kinetic energy of the emitted photo electrons and the frequency of incident radiation is planck constant $h = 6.634 \times 10^{-34}$ J-s which is same for all metals. This slope is constant and does not depend on the intensity of the radiation or nature of the metal used.

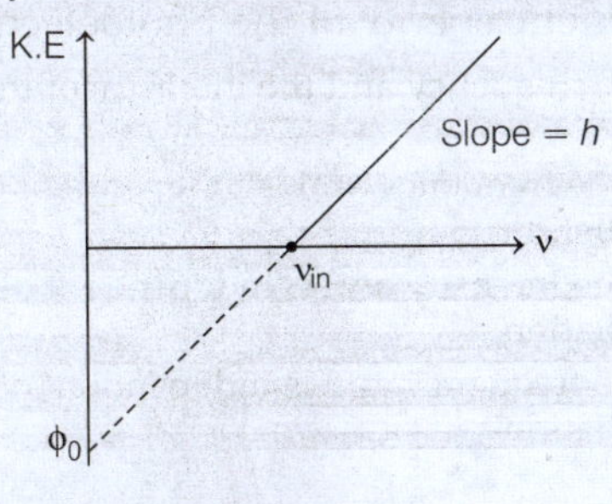

Q.6 When photons of energy, $h\nu$ fall on an aluminium plate having work function ϕ_0, photoelectrons of maximum kinetic enregy K are ejected. If the frequency of radiation is doubled, the maximum kinetc energy of the ejected photoelectrons will be

(a) $2K + \phi_0$ (b) $K + \phi_0$ (c) $2K$ (d) K

Sol. (a) $\because K_1 = h\nu - \phi_0$ (Einstein photoelectric equation)

$$h\nu = K_1 + \phi_0 \quad \ldots(i)$$

$$h2\nu = K_2 + \phi_0 \quad \ldots(ii)$$

$$\frac{\text{Eq. (ii)}}{\text{Eq. (i)}} = \frac{h2\nu}{h\nu} = \frac{K_2 + \phi_0}{K_1 + \phi_0}$$

$$2 = \frac{K_2 + \phi_0}{K_1 + \phi_0}$$

$$K_2 + \phi_0 = 2K_1 + 2\phi_0$$

$$K_2 = 2K_1 + \phi_0$$

Q.7 Which of the following properties of light cannot be explained using wave theory ?

(a) Light waves can be polarized.
(b) Light obeys laws of reflection and refraction.
(c) Light waves show interference.
(d) Light shows photoelectric effect.

Sol. (d) Light shows photoelectric effect.

Q.8 Photoelectric effect supports quantum nature of light because

(a) there is a minimum frequency of light below which no photoelectrons are emitted
(b) even when the metal surface is faintly illuminated, the photoelectrons leave the surface instantaneously
(c) the maximum kinetic energy of photoelectrons depends only on the frequency of light and not on its intensity.
(d) All of the above

Sol. (d) All of the above

Q.9 The maximum kinetic energy of the photoelectrons varies

(a) linearly with the frequency and the intensity of the incident radiation
(b) inversely with the frequency and is independent of the intensity of the incident radiation
(c) inversely with the intensity and is independent of the frequency of the incident radiation
(d) linearly with the frequency and is independent of the intensity of the incident radiation

Sol. (d) As $K_{max} = h\nu - \phi$ (Einstein photoelectric equation)

Where, ϕ is the work function of the material.
ν is the frequency of the incident radiation.
The equation shows that the maximum kinetic energy depends linearly on the frequency v and is independent of the intensity of the incident radiation. Intensity affects the number of photoelectrons emitted, not their kinetic energy.

□ Short Answer Type

Q.1 A metal having work function of 2 eV is illuminated by monochromatic light of wavelength 500 nm. Calculate

(a) the threshold wavelength
(b) the maximum energy of the photoelectrons
(c) the stopping potential

Sol. $W = 2\text{ eV} = 2 \times 1.6 \times 10^{-19}$ J

$$\lambda = 500\text{ nm} = 500 \times 10^{-9}\text{ m}$$

(a) $W_0 = hc / \lambda_0$ or $\lambda_0 = hc / W_0 = 6.6 \times 10^{-34} \times 3 \times 10^8 / 2 \times 1.6 \times 10^{-19}$

$$= 6.1875 \times 10^{-7}\text{ m}$$

(b) $K_{max} = (hc / \lambda) - W_0$ J

$$K_{max} = \left(\frac{hc}{e\lambda} - W_0\right)\text{eV}$$

$$= (6.6 \times 10^{-34} \times 3 \times 10^8 / 500 \times 10^{-9} \times 1.6 \times 10^{-19}) - 2$$

$$= 2.475 - 2 = 0.475\text{ eV}$$

(c) $\because \quad K_{max} = eV_0$

$$V_0 = K_{max} / e = 0.475\text{ V}$$

Q.2 Light of intensity 'I' and frequency 'ν' is incident on a photosensitive surface and causes photoelectric emission. What will be the effect on anode current when (i) the intensity of light is increased, (ii) the frequency of incident radiation is increased, and (iii) the anode potential is increased ? In each case, all the other factors remain the same. Justify your answer.

Sol.

(i) Larger the intensity of incident radiation, larger is the number of incident photons and hence larger is the number of electrons ejected from the photosensitive surface. Therefore anode current increases.

(ii) The incident photon of increased energy cannot eject more than one electron from the metal surface. It only increases the maximum KE of the ejected electron hence anode current remains same.

(iii) All the photoelectrons emitted from the metal surface do not have the same KE.The increase in anode potential accelerates more and more electrons. A stage is reached when the anode current attains a saturation value.

Q.3 The following graph shows the variation of stopping potential (V_0) with the frequency (f) for the two photosensitive materials A and B.

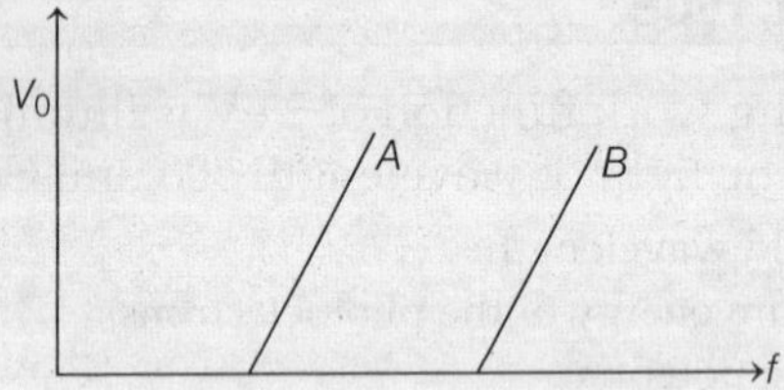

(a) Why is the slope same for both the lines ?

(b) For which material will the emitted electrons have greater kinetic energy, for the incident radiation of the same frequency ? Justify your answer.

Sol.

(a) The slope of the graph gives the value of h/e, which is same for both the materials A and B.

(b) As cut off graph on frequency axis is threshold frequency. The material A has a lower value of threshold frequency. So, A will emit photoelectrons of greater kinetic energy according to $K_{max} = h\nu - W_0 = h\nu - h\nu_0$

Q.4 A negative potential of 0.59 V is required to stop the emission of photoelectrons, when UV light of wavelength 300 nm is incident on a metal plate. Calculate the energy of the incident photon and the work function for the metal in eV.

Sol. $\lambda = 300 \text{ nm} = 300 \times 10^{-9}$ m

$$V_0 = 0.59 \text{ V}$$

$$\because \quad E = \frac{hc}{\lambda} \text{J} = \left(\frac{hc}{e\lambda}\right) \text{eV}$$

$$= \frac{6.6 \times 10^{-34} \times 3 \times 10^8}{300 \times 10^{-9} \times 1.6 \times 10^{-19}} = 4.125 \text{ eV}$$

$$\because \quad K_{max} = eV_0 = 0.59 \text{ eV}$$

Einstein photoelectric equation is

$$K_{max} = h\nu - W_0$$

$$W_0 = h\nu - K_{max} = E - K_{max}.$$

$$W_0 = 4.125 - 0.59 = 3.535 \text{ eV}$$

Atoms

CHAPTER 12

Important Points

01 The distance of closest approach (r_0) is calculated by the formula of kinetic energy of α-particle is given by

$$KE = \frac{1}{2}mv^2 = \frac{1}{4\pi\varepsilon_0} \cdot \frac{Ze(2e)}{r_0}$$

02 Impact parameter is given by $b = \dfrac{Ze^2 \cot \frac{\theta}{2}}{4\pi\varepsilon_0\left(\frac{1}{2}mv^2\right)}$

03 For Bohr's atomic model

(a) $\dfrac{K \cdot Ze^2}{r^2} = \dfrac{mv^2}{r}$ where, $\left[K = \dfrac{1}{4\pi\varepsilon_0}\right]$

(b) Angular momentum of the electron $mvr = \dfrac{nh}{2\pi}$ where $n = 1, 2, 3, 4, \ldots$

(c) $h\nu = E_f - E_i$

(d) Radius of Bohr's orbit, $r_n = \dfrac{n^2h^2}{4\pi^2 mKZe^2}$, $r_n = n^2 r_1$ and $[r_1 = 0.53 \text{ Å}]$

(e) (i) Velocity of electron, $v_n = \dfrac{2\pi Ke^2}{nh} = \dfrac{c}{n}\left(\dfrac{2\pi Ke^2}{ch}\right)$

(ii) Time period of electron in Bohr's orbit $T_n = \dfrac{2\pi r_n}{v_n}$

(f) Total energy of electron in an orbit, $E = -\dfrac{2\pi^2 mK^2e^4Z^2}{n^2h^2}$

(g) $KE = \dfrac{KZe^2}{2r} = -E$, $PE = -\dfrac{KZe^2}{r} = 2E$

(h) Total energy of electron in an orbit is calculated as

$$E_n = -\frac{13.6}{n^2}\text{ eV}$$

(i) The origin of spectral lines of hydrogen atom

Wave number $\bar{\nu} = \dfrac{1}{\lambda} = R\left[\dfrac{1}{n_1^2} - \dfrac{1}{n_2^2}\right]$

where, $R = 1.0973 \times 10^7\ \text{m}^{-1}$ is the Rydberg's constant.

Exercises

Question 1 Choose the correct alternative from the clues given at the end of the each statement:

(a) The size of the atom in Thomson's model is .... the atomic size in Rutherford's model. (much greater than/no different from/much less than)

(b) In the ground state of .... electrons are in stable equilibrium, while in .... electrons always experience a net force. (Thomson's model/ Rutherford's model)

(c) A classical atom based on .... is doomed to collapse. (Thomson's model/ Rutherford's model)

(d) An atom has a nearly continuous mass distribution in a .... but has a highly non-uniform mass distribution in .... (Thomson's model/ Rutherford's model)

(e) The positively charged part of the atom possesses most of the mass in .... (Rutherford's model/both the models)

Sol. (a) No different from

(b) Thomson's model, Rutherford's model

(c) Rutherford's model

(d) Thomson's model, Rutherford's model

(e) Both the models

Question 2 Suppose you are given a chance to repeat the alpha particle scattering experiment using a thin sheet of solid hydrogen in place of the gold foil. (Hydrogen is a solid at temperatures below 14 K.) What results do you expect?

Sol. The basic purpose of scattering experiment is not completed because solid hydrogen will be a much lighter target as compared to the alpha particle acting as a projectile. By using the conditions of elastic collisions, the hydrogen of mass 1.67×10^{-27} kg will move much faster as compared to alpha particle of mass 6.64×10^{-27} kg after the collision. We cannot determine the size of hydrogen nucleus, because α-particle would not bounce back thus there would be no appreciable scattering.

Note The nucleus of gold is 50 times heavier than α-particles.

Question 3 A difference of 2.3 eV separates two energy levels in an atom. What is the frequency of radiation emitted when the atom makes a transition from the upper level to the lower level?

Sol. Given, difference in energy level $\Delta E = 2.3$ eV

$$= 2.3 \times 1.6 \times 10^{-19} \text{ J}$$

Planck's constant $h = 6.63 \times 10^{-34}$ J-s

Let ν be the frequency, then $\Delta E = h\nu$

or
$$\nu = \frac{E}{h} = \frac{2.3 \times 1.6 \times 10^{-19}}{6.63 \times 10^{-34}}$$
$$= 5.6 \times 10^{14} \text{ Hz}$$

Question 4 The ground state energy of hydrogen atom is –13.6 eV. What are the kinetic and potential energies of the electron in this state?

Sol. Given, the ground state energy of hydrogen atom

$$E = -13.6 \text{ eV}$$

We know that

Kinetic Energy (KE) $= -E = -(-13.6) = 13.6$ eV

Potential Energy (PE) $= -2\text{KE} = -2 \times 13.6 = -27.2$ eV

Question 5 A hydrogen atom initially in the ground level absorbs a photon, which excites it to the $n = 4$ level. Determine the wavelength and frequency of photon.

◎ *Thinking Process* To find the wavelength and frequency of photon, use the relation of energy of electron in n^{th} state of hydrogen atom $E_n = -\frac{13.6}{n^2}$ eV.

Sol. For ground state $n_1 = 1$ to $n_2 = 4$

Energy absorbed by photon, $\Delta E = E_2 - E_1$

$$= +13.6\left(\frac{1}{n_1^2}-\frac{1}{n_2^2}\right)\times 1.6\times 10^{-19}\text{ J}$$

$$= 13.6\left(\frac{1}{1^2}-\frac{1}{4^2}\right)\times 1.6\times 10^{-19}$$

$$= 13.6 \times 1.6\times 10^{-19}\left(\frac{15}{16}\right)$$

$$= 20.4\times 10^{-19}\text{ J}$$

or $\because \Delta E = h\nu = 20.4\times 10^{-19}$

$$\text{Frequency } \nu = \frac{20.4\times 10^{-19}}{h}$$

$$= \frac{20.4\times 10^{-19}}{6.63\times 10^{-34}}$$

$$= 3.076\times 10^{15}$$

$$= 3.1\times 10^{15}\text{ Hz}$$

$$\text{Wavelength of photon } \lambda = \frac{c}{\nu}$$

$$= \frac{3\times 10^{8}}{3.076\times 10^{15}}$$

$$= 9.75\times 10^{-8}\text{ m}$$

Thus, the wavelength is 9.7×10^{-8} m and frequency is 3.1×10^{15} Hz.

Question 6 (a) Using the Bohr's model calculate the speed of the electron in a hydrogen atom in the $n = 1$, 2, and 3 levels.

(b) Calculate the orbital period in each of these levels.

Sol.

(a) Speed of the electron in Bohr's nth orbit.

$$v_n = \frac{2\pi K' e^2}{nh} = \frac{v_1}{n}$$

For $n = 1$, $v_1 = \frac{2\pi K' e^2}{h}\left[K' = \frac{1}{4\pi\varepsilon_0} = 9\times 10^9\right]$

$$v_1 = \frac{2\times 3.14\times 9\times 10^9\times (1.6\times 10^{-19})^2}{6.634\times 10^{-34}}$$

$$v_1 = 2.18\times 10^6\text{ m/s}$$

For $n = 2, v_2 = \frac{v_1}{2} = \frac{2.18\times 10^6}{2} = 1.09\times 10^6$ m/s

For $n = 3, v_3 = \frac{v_1}{3} = \frac{2.18\times 10^6}{3}$

$$= 7.3\times 10^5\text{ m/s}$$

(b) Orbital period for nth Bohr's orbit

$$T_n = \frac{2\pi r_n}{v_n} = \frac{2\pi n^2 r_1}{\frac{v_1}{n}} \qquad \left[\because r_n = n^2 r_1, v_n = \frac{v_1}{n}\right]$$

$$T_n = n^3 \frac{2\pi r_1}{v_1}$$

For $n = 1$,

$$T_1 = \frac{2\pi r_1}{v_1}$$

$$= \frac{2 \times 3.14 \times 0.53 \times 10^{-10}}{2.18 \times 10^6} = 1.52 \times 10^{-16} \text{ s}$$

$$[r_1 = 0.53 \times 10^{-10} \text{m}, v_1 = 2.18 \times 10^6 \text{ m/s}]$$

For $n = 2$,

$$T_2 = (2)^3 T_1$$

$$= 8 \times 1.52 \times 10^{-16} = 1.216 \times 10^{-15} \text{ s}$$

For n, = 3

$$T_3 = (3)^3 T_1 = 27 \times 1.52 \times 10^{-15} = 4.1 \times 10^{-15} \text{ s}$$

Mistake Alert The principal quantum number n must always be a positive integer. Values like $n = -1$ are physically meaningless in Bohr's model. Ensure you are using positive integer values for n only.

Question 7 The radius of the innermost electron orbit of a hydrogen atom is 5.3×10^{-11} m. What are the radii of the $n = 2$ and $n = 3$ orbits?

Thinking Process The Bohr radius formula $r_n = n^2 . r_1$ reflects the idea that electron orbits are quantized, meaning the electron can only occupy specific orbits, each with a fixed radius corresponding to a specific quantum number n.

Sol. Given, the radius of the innermost electron orbit of a hydrogen $= 5.3 \times 10^{-11}$ m

As we know that the radius of nth orbit of H atom is given by : $r_n = n^2 r_1$

where $r_1 = 5.3 \times 10^{-11}$ m $\qquad r_n = n^2 r_1$

For $n = 2$, $\quad$ radius $r_2 = 2^2 r_1 = 4 \times 5.3 \times 10^{-11} = 2.12 \times 10^{-10}$ m

For $n = 3$, $\quad$ radius $r_3 = 3^2 r_1 = 9 \times 5.3 \times 10^{-11} = 4.77 \times 10^{-10}$ m

Question 8 A 12.5 eV electron beam is used to bombard gaseous hydrogen at room temperature. What series of wavelengths will be emitted?

Sol. Formula to get wavelength for the transition in a hydrogen atom is given by

$$\frac{1}{\lambda} = R\left(\frac{1}{n_1^2} - \frac{1}{n_2^2}\right) \qquad \ldots(i)$$

where, $R = 1.097 \times 10^7 \text{ m}^{-1}$, is the Rydberg constant.

The nth energy level of a H-atom has energy given by $E_n = \frac{-13.6}{n^2}$ eV

The difference between energy level $n = 2$ and $n = 1$

$$E_2 - E_1 = -13.6\left(\frac{1}{2^2} - \frac{1}{1^2}\right) \approx 10.2\,\text{eV}$$

Similarly for $n = 3$ and $n = 1$

$$E_3 - E_1 = -13.6\left(\frac{1}{3^2} - \frac{1}{1^2}\right) \approx 12.09\,\text{eV}$$

From question we have 12.5 eV energy of hydrogen atom, which is sufficient to excite the H-atom to the level with $n = 3$, thus we will get 3 wavelengths corresponding to the following transition

(1) $n = 3$ to $n = 1$ (2) $n = 2$ to $n = 1$

(3) $n = 3$ to $n = 2$

For $n = 3$ to $n = 1$ we obtain λ as

$$\frac{1}{\lambda} = 1.097 \times 10^7\left(\frac{1}{1^2} - \frac{1}{3^2}\right) \quad \text{[from Eq. (i)]}$$

$$= 1.097 \times 10^7\left(1 - \frac{1}{9}\right) = 1.097 \times 10^7 \times \frac{8}{9}$$

$$\Rightarrow \lambda = \frac{9}{8 \times 1.097 \times 10^7} = 102.55\,\text{nm}$$

For $n = 2$ to $n = 1$,

$$\frac{1}{\lambda} = 1.097 \times 10^7\left(\frac{1}{1^2} - \frac{1}{2^2}\right)$$

$$= 1.097 \times 10^7\left(1 - \frac{1}{4}\right) = 1.097 \times 10^7 \times \frac{3}{4}$$

$$\Rightarrow \lambda = \frac{4}{1.097 \times 10^7 \times 3} = 121.54\,\text{nm}$$

For $n = 3$ to $n = 2$

$$\frac{1}{\lambda} = 1.097 \times 10^7\left(\frac{1}{3^2} - \frac{1}{2^2}\right) = 1.097 \times 10^7 \times \frac{5}{36}$$

$$= \frac{0.36}{5 \times 1.097 \times 10^7} = 656.33\,\text{nm}$$

(1) $\lambda = 102.55$ nm (2) 121.54 nm (3) 656.33 nm

In Lyman series two wavelengths *i.e.*, 102.55 nm and 121 nm are emitted and in Balmer series one wavelength *i.e.*, 656.33 nm is emitted.

Question 9 In accordance with the Bohr's model, find the quantum number that characterises the earth's revolution around the sun in an orbit of radius 1.5×10^{11} m with orbital speed 3×10^4 m/s. (Mass of earth $= 6.0 \times 10^{24}$ kg.)

Sol. Given, radius of orbit $r = 1.5 \times 10^{11}$ m

Orbital speed $v = 3 \times 10^4$ m/s; Mass of earth $M = 6 \times 10^{24}$ kg

Angular momentum, $mvr = \dfrac{nh}{2\pi}$ (Bohr's 2nd postulate of quantization of angular momentum)

or $$n = \frac{2\pi vrm}{h}$$

[where, n is the quantum number of the orbit]

$$= \frac{2 \times 3.14 \times 3 \times 10^4 \times 1.5 \times 10^{11} \times 6 \times 10^{24}}{6.63 \times 10^{-34}}$$

$$= 2.57 \times 10^{74}$$

or $$n = 2.6 \times 10^{74}$$

Thus, the quantum number is 2.6×10^{74} which is too large.

DIKSHA APP Questions

Multiple Choice Questions

Q.1 According to Bohr's model of hydrogen atom, an electron can revolve round a nucleus indefinitely. If its path is

(a) a perfect circle of any radius
(b) a circle of constantly decreasing radius
(c) a circle of an allowed radius
(d) an ellipse

Sol. (c) According Bohr's postulate electrons can revolve in fixed orbits. In Bohr's model, an electron can revolve indefinitely in a circle of an allowed radius, because these orbits have specific fixed energy levels. In these orbits, the electron does not emit energy. So, it remains stable and does not spiral into the nucleus.

Q.2 De Broglie's hypothesis gave an explanation for Bohr's quantized orbits by bringing in the wave particle duality. According to this, the orbits correspond to circular standing waves in which the circumference of the orbit is

(a) an integral multiple of wavelength
(b) always equal to wavelength
(c) independent of wavelength
(d) an integral multiple of frequency

Sol. (a) According to second postulate of Bohr's model of an atom

$$mvr = \frac{nh}{2\pi}, \; mv = \frac{nh}{2\pi r} \quad \text{...(i)}$$

de Broglie wavelength $\lambda = \frac{h}{mv}$ Put value of mv from Eq. (i)

$$\lambda = \frac{h}{\frac{nh}{2\pi r}} \Rightarrow 2\pi r = n\lambda$$

Q.3 The energy level diagram of an element is given in the figure. Identify, by doing necessary calculations, which transition corresponds to the emission of a spectral line of wavelength 487 nm.

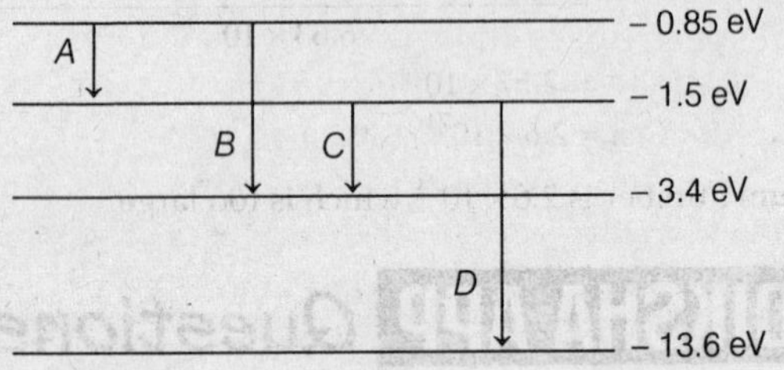

(a) A (b) B (c) C (d) D

Sol. (b) For (B)

$$\therefore \qquad \Delta E = E_2 - E_1 = h\nu = \frac{hc}{\lambda}$$

$$\lambda = \frac{hc}{E_2 - E_1} = \frac{6.63 \times 10^{-34} \times 3 \times 10^8}{[-0.85-(-3.4)] \times 1.6 \times 10^{-19}}$$

$$\lambda = 487 \text{ nm}$$

Q.4 As an electron makes a transition from an excited state to the ground state of a hydrogen like atom/ion.

(a) its kinetic energy increases but potential energy and total energy decreases

(b) kinetic energy, potential energy and total energy decreases

(c) kinetic energy decreases but potential energy and total energy increases

(d) kinetic and total energy decreases but potential energy increases.

Sol. (a) When electron makes transistion from ground state to excited state.

Total energy, $E_n = \frac{-13.6}{n^2}$ eV, decreases because the value of n is less for ground state than excited state.

Kinetic energy $K = -E$, increases Potential energy $U = 2E$, decreaes.

Q.5 Bohr's theory of hydrogen atom could not completely explain the

(a) diameter of H-atom (b) emission spectra

(c) ionization energy (d) fine structure of hydrogen spectrum

Sol. (d) Fine structure of hydrogen spectrum.

Q.6 The angular momentum of an electron in the third orbit of an atom is

(a) 3.15×10^{-34} Js (b) 2.15×10^{-34} Js

(c) 3.15×10^{-32} Js (d) 2.15×10^{-33} Js

Sol. (a) $L = mvr = \frac{nh}{2\pi}$ (Bohr's 2nd postulate)

$$L = \frac{3 \times 6.634 \times 10^{-34}}{2 \times 3.14} = 3.16 \times 10^{-34} \text{ Js}$$

Q.7 The wavelength of second line of the Balmer series in the hydrogen spectrum is 486.1 nm. The wavelength of the first line of the Balmer series will be

(a) 656.2 nm (b) 527.4 nm (c) 686.9 nm (d) 753.6 nm

Sol. (a) Use formula $\frac{1}{\lambda} = R\left[\frac{1}{n_1^2} - \frac{1}{n_2^2}\right]$

Wavelength of 2nd line Balmer series corresponds to transition from $n_2 = 4$ to $n_1 = 2$

$$\frac{1}{\lambda_2} = R\left[\frac{1}{2^2} - \frac{1}{4^2}\right] = R\left[\frac{1}{4} - \frac{1}{16}\right] = \frac{3R}{16} \quad \text{...(i)}$$

Wavelength of 1st line of Balmer series corresponds to transistion from $n_2 = 3$ to $n_1 = 2$

$$\frac{1}{\lambda_1} = R\left[\frac{1}{2^2} - \frac{1}{3^2}\right] = R\left[\frac{1}{4} - \frac{1}{9}\right] = \frac{5R}{36} \quad \text{...(ii)}$$

Diving Eq. (i) and Eq. (ii)

$$\frac{\frac{1}{\lambda_2}}{\frac{1}{\lambda_1}} = \frac{\frac{3R}{16}}{\frac{5R}{36}} = \frac{3 \times 36}{5 \times 16} = \frac{27}{20} \Rightarrow \frac{\lambda_1}{\lambda_2} = \frac{27}{20}$$

$$\lambda_1 = \frac{27}{20} \times \lambda_2 = \frac{27}{20} \times 486.1 = 656.23 \text{ nm}$$

Q.8 Which of the following transitions in hydrogen atom, emits photon of highest frequency?

(a) $n = 1$ to $n = 2$ (b) $n = 2$ to $n = 6$

(c) $n = 6$ to $n = 2$ (d) $n = 2$ to $n = 1$

Sol. (d) $\because \Delta E = h\nu$

$$\nu = \frac{\Delta E}{h}$$

Transition in hydrogen atom from $n = 2$ to $n = 1$ has highest energy difference

$$\Delta E = E_2 - E_1$$
$$= -3.4 - (-13.6) = 10.2 \text{ eV}$$

Q.9 If an alpha particle collides head on with the nucleus, the impact parameter will be

(a) zero (b) infinite (c) 10^{-10} m (d) 10^{10} m

Sol. (a) For head on collision the impact parameter is zero as it refraces the path.

□ Short Answer Types

Q.1 Calculate the energy required to excite an electron from ground state to second excited state.

Sol. Energy in ground state ($n = 1$)

$$E_1 = -13.6/1^2 = -13.6 \text{ eV.}$$

Energy in second excited state ($n = 3$)

$$E_3 = -13.6/3^2 = -1.51 \text{ eV}$$

Required energy $= E_3 - E_1 = -1.51-(-13.6) = 12.09 \text{ eV}$

Q.2 Calculate the impact parameter of a 6 MeV particle scattered by 90° when it approaches a gold nucleus.

Sol. Here, $K = \frac{1}{2}mv^2 = 6 \text{ MeV} = 6 \times 1.6 \times 10^{-13}$ J

and $\theta = 90°$, $Z = 79$ for gold

Impact parameter

$$b = \frac{k \cdot Ze^2 \cot\frac{\theta}{2}}{\frac{1}{2}mv^2} = \frac{9 \times 10^9 \times 79 \times (1.6 \times 10^{-19})^2 \times \cot\left(\frac{90°}{2}\right)}{6 \times 1.6 \times 10^{-13}}$$

$\Rightarrow$ $b = 189.6 \times 10^{-16}$ m $\Rightarrow b = 1.89 \times 10^{-14}$ m

□ Long Answer Type

Q.1 (a) The kinetic energy of α-particle incident on gold foil is doubled. How does the distance of closest approach change ?

(b) the trajectories, traced by different α-particles were observed as shown in figure given below.

(i) What names are given to b and θ ?

(ii) What can we say about b, for $\theta = 0°$ and $\theta = 180°$?

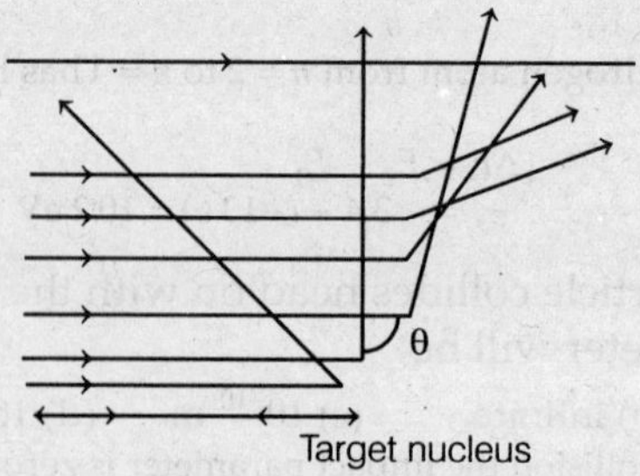

Sol. (a) As the distance of closest approach is inversely proportional to the kinetic energy of the incident α-particle, so the distance of closest approach is halved when kinetic energy of α-particle incident on gold foil is doubled.

As kinetic energy of α-particle,

$$KE = \frac{1}{2}mv^2 = \frac{2kZe^2}{r_0}$$

$$r_0 = \frac{2kZe^2}{KE}$$

where, r_0 is distance of closest approach and KE is kinetic energy of α-particle, $k = 9 \times 10^9\ Nm^2C^{-2}$

So, the distance of closest approach is halved when kinetic energy of α-particle incident on gold foil is doubled.

(b) (i) The symbol b represents impact parameter and θ represents the scattering angle.

(ii) When θ = 0°, the impact parameter b is large.

When θ = 180°, the impact parameter $b = 0$

Q.2 The ground state energy of hydrogen atom is –13.6 eV.

(i) What is the kinetic energy of an electron in the 2nd excited state ?

(ii) What is the potential energy of an electron in the 3rd excited state ?

(iii) If the electron jumps to the ground state from the 3rd excited state, calculate the wavelength of the photon emitted.

Sol. Here $E_1 = -13.6$ eV

$$E_3 = -13.6/3^2 = -1.51\ eV$$

$$E_4 = -13.6/4^2 = -0.85\ eV$$

(i) Kinetic energy of an electron in the 2nd excited state

$$K = -E_3 = 1.51\ eV$$

(ii) Potential energy of an electron in the 3rd excited state

$$U = 2E_4 = -1.70\ eV$$

(iii) $E_4 - E_1 = -0.85 - (-13.6) = 12.75$ eV

$$= 12.75 \times 1.6 \times 10^{-19}\ J$$

As $E_4 - E_1 = hc/\lambda$

Now $\lambda = hc/(E_4 - E_1) = 6.6 \times 10^{-34} \times 3 \times 10^8 / 12.75 \times 1.6 \times 10^{-19}$

$$= 970 \times 10^{-10}\ m$$

Nuclei

CHAPTER 13

Important Points

01 The radius of nucleus is given by $R = R_0 A^{1/3}$

where, R_0 = emperical constant = 1.2 fm, A = mass number

02 Density of nucleus is given by $\rho = \dfrac{3m}{4\pi R_0^3} = 2.30 \times 10^{17}\ \text{kg/m}^3$, which is same for all nuclei.

03 1 amu = 1.66×10^{-27} kg, m = mass of neucleons = 1.66×10^{-27} kg

04 1 MeV = 1.6×10^{-13} J

05 1 amu = 931.5 MeV

06 Mass defect is given by Δm (mass of neucleons – mass of nucleus) $= [Z(m_p) + (A - Z)\, m_n] - m_N$

07 Total binding energy = $\Delta m \times 931.5$ MeV

08 Average binding energy per nucleon = $\dfrac{\Delta m \times 931.5}{A}\ \dfrac{\text{MeV}}{\text{nucleon}}$

09 The Q value of nuclear process

Q = final kinetic energy – initial kinetic energy

or $Q = (m_{\text{reactant}} - m_{\text{product}})c^2$

10 **Nuclear Fission**

$${}_0^1n + {}_{92}^{235}\text{U} \rightarrow {}_{92}^{236}\text{U} \rightarrow {}_{56}^{144}\text{Ba} + {}_{36}^{89}\text{Kr} + 3\,{}_0^1n + 200\ \text{MeV}$$

11 Nuclear fusion (energy generation in stars)

$${}_1^1\text{H} + {}_1^1\text{H} \longrightarrow + {}_1^2\text{H} + e^+ + \nu + 0.42\ \text{MeV}$$

Exercises

Question 1 Obtain the binding energy (in MeV) of a nitrogen nucleus $\left({}^{14}_{7}\text{N}\right)$, given $m\left({}^{14}_{7}\text{N}\right) = 14.00307$ u.

Sol. Given, mass of proton, $m_p = 1.00783u$,

Mass of neutron, $m_n = 1.00867$ u

${}^{14}_{7}$N nucleus contains 7 protons and 7 neutrons.

Mass defect (Δm) = mass of nucleons – mass of nucleus

$$= 7m_p + 7m_n - m_N$$
$$= 7 \times 1.00783 + 7 \times 1.00867 - 14.00307$$
$$= 7.05481 + 7.06069 - 14.00307 = 0.11243 \text{ u}$$

Binding energy of nitrogen nucleus $= \Delta m \times 931.5$ MeV

$$= 0.11243 \times 931.5 \text{ MeV}$$
$$= 104.72 \text{ MeV}$$

Thus, the binding energy is 104.67 MeV.

Question 2 Obtain the binding energy of the nuclei ${}^{56}_{26}$Fe and ${}^{209}_{83}$Bi in units of MeV from the following data

$$m\left({}^{56}_{26}\text{Fe}\right) = 55.934939 \text{ u}, \; m\left({}^{209}_{83}\text{Bi}\right) = 208.980388 \text{ u}.$$

Sol. Given, mass of proton $m_p = 1.00783$ u

Mass of neutron, $m_n = 1.00867$ u

(i) **For ${}^{56}_{26}$Fe**

${}^{56}_{26}$Fe contains 26 protons and $(56 - 26) = 30$ neutrons

Mass defect (Δm) = mass of nucleons – mass of nucleus of ${}^{56}_{26}$Fe

Mass defect $(\Delta m) = 26 \times m_p + 30 \times m_n - m_N$

$$= 26 \times 1.00783 + 30 \times 1.00867 - 55.934939$$
$$= 26.20345 + 30.25995 - 55.934939 = 0.528461 \text{ u}$$

Total binding energy $= \Delta m \times 931.5$ MeV

$$= 0.528461 \times 931.5 = 492.26 \text{ MeV}$$

Average binding energy per nucleon of ${}^{56}_{26}$Fe

$$= \frac{\text{Binding energy}}{\text{Total number of nucleons}} = \frac{492.26}{56} = 8.790 \text{ MeV}$$

(ii) **For ${}_{83}\text{Bi}^{209}$**

It contains 83 protons and $(209 - 83) = 126$ neutrons

defect (Δm) = mass of nucleons – mass of nucleus of ${}^{209}_{83}$Bi

$$= 83 \times m_p + 126 \times m_n - m_N$$
$$= 83 \times 1.007825 + 126 \times 1.008665 - 208.980388$$
$$= 83.649475 + 127.091790 - 208.980388 = 1.760877 \text{ u}$$

Binding Energy $= \Delta m \times 931.5$ MeV $= 1.760877 \times 931.5 = 1640.26$ MeV

Average binding energy per nucleon of $^{209}_{83}Bi$

$$= \frac{\text{Binding energy}}{\text{Total number of nucleon}} = \frac{1640.26}{209} = 7.848 \text{ MeV}$$

Thus, the binding energy per nucleon of Fe is more than Bi.

Question 3 A given coin has a mass of 3.0 g. Calculate the nuclear energy that would be required to separate all the neutrons and protons from each other. For simplicity, assume that the coin is entirely made of $^{63}_{29}Cu$ atoms (of mass 62.92960 u).

Sol. Given, mass of coin = 3 g

$$\text{Number of atoms in 1 g of Cu} = \frac{6.023 \times 10^{23}}{63}$$

$$\text{Number of atoms in 3 g of Cu} = \frac{6.023 \times 10^{23}}{63} \times 3 = 2.868 \times 10^{22}$$

Number of protons in Cu atom, = 29

Number of neutrons in Cu atom = 63 − 29 = 34

mass defect in each atom, $\Delta m = 29 \times m_p + 34 \times m_n - m_{Cu}$

$$= 29 \times 1.00783 + 34 \times 1.00867 - 62.9260 = 0.59585 \text{ u}$$

$\therefore$ Total mass defect in all atoms $= 0.59585 \times 2.868 \times 10^{22} = 1.7088 \times 10^{22}$ u

Binding energy = Mass defect × 931.5 MeV

$$= 1.7088 \times 10^{22} \times 931.5 \text{ MeV} = 1.59 \times 10^{25} \text{ MeV}$$

Thus, the energy required to separate all the neutrons and protons is 1.59×10^{25} MeV *i.e.*, equal to binding energy.

Question 4 Obtain approximately the ratio of the nuclear radii of the gold isotope $^{197}_{79}Au$ and the silver isotope $^{107}_{47}Ag$.

Sol. Radius of nuclei, $R = R_0 \ A^{1/3}$

where A is the mass number of nucleus and R_0 is an empirical constant.

$$\therefore \quad R \propto A^{1/3}$$

$$\therefore \quad \frac{R_{\text{gold}}}{R_{\text{silver}}} = \left(\frac{A_{\text{gold}}}{A_{\text{silver}}}\right)^{1/3} = \left(\frac{197}{107}\right)^{1/3} = 1.225 = 1.23:1$$

Question 5 The Q-value of a nuclear reaction $A + b \rightarrow C + d$ is defined by $Q = [m_A + m_b - m_C - m_d]c^2$, where the masses refer to the respective nuclei. Determine from the given data, the Q-value of the following reactions and state whether the reactions are exothermic or endothermic.

(a) $^1_1H + ^3_1H \longrightarrow ^2_1H + ^2_1H$ (b) $^{12}_6C + ^{12}_6C \longrightarrow ^{20}_{10}Ne + ^4_2He$

Atomic masses are given to be

$m(^2_1H) = 2.014102$ u, $m(^3_1H) = 3.016049$ u,

$m(^{12}_6C) = 12.000000$ u, $m(^{20}_{10}Ne) = 19.992439$ u.

Sol. The given reaction

(a) ${}_1^1\text{H} + {}_1^3\text{H} \longrightarrow {}_1^2\text{H} + {}_1^2\text{H}$

Mass defect Δm = mass of reactant - mass of product

$= [m({}_1^1\text{H}) + m({}_1^3\text{H})] - 2m({}_1^2\text{H})$

$= 1.007825 + 3.016049 - 2\ (2.014102) = -0.00433$ u

Q-value of the reaction

$$Q = \Delta m \times 931.5 = -0.00433 \times 931.5 = -4.033 \text{ MeV}$$

As the energy is negative so, the reaction is endothermic.

(b) The given reaction ${}_6^{12}\text{C} + {}_6^{12}\text{C} \longrightarrow {}_{10}^{20}\text{Ne} + {}_2^4\text{He}$

Δm = mass of reactant - mass of product $= 2m\ ({}_6^{12}\text{C}) - m({}_{10}^{20}\text{Ne}) - m({}_2^4\text{He})$

$= 2 \times 12 - 19.992439 - 4.002603 = 0.00495$ u

$Q = \Delta m \times 931.5 = 0.00495 \times 931.5 = 4.61$ MeV

Since, the energy is positive thus, the reaction is exothermic.

Mistake Alert Ensure mass units are correctly used. Small errors in units (like using atomic masses instead of nuclear masses) can lead to wrong Q-values.

Question 6 Suppose, we think of fission of a ${}_{26}^{56}\text{Fe}$ nucleus into two equal fragments, ${}_{13}^{28}\text{Al}$. Is the fission energetically possible? Argue by working out Q of the process. Given $m({}_{26}^{56}\text{Fe}) = 55.93494$ u and $m({}_{13}^{28}\text{Al}) = 27.98191$ u.

Sol. The given reaction for the decay process

$${}_{26}^{56}\text{Fe} \longrightarrow {}_{13}^{28}\text{Al} + {}_{13}^{28}\text{Al}$$

Mass defect Δm = mass of reactant − mass of product

$= m\ ({}_{26}^{56}\text{Fe}) - 2m\ ({}_{13}^{28}\text{Al})$

$= 55.93494 - 2(27.98191) = -0.02888$ u

$Q = \Delta m \times 931.5 = -26.90172$ MeV

Because the energy is negative, so the fission is not possible energetically.

Question 7 The fission properties of ${}_{94}^{239}\text{Pu}$ are very similar to those of ${}_{92}^{235}\text{U}$. The average energy released per fission is 180 MeV. How much energy, in MeV, is released if all the atoms in 1 kg of pure ${}_{94}^{239}\text{Pu}$ undergo fission?

Sol. According to the concept of Avogadro number

The number of atoms in 239 g of ${}_{94}^{239}\text{Pu} = 6.023 \times 10^{23}$

Number of atoms in 1 kg of ${}_{94}^{239}\text{Pu} = \dfrac{6.023 \times 10^{23} \times 1000}{239}$ [$\because$ 1 kg = 1000 gram]

$= 2.52 \times 10^{24}$

The average energy released in one fission = 180 MeV

So, total energy released in fission of 1 kg of ${}_{94}^{239}\text{Pu} = 180 \times 2.52 \times 10^{24}$

$= 4.53 \times 10^{26}$ MeV

Note • The energy released per fission is given in MeV per atom, so multiplication with the number of atoms is necessary for the total energy.
• Be careful with significant figures.
• The atomic mass of plutonium ($P^{239}_{u_{94}}$) and other constants should be treated with the correct number of significant figures, it based on the data provided.

Question 8 How long can an electric lamp of 100 W be kept glowing by fusion of 2.0 kg of deuterium? Take the fusion reaction as

$$^2_1\text{H} + ^2_1\text{H} \longrightarrow ^3_1\text{He} + n + 3.27 \text{ MeV}$$

Sol. Let t be the time.

According to the Avogadro number concept

Number of atoms in 2 g of deuterium = 6.023×10^{23}

Number of atoms in 2 kg (2×10^3 gram) of deuterium $= \dfrac{6.023 \times 10^{23} \times 2 \times 10^3}{2}$

$= 6.023 \times 10^{26}$

From given equation, energy released during fusion of two deuterium

$= 3.27$ MeV

$\therefore$ Energy released by one deuterium $= \dfrac{3.27}{2} = 1.635$ MeV

Energy relesed in 6.023×10^{26} deuterium atoms

$= 1.635 \times 6.023 \times 10^{26} = 9.848 \times 10^{26}$ MeV

$= 9.848 \times 10^{26} \times 1.6 \times 10^{-13} = 15.75 \times 10^{13}$ J

[$\because$ 1 MeV $= 1.6 \times 10^{-13}$ J]

Energy used by bulb in 1s = 100 J

100 J energy used in time = 1 s

15.75×10^{13} J energy used in time $= \dfrac{1 \times 15.75 \times 10^{13}}{100} = 15.75 \times 10^{11}$ s

($\because$ We know that 1 yr = $(365 \times 24 \times 60 \times 60)$ s)

$= \dfrac{15.75 \times 10^{11}}{60 \times 24 \times 60 \times 365}$ yr $= 4.99 \times 10^4$ yr

Thus, the bulbs glow for 4.99×10^4 yr.

Mistake Alert Only two deuterium atoms fuse in each reaction, so dividing the total number of atoms by two is necessary to calculate the number of atoms in 1g.

Always check the units of time, power, and energy to ensure correct conversions, especially when switching from seconds to years.

Question 9 Calculate the height of the potential barrier for a head on collision of two deuterons. [Hint : The height of the potential barrier is given by the Coulomb repulsion between the two deuterons when they just touch each other. Assume that they can be taken as hard spheres of radius 2.0 fm.]

Sol. Given, radius $r = 2\text{ fm} = 2 \times 10^{-15}$ m

For head on collision, the distance between the centres of two deuterons

$$d = 2r$$

$$d = 2 \times 2 \times 10^{-15} = 4 \times 10^{-15} \text{ m}$$

Charge on each deuteron, $e = 1.6 \times 10^{-19}$ C

$$\text{Potential energy} = \frac{1}{4\pi\varepsilon_0} \cdot \frac{q_1 q_2}{d} = \frac{9 \times 10^9 \times 1.6 \times 10^{-19} \times 1.6 \times 10^{-19}}{4 \times 10^{-15}} \text{ J}$$

$$\left(\because \frac{1}{4\pi\varepsilon_0} = 9 \times 10^9\right)$$

$$\text{Potential energy} = \frac{5.76 \times 10^{-14}}{1.6 \times 10^{-19}} = 3{,}60{,}000 \text{ eV} \qquad [\because 1 \text{ eV} = 1.6 \times 10^{-19} \text{ J}]$$

Mistake Alert When converting from joules to MeV, be careful with the Coulomb formula, make sure the distance is in meters and charges are in coulombs.

The assumption that the deuterons are hard spheres is an idealization, so the actual repulsion might differ slightly in more complex models. However, this assumption is standard for such calculations.

Question 10 From the relation $R = R_0 A^{1/3}$, where R_0 is a constant and A is the mass number of a nucleus, show that the nuclear matter density is nearly constant (*i.e.*, independent of A).

Thinking Process **The first step involves recognizing that the radius of a nucleus grows as $A^{1/3}$, which is a crucial characteristic of nuclear structure. The volume of a nucleus scales with A and this is key to realizing that the density is inversely proportional to volume, which cancels out the dependence on A.**

Sol. Given, the expression of the radius of nucleus is given by $R = R_0 A^{1/3}$ where R_0 is a constant and A is the mass number of nucleus.

$$\text{Density of nucleus} = \frac{\text{Mass of nucleus}}{\text{Volume of nucleus}}$$

$$= \frac{\text{Mass of each neucleon} \times \text{Number of neucleons}}{\frac{4}{3}\pi R^3}$$

$$= \frac{m \times A \times 3}{4\pi R^3} = \frac{Am\,3}{4\pi R_0^3 A} = \frac{3m}{4\pi R_0^3} \quad [\text{as } R = R_0 A^{\frac{1}{3}}]$$

As R_0 is a constant so, density is constant or independent of A.

Note $\rho = \dfrac{3 \times 1.66 \times 10^{-27}}{4 \times 3.14 \times (1.1 \times 10^{-15})^3} = 2.29 \times 10^{17} \text{ kg/m}^3$

DIKSHA APP Questions

Multiple Choice Questions

Q.1 Fusion reaction takes place at high temperature because

(a) atoms get ionized at high temperature
(b) kinetic energy is high enough to overcome the coulomb repulsion between nuclei
(c) molecules break up at high temperature
(d) nuclei break up at high temperature

Sol. (b) When the coulomb repulsion between the nuclei is overcome, then nuclear fusion reaction takes place. This is possible when temperature is too high.

Q.2 In a nuclear reactor, moderators slow down the neutrons which come out in a fission process. The moderators used have light nuclei. Heavy nuclei will not serve the purpose because

(a) they will break up.
(b) elastic collision of neutrons with heavy nuclei will not slow them down.
(c) the net weight of reactor would be unbearably high.
(d) substances with heavy nuclei do not occur in liquid or gaseous state at room temperature.

Sol. (b) During an elastic collision between two particles, the maximum kinetic energy is transferred from one particle to the other when they have the same mass. Therefore, heavy nuclei will not serve the purpose because elastic collision of neutrons with heavy nuclei will not slow them down.

Q.3 Potential energy of a pair of nucleons as a function of their separation is minimum at a distance of about

(a) 0.2 fm (b) 0.8 fm
(c) less than 0.8 fm (d) greater than 0.8 fm

Sol. (b) The potential energy between a pair of nucleons is minimum at around 0.8 fm. This distance represents the equilibrium separation where the strong nuclear attraction balances the short-range repulsive force, leading to a stable configuration. At distances greater or less than this, the net potential energy increases.

Q.4 Which of the following statements is true for nuclear forces?

(a) They obey the inverse square law of distance
(b) They obey the inverse third power law of distance
(c) They are short-range forces
(d) They are equal in strength to electromagnetic forces.

Sol. (c) Nuclear forces are short range forces.

Q.5 Heavy stable nuclei have more neutrons than protons. This is because of the fact that

(a) neutrons are heavier than protons
(b) electrostatic forces between protons are repulsive
(c) neutrons decay into protons through beta decay
(d) nuclear forces between neutrons are weaker than that between protons

Sol. (b) Electrostatic force between proton is repulsive which causes the unstability of nucleus. So, neutrons are larger in number than proton.

Q.6 What is the nuclear radius of Fe^{125}, if nuclear radius of Al^{27} is 3.6 fm ?

(a) 3 fermi (b) 3.6 fermi
(c) 6 fermi (d) 6.3 fermi

Sol. (c) $\because R \propto A^{\frac{1}{3}}$

$$\frac{R_{Fe}}{R_{Al}} = \left(\frac{125}{27}\right)^{\frac{1}{3}} = \frac{5}{3} \Rightarrow \frac{R_{Fe}}{3.6} = \frac{5}{3}$$

$$R_{Fe} = 6.0 \text{ fermi}$$

Q.7 Given the mass of the iron nucleus as 55.85 u and $A = 56$, find nuclear density.

(a) 2.29×10^{26} kg m^{-3} (b) 2.92×10^{16} kg m^{-3}
(c) 4.59×10^{-15} kg m^{-3} (d) 2.29×10^{17} kg m^{-3}

Sol. (d) Mass of nucleus $= 55.85 = 55.85 \times 1.66 \times 10^{-27}$ kg $= 92.71 \times 10^{-27}$ kg

$$\text{Volume of nucleus} = \frac{4}{3}\pi R^3 = \frac{4}{3}\pi(R_0 A^{\frac{1}{3}})^3 \; [\because R = R_0 A^{\frac{1}{3}}]$$

$$= \frac{4}{3}\pi R_0^3 A = \frac{4}{3} \times 3.14 \times (1.2 \times 10^{-15})^3 \times 56$$

$$= 4.05 \times 10^{-43} \text{ m}^3 \qquad [\because R_0 = 1.2 \times 10^{-15}]$$

$$\because \text{Nuclear density} = \frac{\text{Nuclear mass}}{\text{Nuclear volume}} = \frac{92.71 \times 10^{-27}}{4.05 \times 10^{-43}} = 2.29 \times 10^{17} \text{ kg m}^{-3}$$

Q.8 Nuclides with same neutron number N but different atomic number Z, are called

(a) isobars (b) isotones
(c) isotopes (d) isomers

Sol. (b) If two nuclides have the same neutron number N but different atomic number Z, they are isotones.

☐ Short Answer Type

Q.1 Are the equations of nuclear reactions 'balanced' in the sense a chemical equation (*e.g.*, $2H_2 + O_2 \longrightarrow 2H_2O$) is? If not, in what sense are they balanced on both sides ?

Sol. A chemical equation is balanced in the sense that the number of atoms of each element is the same on both sides of the equation. In a nuclear reaction, the number of atoms of each element is not necessarily conserved. In nuclear reactions, the number of protons and the number of neutrons are the same on the two sides of the equation.

☐ Long Answer Type

Q.1 Explain the processes of nuclear fission and nuclear fusion by using the plot of binding energy per nucleon (BE/A) *versus* the mass number A.

Sol. (a) **Nuclear Fission** When a heavy nucleus ($A > 235$ say) breaks into two lighter nuclei (nuclear fission), the binding energy per nucleon increases i.e. nucleons get more tightly bound. This implies that energy would be released in nuclear fission.

Example. ${}_0^1n + {}_{92}^{235}\text{U} \longrightarrow {}_{92}^{236}\text{U} \longrightarrow {}_{56}^{144}\text{Ba} + {}_{36}^{89}\text{Kr} + 3{}_0^1n + Q.$

Nuclear Fusion When two very light nuclei join to form a heavy nucleus, the binding energy per nucleon of fused heavier nucleus is more than the binding energy per nucleon of lighter nuclei, so again energy would be released in nuclear fusion.

Binding energy per nucleon versus mass number graph

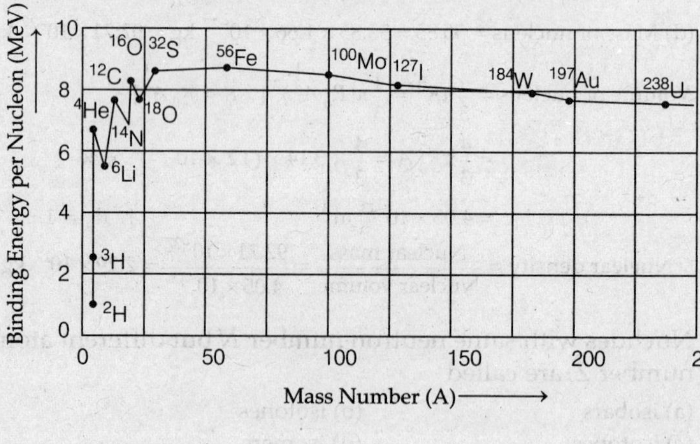

Semiconductor Electronics : Materials, Devices and Simple Circuits

CHAPTER 14

Important Points

01 Classification of metals, conductors and semiconductors

(a) **On the basis of conductivity (σ)**

(i) Metals
Low resistivity $\rho \approx 10^{-2} - 10^{-8}\ \Omega\text{m}$
High conductivity $\sigma \approx 10^{2} - 10^{8}\ \text{Sm}^{-1}$

(ii) Semiconductor restivity (ρ) is more than metals but less than insulators. $\rho \approx 10^{-5} - 10^{6}\ \Omega\text{m}$
Their conductivity (σ) is less than metals but more than insulators.

$$\sigma \approx 10^{5} - 10^{-6}\ \text{Sm}^{-1}$$

(iii) Insulators resistivity $\rho \approx 10^{11} - 10^{19}\ \Omega\text{m}$.
Conductivity $\sigma \approx 10^{-11} - 10^{-19}\ \text{Sm}^{-1}$

(b) **On the basis of energy bands**

(i) **Metals Completely** filled valance band overlaps with completely empty conduction band *i.e.*, band gap, $E_g = 0$

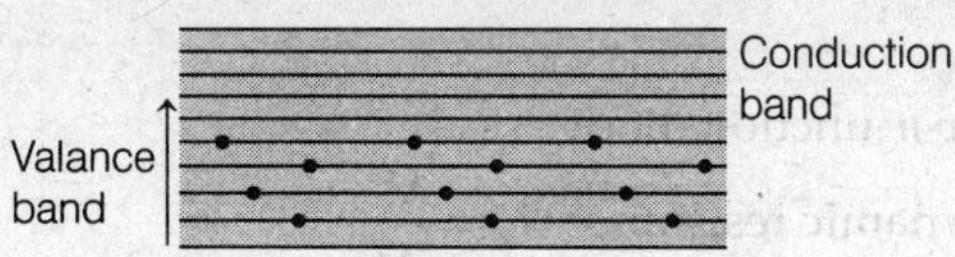

(a)

(ii) **Semiconductors** At absolute zero temperature, valance band is completely filled and conduction band is completely empty with small band gap, $E_g < 3$ eV between them.

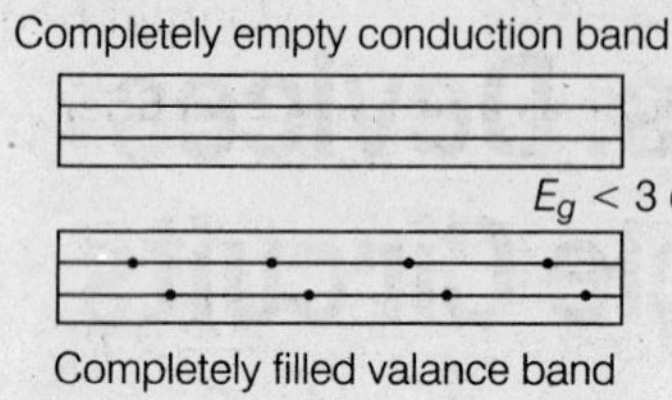

(b) i

At room temperature, some electrons from valence band can acquire enough energy to cross energy gap and reach conduction band.

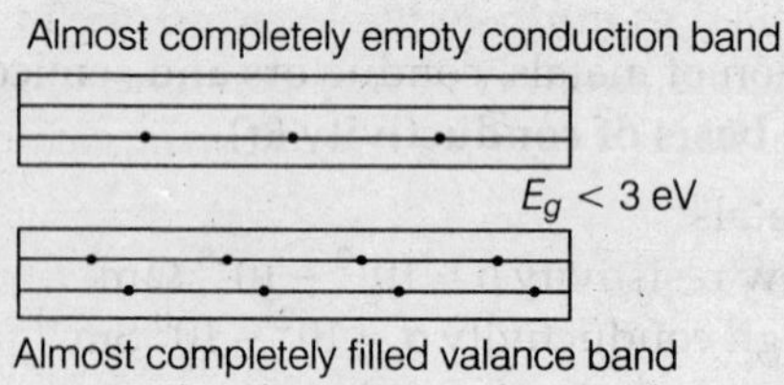

(b) ii

(iii) **Insulators** Completely filled valance band and completely empty conduction band with large band gap $E_g > 3$ eV between them.

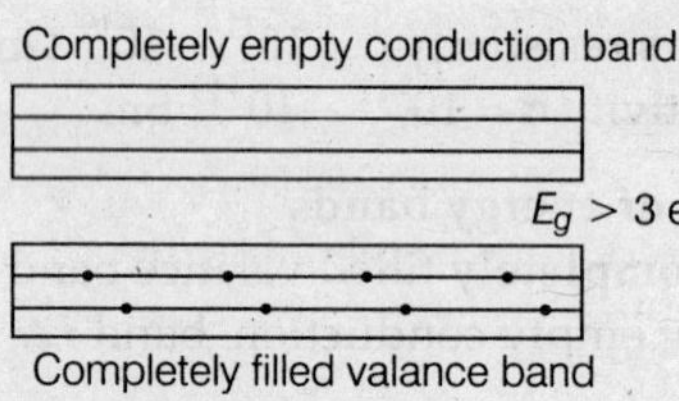

(c)

02 For a *p-n* junction diode

(a) Dynamic resistance $R_d = \dfrac{\Delta V}{\Delta I}$

(b) Wattage of diode = Voltage drop × Current

03 In a *p-n* junction diode as a half-wave rectifier

(a) $I_{DC} = \frac{I_0}{\pi}, I_{rms} = \frac{I_0}{2}$ (b) Output rms voltage = $V_0/2$

(c) Input fequency = 50 Hz (d) Output frequency = 50 Hz

04 In a *p-n* junction diode as a full-wave rectifier

(a) $I_{DC} = \frac{2 I_0}{\pi}, I_{rms} = \frac{I_0}{\sqrt{2}}$

(b) Output DC voltage = $I_{DC} \times R_L = \frac{2 I_0}{\pi} \times R_L$

(c) Input fequency = 50 Hz

(d) Output frequency = 100 Hz

05 **Intrinsic Semiconductors** Semiconductors in its pure form or state are called as intrinsic semiconductors. In intrinsic semiconductors, number of free electrons, n_e and number of holes n_h are equal *i.e.*, $n_e = n_h = n_i$, n_i is intrinsic carrier concentration.

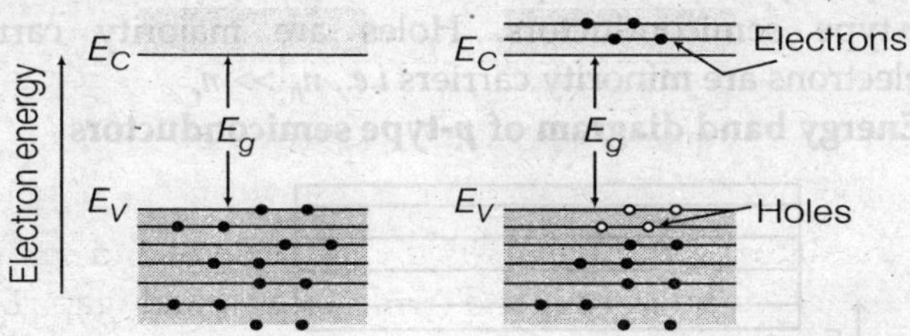

Fig. (a) Fig. (b)

▲ (a) An intrinsic semiconductor at $T = 0$ K behaves like insulator
(b) At $T > 0$ K, four thermally generated electron-hole pairs. The filled circles (·) represent electrons and empty circles (0) represent holes.

06 **Doping** Addition of a desirable impurity in small amount say a few parts per million (ppm) to pure semiconductor is called doping.

07 **Extrinsic Semiconductors** Doped semiconductors are known as extrinsic semiconductors. These are of two types as follows.

(i) ***n*-type Semiconductors** Semiconductors doped with pentavalent impurity atoms (donor atoms) such as, P, As, Sb etc, known as *n*-type semiconductors. Electrons are majority carriers and holes are minority carriers, *i.e.*

$$n_e >> n_h$$

Energy band diagram of *n*-type semiconductor

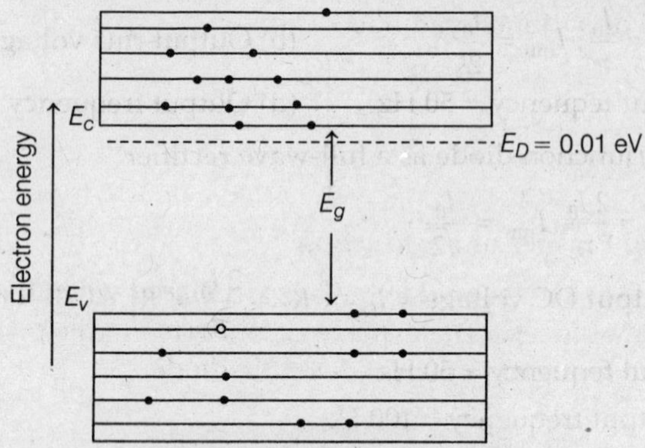

▲ (a) $T >$ OK one theremally generated electron-hole pair +9 electrons from donor atoms

(ii) ***p*-type semiconductor** Semiconductors doped with trivalent impurity atoms (acceptor atoms) like Al, B, In etc., are called *p*-type semiconductors. Holes are majority carriers and electrons are minority carriers *i.e.*, $n_h >> n_e$

Energy band diagram of *p*-type semiconductors

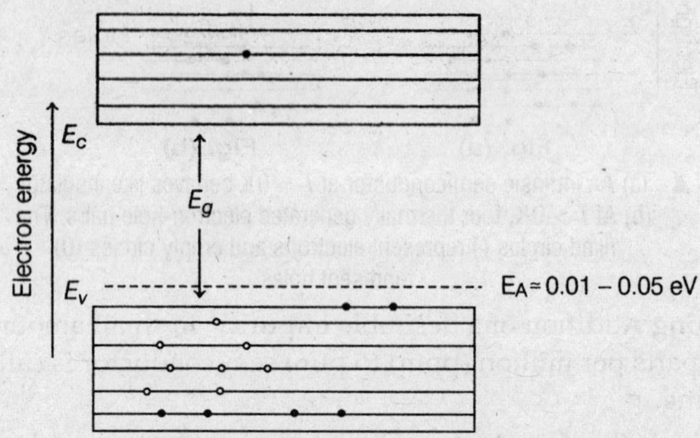

▲ (b) Energy band of *p*-type semiconductor at $T >$ OK

08 In Extrinsic semiconductors

In thermal equilibrium $n_e n_h = n_i^2$

09 *p-n* Junction In a *p*-type semiconductor wafer add small quantity of pentavalent impurity so that a part of this wafer can be converted into *n*-type and *p-n* junction is formed.

Symbol of p-n junction diode

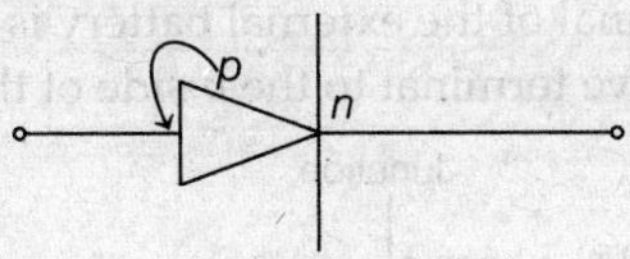

10 Forward Biasing of p-n junction

A junction diode is said to be forward biased when the positive terminal of the external battery is connected to the p-side and negative terminal to the n-side of the diode.

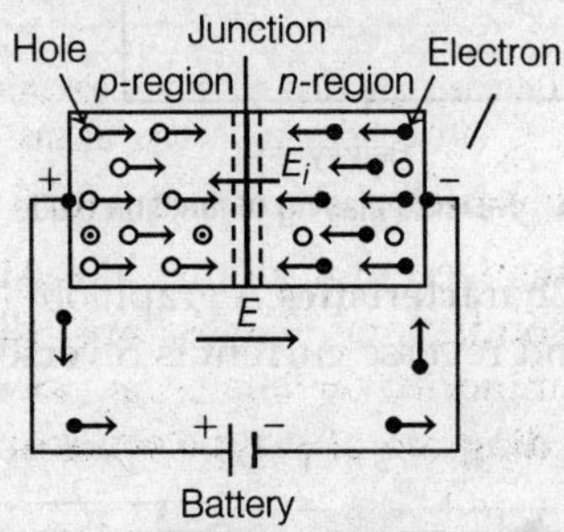

▲ Forward biasing of junction diode

11 In forward biased width of depletion layer and also height of potential barrier decreases.

12 Forward Biased Characteristics A graph between forward voltage and forward current is forward characteristic.

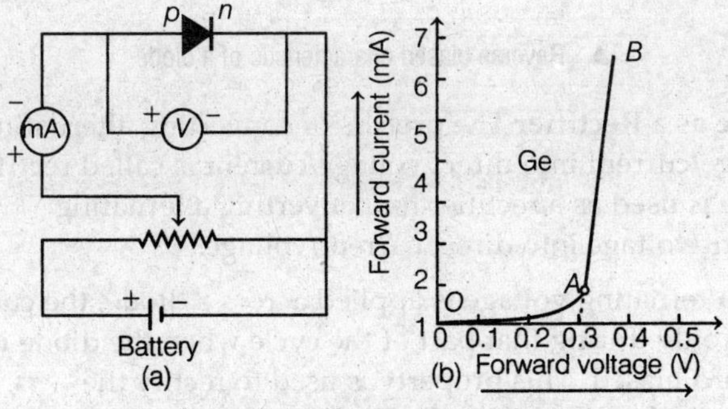

▲ Forward biased characteristic of a diode

13 **Reverse Biasing** A junction diode is said to be reverse biased when the positive terminal of the external battery is connected to the n-side and negative terminal to the p-side of the diode.

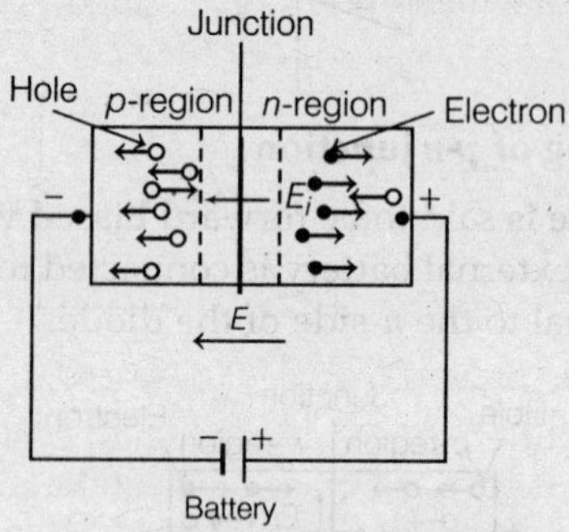

▲ Reverse biasing of junction diode

14 **Reverse Biased Characteristics** A graph obtained between reverse voltage and reverse current is reverse biased characteristic.

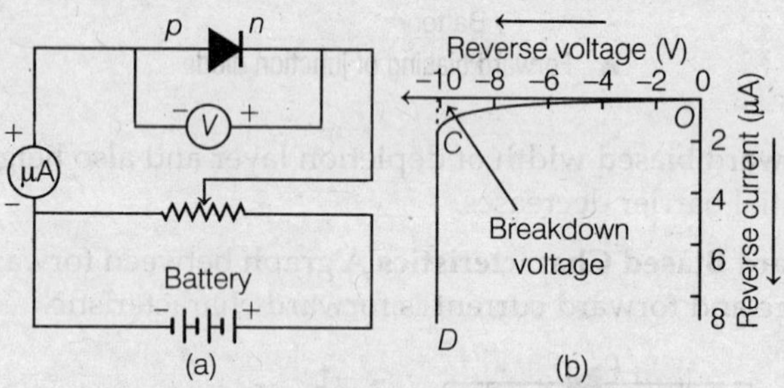

▲ Reverse biased characteristic of a diode

15 **Diode as a Rectifier** The process of converting alternating voltage/current into direct voltage/current is called **rectification.** Diode is used as a rectifier for converting alternating current/voltage into direct current/voltage.

16 If an alternating voltage is applied across a diode, the current flows only during that part of the cycle when the diode is forward biased. This property is used to rectify the current/voltage.

17 Diode as a Half-Wave Rectifier In this rectifier the AC voltage to be rectified is connected to the primary coil of a step-down transformer and secondary coil is connected to the diode through resistor R_L across which output is obtained.

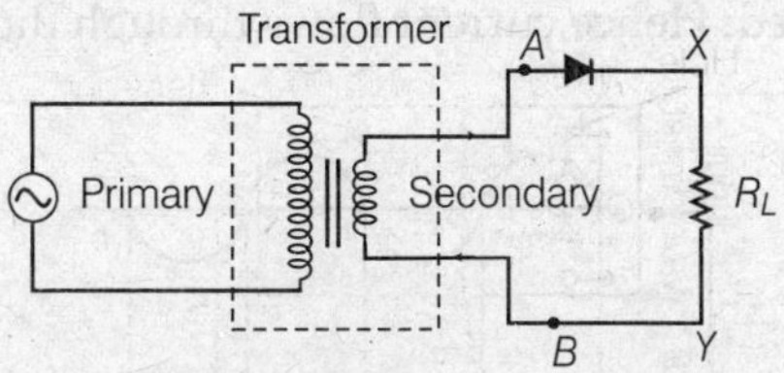

▲ Circuit diagram of half-wave rectifier

18 In half-wave rectifier, during positive half cycle of the input AC, the *p-n* junction is forward biased. Thus, the resistance in *p-n* junction becomes low and current flows while during negative half cycle, the *p-n* junction is reverse biased. Hence, we get output in the load only during positive half cycle.

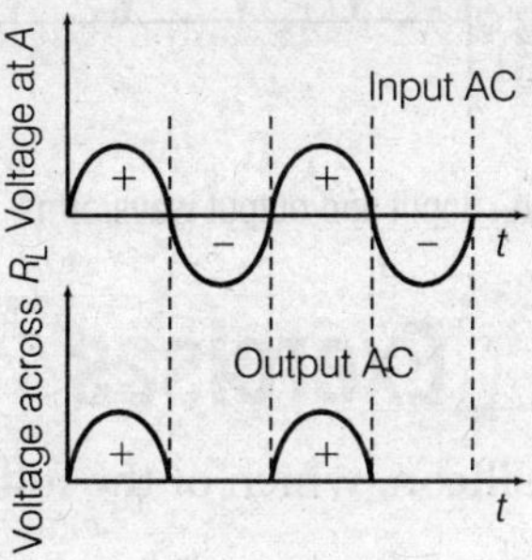

▲ Input and output waveforms

19 Diode as a Full Wave Rectifier In the full wave rectifier, two *p-n* junction diodes, D_1 and D_2 are used. This arrangement is shown in the diagram below.

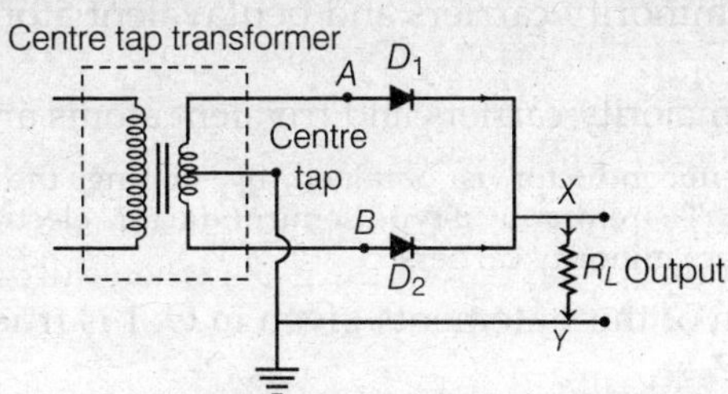

▲ Circuit diagram of full wave rectifier

20 In full wave rectifier, during the positive half cycle of the input AC, the diode D_1 is forward biased and the diode D_2 is reverse biased. The forward current flows through diode D_1. During negative half cycle, the diode D_1 is reverse biased and D_2 is forward biased. Hence current flows through diode D_2.

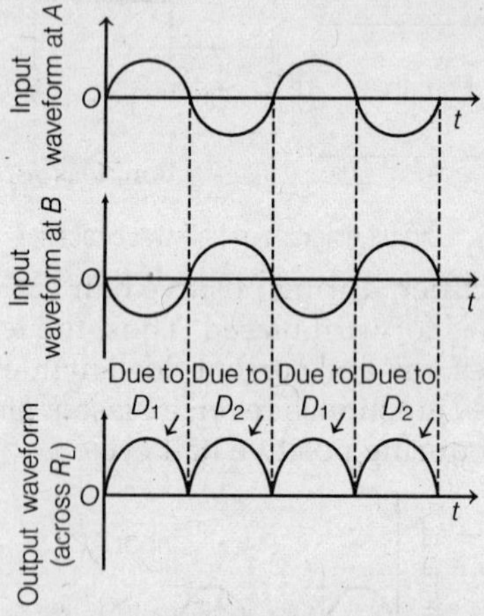

▲ Input and output waveforms

Exercises

Question 1 In an n-type silicon, which of the following statements is true?

(a) Electrons are majority carriers and trivalent atoms are the dopants.
(b) Electrons are minority carriers and pentavalent atoms are the dopants.
(c) Holes are minority carriers and pentavalent atoms are the dopants.
(d) Holes are majority carriers and trivalent atoms are the dopants.

Sol. (c) n-type semiconductor is obtained by doping the Ge or Si with pentavalent atoms. Therefore, in n-type semiconductor, electrons are majority carriers and holes are minority carriers.

Question 2 Which of the statements given in Q. 1 is true for p-type semiconductors?

Sol. (d) A p-type semiconductor is obtained by doping Ge or Si with trivalent atoms. Therefore, in p-type semiconductor holes are majority carriers and electrons are minority carriers.

Question 3 Carbon, silicon and germanium have four valence electrons each. These are characterised by valence and conduction bands separated by energy band-gap respectively equal to $(E_g)_C, (E_g)_{Si}$ and $(E_g)_{Ge}$. Which of the following statements is true?

(a) $(E_g)_{Si} < (E_g)_{Ge} < (E_g)_C$

(b) $(E_g)_C < (E_g)_{Ge} > (E_g)_{Si}$

(c) $(E_g)_C > (E_g)_{Si} > (E_g)_{Ge}$

(d) $(E_g)_C = (E_g)_{Si} = (E_g)_{Ge}$

Sol. (c) The energy band-gap is largest for carbon, less for silicon and least for germanium.

Question 4 In an unbiased *p-n* junction, holes diffuse from the *p*-region to *n*-region because

(a) free electrons in the *n*-region attract them

(b) they move across the junction by the potential difference

(c) hole concentration in *p*-region is more as compared to *n*-region

(d) All of the above

Sol. (c) In an unbiased *p-n* junction, the diffusion of charge carriers across the junction takes place from higher concentration to lower concentration. Therefore, hole concentration in *p*-region is more as compared to *n*-region.

Question 5 When a forward bias is applied to a *p-n* junction. It

(a) raises the potential barrier

(b) reduces the majority carrier current to zero

(c) lowers the potential barrier

(d) None of the above

Sol. (c) When a forward bias is applied across the *p-n* junction, the applied voltage opposes the barrier voltage. Due to this, the potential barrier across the junction is lowered.

Question 6 In half-wave rectification, what is the output frequency, if the input frequency is 50 Hz. What is the output frequency of a full-wave rectifier for the same input frequency?

Sol. A half wave rectifier rectifies only the half of AC input *i.e.,* it conducts once during an AC input cycle while a full-wave rectifier rectifies both the half cycles of the AC input *i.e.,* it conducts twice during a cycle.

$\therefore$ The output frequency for half-wave is 50 Hz.

The output frequency of a full-wave rectifier is $2 \times 50 = 100$ Hz.

DIKSHA APP Questions

☐ Multiple Choice Questions

Q.1 A *p-n* photodiode is fabricated from a semiconductor with a band gap of 2.5 eV. It can detect a signal of wavelength

(a) 4000 nm (b) 6000 nm

(c) 4000×10^{-10} m (d) 6000×10^{-10} m

Sol. (c) Given, $E = 2.5\,\text{eV} = 2.5 \times 1.6 \times 10^{-19}$ J

$$E = \frac{hc}{\lambda} \Rightarrow \lambda_{max} = \frac{hc}{E} = \frac{6.63 \times 10^{-34} \times 3 \times 10^{8}}{2.5 \times 1.6 \times 10^{-19}}$$

$$= 4972 \times 10^{-10} \text{ m}$$

This is maximum wavelength.

So photodiode can detect less or equal to this wavelength.

Q.2 In half-wave rectification, if input frequency is 60 Hz. The output frequency will be

(a) 120 Hz (b) 60 Hz (c) 30 Hz (d) 20 Hz

Sol. (b) Output frequency = Input frequency

Q.3 The unidirectional flow of current through *p-n* junction makes it ideal to be used as

(a) an oscillator (b) a rectifier

(c) a modulator (d) a resistor

Sol. (b) As a rectifier convert AC to DC

Q.4 In forward bias, the width of potential barrier in *p-n* juction diode

(a) remains constant (b) decreases

(c) increases (d) first decreases then increases

Sol. (b) In forward bias the external voltage reduces the built-in potential barrier of the p-n junction. This decreases the width of the depletion region, allowing charge carriers to flow more easily across the junction.

Q.5 When a junction diode is reverse biased, the flow of current across the junction

(a) is mainly due to diffusion of charges

(b) depends upon the nature of material

(c) is mainly due to drift of charges

(d) is due to both drift and diffusion of charges

Sol. (c) In reverse bias, the applied voltage increases the depletion region and the minority carriers (electrons in *p*-region and holes in *n*-region) are swept across the junction by the electric field, causing a small reverse current. This current is due to the drift of minority carriers.

Q.6 In an unbiased *p-n* jucntion,

(a) *n*-side is at higher potential and *p*-side is at lower potential
(b) *p*-side is at higher potential and *n*-side is at lower potential
(c) *p*-and *n*-both are at the same potential
(d) undetermined

Sol. (a) As in depletion layer donor atoms (positively charged) are in *n*-side and acceptor atoms (negative charged) are in *p*-side

Q.7 The depletion layer in the *p-n* junction region is caused by

(a) drift of holes (b) diffusion of charge carriers
(c) migration of impurity ions (d) drift of electrons

Sol. (b) In a *p-n* junction, electrons from the *n*-region, diffuse into *p*-region, and holes from the *p*-region diffuse into the *n*-region. This diffusion of charge carriers leads to recombination, creating an electrically neutral depletion layer with immobile ions

Q.8 When *n*-type semiconductor is heated

(a) number of electrons increases while that of holes decreases
(b) number of holes increase while that of electrons decreases
(c) number of electrons and holes remain same
(d) number of electrons and holes increases equally

Sol. (d) When an *n*-type semiconductor is heated, thermal energy excites electrons from the valance band to the conduction band generating electron-hole pairs. Although the majority carriers (electrons) dominate, the number of minority carriers (holes) also increases due to thermal excitation. Thus, both electrons and holes increase equally.

Q.9 In semiconductors, at a room temperature

(a) the valence band is partially empty the conduction band is partially filled.
(b) The valence band is completely filled and the conduction band is partially filled.
(c) the valence band is completely filled.
(d) the conduction band is completely empty.

Sol. (a) In semiconductors at room temperature the electrons get enough energy, so that they are able to overcome the forbidden gap. Thus, at room temperature the valance band is partially empty and conduction band is partially filled.

Q.10 At absolute zero, an intrinsic semiconductor behaves like
(a) an insulator
(b) a superconductor
(c) *n*-type semiconductor
(d) *p*-type semiconductor

Sol. (a) At absolute zero temperature valence band is full of electrons and the conduction band is empty, hence there are no free electrons in the conduction band and holes in the valence band. The charge carrier concentration is zero. Hence intrinsic semiconductor behave like an insulator.

□ Long Answer Type

Q.1 Why is a photodiode operated in reverse bias mode? For a given photodiode, reverse bias current under different illumination intensities I_1, I_2, I_3 and I_4 is shown in the diagram. Arrange the intensities I_1, I_2, I_3 and I_4, in the decreasing order of magnitude.

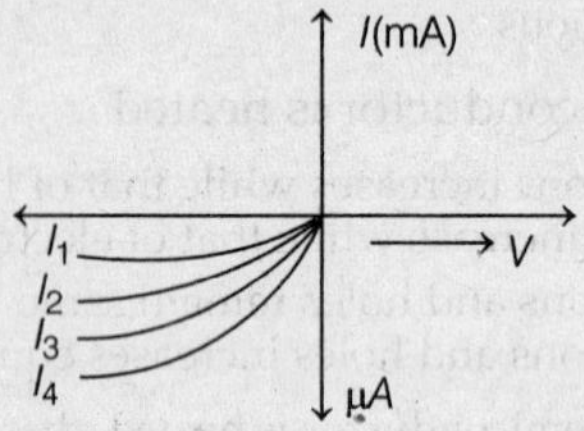

Sol. Due to photo-effects, the fractional increase in minority charge carriers is more than the fractional increase in majority charge carriers, hence the fractional change in minority charge carriers dominates reverse biased. A photodiode is operated in reverse bias mode as reverse bias current is more easily measurable. As the reverse saturation current through a photodiode increases with the increase intensity of the incident radiation, so $I_4 > I_3 > I_2 > I_1$.

Q.2 When the voltage drop across a *p-n* junction diode is increased from 0.70 V to 0.71 V, the change in the diode current is 10 mA. What is the dynamic resistance of the diode?

Sol. Dynamic resistance $r = \Delta V / \Delta I = (0.71 - 0.70) / 10 \times 10^{-3} = 1\,\Omega$